T0304088

Methylmercury Accumulation in Rice

This book presents state-of-the-art knowledge related to concerns about methylmercury (MeHg) in the soil-rice system. It covers increasing concerns about human exposure to methylmercury through the consumption of Hg-contaminated rice and shows the global contamination of soil and how Hg can be mobilized, immobilized, methylated, and demethylated in soils. The authors present the biogeochemical process through which rice plants accumulate Hg. This book comprehensively displays the biogeochemical behavior of Hg in paddy soils and rice plants, as well as the current remediation technologies to mitigate Hg risks from paddy soil ecosystems.

Features:

- Provides cutting-edge knowledge on mercury in paddy field ecosystems.
- Discusses the key biogeochemical transformation processes of mercury in soil.
- Explains the accumulation processes of mercury in rice plants.
- Includes case studies on how to inhibit mercury accumulation in rice plants.
- Shows the application of Hg stable isotope traces in paddy soil-rice field studies.

Intended for researchers, graduate students, and professionals working in fields such as Geochemistry, Agronomy, and Environmental Science and Engineering, this book will be an important resource for anyone interested in Hg contamination in soils and rice and the related risk for human and environmental health.

Emergent Environmental Pollution

Series Editor: Jörg Rinklebe, University of Wuppertal, Germany

The nature of pollutants in the environment depends largely on their interactions in the soil, water, air, and organisms. Understanding the fate and transport of pollutants in the environment is essential for humans and animals, plants, water bodies, air, soils, and sediments. This series provides timely information on the biological, chemical, and physical processes governing the interactions of pollutants in the environment. Such knowledge is needed for minimizing the negative impact of pollutants on human health and the health of ecosystems. Books from this series are of value to professionals and researchers, students, industrial and mining engineers, government regulators, authorities, and consultants in the environmental arena.

Dynamics and Bioavailability of Heavy Metals in the Rootzone
Edited by H. Magdi Selim

Trace Elements in Waterlogged Soils and Sediments
Edited by Jörg Rinklebe, Anna Sophia Knox, and Michael Paller

Competitive Sorption and Transport of Heavy Metals in Soils and Geological Media
Edited by H. Magdi Selim

Nickel in Soils and Plants
Edited by Christos Tsadilas, Jörg Rinklebe, and Magdi Selim

Phosphate in Soils
Interaction with Micronutrients, Radionuclides and Heavy Metals
Edited by H. Magdi Selim

Permeable Reactive Barrier
Sustainable Groundwater Remediation
Edited by Ravi Naidu and Volker Birke

Nitrate Handbook
Environmental, Agricultural, and Health Effects
Edited by Christos Tsadilas

Vanadium in Soils and Plants
Edited by Jörg Rinklebe

Maritime Accidents and Environmental Pollution – The X-Press Pearl Disaster
Causes, Consequences, and Lessons Learned
Edited by Meththika Vithanage, Ajith Priyal de Alwis, and Deshai Botheju

Methylmercury Accumulation in Rice
Process and Regulation
Edited by Xinbin Feng, Jianxu Wang, and Jörg Rinklebe

For more information on this series, please visit: https://www.routledge.com/Emergent-Environmental-Pollution/book-series/CRCEEP

Methylmercury Accumulation in Rice
Process and Regulation

Edited by
Xinbin Feng, Jianxu Wang,
and Jörg Rinklebe

CRC Press
Taylor & Francis Group
Boca Raton London New York

CRC Press is an imprint of the
Taylor & Francis Group, an **informa** business

Designed cover image: © Jianxu Wang

First edition published 2025
by CRC Press
2385 NW Executive Center Drive, Suite 320, Boca Raton FL 33431

and by CRC Press
4 Park Square, Milton Park, Abingdon, Oxon, OX14 4RN

CRC Press is an imprint of Taylor & Francis Group, LLC

© 2025 selection and editorial matter, Xinbin Feng, Jianxu Wang, and Jörg Rinklebe; individual chapters, the contributors

Library of Congress Cataloging-in-Publication Data
Names: Feng, Xinbin, 1968- editor. | Wang, Jianxu, editor. | Rinklebe, Jörg, editor.
Title: Methylmercury accumulation in rice : process and regulation / edited by Xinbin Feng, Jianxu Wang, and Jörg Rinklebe
Description: First edition | Boca Raton, FL : CRC Press, 2025 | Includes bibliographical references and index
Identifiers: LCCN 2024009681 (print) | LCCN 2024009682 (ebook) |
ISBN 9781032520254 (hardback) | ISBN 9781032520261 (paperback) |
ISBN 9781003404941 (ebook)
Subjects: LCSH: Methylmercury--Bioaccumulation. | Rice--Processing. |
Soils--Mercury content.
Classification: LCC QH545.M4 M48 2025 (print) | LCC QH545.M4 (ebook) |
DDC 633.1/8919--dc23/eng/20240617
LC record available at https://lccn.loc.gov/2024009681
LC ebook record available at https://lccn.loc.gov/2024009682

ISBN: 978-1-032-52025-4 (hbk)
ISBN: 978-1-032-52026-1 (pbk)
ISBN: 978-1-003-40494-1 (ebk)

DOI: 10.1201/9781003404941

Typeset in Times
by KnowledgeWorks Global Ltd.

Contents

Preface

Mercury (Hg) is volatile and extremely toxic to humans. Both natural and anthropogenic sources release Hg into the environment, causing contamination. Mercury mainly presents as elemental gaseous Hg, inorganic Hg, and methylmercury (MeHg) in the environment. MeHg is predominantly converted from inorganic Hg by microorganisms in anaerobic environments such as ocean and lake sediments, coastal areas, floodplain soils, marshes, bogs, and fens as well as constructed wetlands and further human-made wetlands. MeHg attracts the greatest concern due to its bioaccumulation and biomagnification in the aquatic food chain, leading to MeHg contamination in fish. The consumption of Hg-contaminated fish products has long been considered the main pathway of human exposure to MeHg. At heavily Hg-contaminated sites, the consumption of MeHg-contaminated fish can lead to acute MeHg poisoning—i.e., Minamata disease.

A paddy field is a type of human-made wetland that is seasonally flooded for rice cultivation. Such a kind of anaerobic environment is favorable for MeHg formation. In the 2000s, the first author of this book (Xinbin Feng) and his team members discovered elevated MeHg concentrations in rice and found that rice consumption is the primary MeHg exposure pathway in Hg mining areas in Guizhou. This discovery has raised global concern, as rice is the most important staple food for the population in Asia, where a large number of sites are polluted with Hg. Hence, it is particularly important to manage the transfer of Hg from paddy soil to rice plant, thereby minimizing human Hg exposure risks. A principle that is paramount in managing paddy field Hg risk is the understanding of biogeochemical transfer of Hg in the soil-rice-human continuum. Therefore, knowledge of Hg transformation mechanisms in paddy fields, the Hg accumulation process in the rice plant, and human Hg exposure risks via rice consumption is essential for developing strategies for management of Hg risks in paddy fields.

This book covers important aspects of the biogeochemical transfer of Hg in the soil-rice-human continuum, including (1) a summary of current understanding and future research needs (Chapter 1); (2) Hg contamination in regional and global soils (Chapters 2 and 3); (3) human Hg exposure risks (Chapter 4); (4) the biogeochemical transformation of Hg in soils (Chapters 5, 6, 7, and 8) and the Hg accumulation process in rice plants (Chapters 9 and 10); and (5) methods used to mitigate Hg from rice plants (Chapters 11 and 12).

In covering a range of aspects and in emphasizing the new approaches for understanding the underlying processes of the biogeochemical transfer of Hg in the soil-rice-human continuum, this book will support scientists and practitioners who work on the management of Hg risks in paddy field ecosystems. Furthermore, this book was written for scientists with an interest in Environmental Geochemistry, Environmental Science, and Isotope Chemistry.

We would like to thank the contributing authors for preparing the chapters and revising them to improve their quality. We would also like to express our thanks to the editors, Chelsea Reeves, and Irma Shagla Britton of CRC Press/Taylor & Francis Group for their dedication, patience, and diligence in the production of this book.

About the Editors

Prof. Xinbin Feng obtained his PhD degree from the Institute of Geochemistry, Chinese Academy of Sciences (IGCAS) in 1997. Since 2020, he has served as the Director of IGCAS. He is now serving as an associate editor of reputed journals such as *Science of the Total Environment*, the *Journal of Geochemical Exploration*, the *Journal of Asian Earth Sciences*, and *Acta Geochimica*, as well as an editorial board member of *Journal of Environmental Science* and *Atmospheres and Environmental Science and Technology*. His research interests include the biogeochemical cycling of heavy metals, such as mercury, cadmium, antimony, and lead, in the environment and their human health impacts; Hg stable isotope fractionation in the environmental compartments; and utilization of Hg isotope ratios as a tool to trace the sources of Hg contamination in the environment, as well as remediation of Hg-contaminated environments. He has guided more than 100 postgraduate students and published more than 440 papers in peer-reviewed high-quality SCI journals.

Dr. Jianxu Wang has served as a professor at the Institute of Geochemistry, Chinese Academy of Sciences. He worked on the biogeochemical cycle of trace elements in the environment and the remediation of heavy metal-polluted soils. He has published more than 40 papers in peer-reviewed high-quality SCI journals.

Dr. Jörg Rinklebe is Professor for Soil- and Groundwater-Management at the University of Wuppertal, Germany. He has been selected as ISI Web of Science Highly Cited Researcher in 2019, 2020, 2021, and 2022. Prof. Rinklebe is President of the International Society of Trace Element Biogeochemistry (ISTEB). His academic background covers environmental science, bioavailability of emerging contaminants, and remediation of contaminated sites. His main research is on soils, sediments, waters, plants, and their pollutions and linked biogeochemical issues, with a special focus on redox chemistry. He also has a certain expertise in soil microbiology. Among his published works are 510 research papers and four books entitled *Trace Elements in Waterlogged Soils and Sediments* (Taylor & Francis, 2016), *Nickel in Soils and Plants* (Taylor & Francis, 2018), *Soil and Groundwater Remediation Technologies* (Taylor & Francis, 2020), and *Vanadium in Soils and Plants* (Taylor & Francis, 2022), as well as numerous book chapters.

Contributors

Qingliang Chen
Key Laboratory for Biomedical Effects
  of Nanomaterials and Nanosafety
Institute of High Energy Physics
Chinese Academy of Sciences
Beijing, P.R. China
and
University of Chinese Academy
  of Sciences
Beijing, P.R. China

Buyun Du
State Key Laboratory of Environmental
  Geochemistry
Institute of Geochemistry
Chinese Academy of Sciences
Guiyang, P.R. China

Lin Feng
State Key Laboratory of Environmental
  Geochemistry
Institute of Geochemistry
Chinese Academy of Sciences
Guiyang, P.R. China

Xinbin Feng
State Key Laboratory of Environmental
  Geochemistry
Institute of Geochemistry
Chinese Academy of Sciences
Guiyang, P.R. China
and
University of Chinese Academy
  of Sciences
Beijing, P.R. China

Yuxi Gao
Key Laboratory for Biomedical Effects
  of Nanomaterials and Nanosafety
Institute of High Energy Physics
Chinese Academy of Sciences
Beijing, P.R. China

Haiyan Hu
State Key Laboratory of Environmental
  Geochemistry
Institute of Geochemistry
Chinese Academy of Sciences
Guiyang, P.R. China

Ping Li
State Key Laboratory of Environmental
  Geochemistry
Institute of Geochemistry
Chinese Academy of Sciences
Guiyang, P.R. China

Yufeng Li
Key Laboratory for Biomedical
  Effects of Nanomaterials and
  Nanosafety
Institute of High Energy Physics
Chinese Academy of Sciences
Beijing, P.R. China

Jiang Liu
College of Resources
Sichuan Agricultural University
Chengdu, P.R. China
and
State Key Laboratory of Environmental
  Geochemistry
Institute of Geochemistry
Chinese Academy of Sciences
Guiyang, P.R. China

Jinling Liu
School of Earth Sciences
China University of Geosciences
Wuhan, P.R. China

Xile Liu
State Key Laboratory of Environmental
  Geochemistry
Institute of Geochemistry
Chinese Academy of Sciences
Guiyang, P.R. China

Zhe Liu
School of Earth Sciences
China University of Geosciences
Wuhan, P.R. China

Bo Meng
State Key Laboratory of Environmental
  Geochemistry
Institute of Geochemistry
Chinese Academy of Sciences
Guiyang, P.R. China

Ilia Mironov
State Key Laboratory of Environmental
  Geochemistry
Institute of Geochemistry
Chinese Academy of Sciences
Guiyang, P.R. China

Chongyang Qin
Institute of Geochemistry
Chinese Academy of Sciences
Guiyang, P.R. China

Jörg Rinklebe
Laboratory of Soil and Groundwater
  Management
Institute of Foundation Engineering,
  Water and Waste-Management
School of Architecture and Civil
  Engineering
University of Wuppertal
Wuppertal, Germany

Baolin Wang
School of Geography and
  Environmental Science
Guizhou Normal University
Guiyang, P.R. China

Jianxu Wang
State Key Laboratory of Environmental
  Geochemistry
Institute of Geochemistry
Chinese Academy of Sciences
Guiyang, P.R. China

Xun Wang
State Key Laboratory of Environmental
  Geochemistry
Institute of Geochemistry
Chinese Academy of Sciences
Guiyang, P.R. China

Qingqing Wu
State Key Laboratory of Environmental
  Geochemistry
Institute of Geochemistry
Chinese Academy of Sciences
Guiyang, P.R. China

Jicheng Xia
Key Laboratory of Karst Georesources
  and Environment
Ministry of Education
Guizhou University
Guiyang, P.R. China

Xiaohang Xu
Key Laboratory of Karst Georesources
  and Environment
Ministry of Education
Guizhou University
Guiyang, P.R. China

Shaochen Yang
School of Earth Sciences
China University of Geosciences
Wuhan, P.R. China

Runsheng Yin
Institute of Geochemistry
Chinese Academy of Sciences
Guiyang, P.R. China

Wei Yuan
State Key Laboratory of Environmental
   Geochemistry
Institute of Geochemistry
Chinese Academy of Sciences
Guiyang, P.R. China

Jiating Zhao
Department of Environmental Science
Zhejiang University
Hangzhou, P.R. China
and

Key Laboratory for Biomedical Effects
   of Nanomaterials and Nanosafety
Institute of High Energy Physics
Chinese Academy of Sciences
Beijing, P.R. China

Lei Zhao
School of Management Science
Guizhou University of Finance and
   Economics
Guiyang, P.R. China

1 Methylmercury Accumulation in Rice
Process, Risk, and Regulation

Xinbin Feng, Jianxu Wang, and Jörg Rinklebe

1.1 INTRODUCTION

Mercury (Hg) is a highly toxic heavy metal with no known biological functions (Clarkson, 1993; Feng and Qiu, 2008). It is bioaccumulative, volatile, and mobile. Mercury attracts global concern due to its long-range transport in the atmosphere and its transformation to methylmercury (MeHg) both in terrestrial and in aquatic ecosystems (Hsu-Kim et al., 2018). MeHg is the most toxic form of Hg, and it causes Minamata disease in humans at high exposure doses and neurological disease at low doses (Harada, 1995; Zahir et al., 2005). Mercury has been known since prehistorical times and used by alchemists in China since 2000 BC. The concentration of Hg in earth's crust is 0.02–0.09 mg/kg and in global soil is about 0.07 mg/kg. Elevated Hg concentrations in soils were found at anthropogenically polluted sites, such as Hg mining regions, chlor-alkali production factories, vinyl chloride monomer production factories, coal-fired power plants, artisanal gold mining regions, etc., as well as at sites with high Hg background (i.e., the Hg mineral belt) (Bolaños-Álvarez et al., 2016; Wang et al., 2012). The contamination of Hg in soils poses risks to the environment and human health. International/local organizations, policy makers, and scientists have defined the maximum Hg concentration in soils, aiming to protect human health. According to Alina, (2011), the range of maximum allowable concentrations for Hg is 0.5–5 mg/kg and the range of trigger action values is 1.5–10 mg/kg in agricultural soils. As per soil environmental quality (GB15618-2018) as defined by the Chinese government, the risk screening value for soil contamination of agricultural land is 0.6 mg/kg (paddy fields, $6.5 < pH \leq 7.5$) and the risk intervention value for soil contamination of agricultural land is 4.0 mg/kg (paddy fields, $6.5 < pH \leq 7.5$).

In soils, Hg mainly occurs as inorganic Hg, MeHg, and Hg^0, among which inorganic Hg forms are prevalent (Higueras et al., 2003; Yin et al., 2016). Those Hg forms can be subjected to mutual transformations in soils (as will be shown in Figures 1.1 and 1.2). The common form of inorganic Hg is HgS, which has limited bioavailability to organisms (Yin et al., 2016). However, the dissolution of HgS occurs in the presence of sulfide and dissolved organic carbon (DOC) under anaerobic conditions (Graham et al., 2012; Mazrui et al., 2018). Although free mercuric ions and mobilized/soluble Hg complexes represent a small fractional amount of the inorganic Hg in soil, they are of the highest concern due to their active biogeochemical properties (Huang et al., 2020). They can be adsorbed onto carbonate, Fe/Mn(hydro)oxide, and

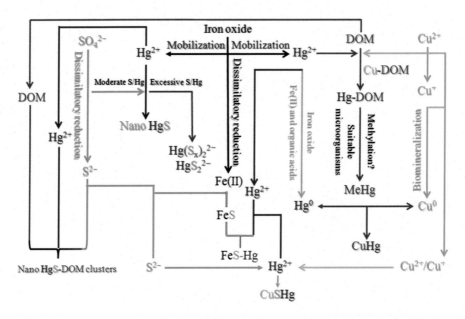

FIGURE 1.1   Biogeochemical transformation of Hg in soils under anaerobic conditions.

organic matter, or they can be converted to MeHg by microorganisms under anaerobic conditions or be converted to Hg^0 via biotic (e.g., photo-reduction) and abiotic processes (Renneberg and Dudas, 2001; Wang et al., 2011). Desorption of Hg from carbonate and Fe/Mn (hydro)oxides occurs under low pH and Eh conditions because of the dissolution of carbonate minerals and Fe/Mn (hydro)oxides and the reductive dissolution of Fe/Mn (hydro)oxides (Frohne et al., 2012; Wang et al., 2021).

MeHg concentrations are at ppb (μg/kg) levels in most soils and can be decomposed to inorganic Hg by Hg demethylation microorganisms and through photodegradation (Li and Cai, 2013). MeHg contamination is the primary concern in paddy fields, as MeHg is bioaccumulated by rice grain and subsequently enters the human body through food webs (Feng et al., 2008). Qiu et al. (2005) studied the concentration of total Hg (THg)and MeHg in different crops collected from Wanshan Hg mining regions in China, and they found that rice grain had MeHg concentrations several orders of magnitude higher than those of other crops. The MeHg concentration in rice grain at Wanshan Hg mining sites exceeds the maximum allowable total Hg concentration in rice grain defined by the Chinese government (20 ng/g, GB2762-2012). Zhang et al. (2010a) evaluated the Hg bioaccumulation in rice grain at Wanshan Hg mining regions and found that bioaccumulation factors (BAFs) ranged from 0.00014 to 0.51 for IHg and from 0.71 to 50 for MeHg. It is clear that rice grain has a strong capacity to accumulate MeHg. Zhang et al. (2010b) studied the main exposure pathway of Hg in populations in different Hg-contaminated regions in China and found that rice consumption accounted for 94–96% of the probable daily intake (PDI) of MeHg. There is no doubt that the consumption of rice is the main pathway of human exposure to MeHg at Hg-contaminated regions in China. Knowledge of Hg speciation transformation in soil, Hg accumulation in rice plants, and human health risks associated with rice consumption is fundamental for developing sustainable strategies and technologies to mitigate MeHg bioaccumulation in rice grain, thereby reducing human Hg exposure risks.

1.2 MERCURY SPECIATION TRANSFORMATION IN SOILS

Most studies have focused on MeHg in soils and sediments due to the high bioaccumulation and the toxicity of MeHg to humans. MeHg is converted from inorganic Hg by microorganisms under anaerobic conditions. Microorganisms capable of methylation of Hg have been identified, including sulfate-reducing bacteria (SRBs), iron-reducing bacteria (IRBs), and methanogens, as well as several fermentative, acetogenic, and cellulolytic microorganisms. It is reported that most Hg methylation microorganisms possess *hgcAB* gene clusters (Parks et al., 2013). Mercury methylation microorganisms in paddy fields in Hg mining regions are dominated by IRBs (i.e., Geobacter) and methanogens (Liu et al., 2018). Vishnivetskaya et al. (2018) reported that *Proteobacteria, Actinobacteria, Chloroflexi, Acidobacteria, Euryarchaeota*, and *Crenarchaeota* are dominant in rice paddies; the abundance and distribution of microorganisms carrying *hgcAB* genes were determined by total Hg and MeHg concentrations in soils in Hg mining regions in China. Later, Wu et al. (2020) reported that in non-Hg-polluted soil, SRBs are the dominant Hg methylators. They also used a combination of the specific microbial inhibitors and stable isotope tracers to reveal a critical role of methanogens in controlling MeHg concentration in Hg-contaminated soils due to their ability for demethylation of MeHg.

Biogeochemical transformation of Hg in soil is affected by microorganisms, pH, Fe/Mn(oxyhydr)oxides, sulfur, dissolved organic matter, thiols, etc. The biogeochemical transformation of Hg in soils under anaerobic and aerobic conditions is shown in Figures 1.1 and 1.2. The mobile/soluble inorganic Hg pool is the primary

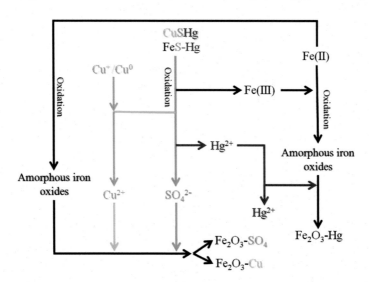

FIGURE 1.2 Biogeochemical transformation of Hg in soils under aerobic conditions.

substrate for methylation. The speciation of the mobile/soluble inorganic Hg is rather important for microbial methylation, as different Hg species are variable in their capacity for crossing cellular boundaries for methylation. The passive diffusion of neutral Hg complexes [$(Hg(SH)_2^0$(aq) and HgS^0(aq)] is regarded as an important mechanism for Hg crossing the barrier of the microorganism (Drott et al., 2007). However, Schaefer and Morel (2009) found that Hg methylation by the bacterium *Geobacter sulfurreducens* is greatly enhanced in the presence of low concentrations of the amino acid cysteine. Further, they reported that microbial cellular Hg uptake and methylation are both affected by specific biochemical mechanisms that led to widely different uptake and methylation rates for different Hg complexes. Lin et al. (2015) also found a cysteine concentration-dependent Hg methylation by *Geobacter sulfurreducens PCA* wild type. Clearly, thiol molecules such as cysteine play a critical role in shaping Hg speciation to Hg(cysteine)$_2$ complexes, which can be actively taken up by microorganisms. The cellular uptake of Hg-cysteine depends on the ratio of Hg to cysteine. It is reported that Hg:cysteine ratios from 1:1 to 1:2 are preferentially taken up by microbial cells (Schaefer et al., 2011; Schaefer and Morel, 2009). The formation of the tris complex Hg(cysteine)$_3$ at high cysteine concentrations (i.e., high Cys:Hg ratios) is unfavorable for microbial uptake and methylation (Schaefer and Morel, 2009). However, the mechanism of inhibition of methylation of Hg(cysteine)$_3$ is unknown.

Low pH is linked to high Hg methylation rate in soils in Hg mining regions in China. This is likely because the lower pH enhances the mobilization of Hg, thereby promoting Hg methylation (Qiu et al., 2005).

Fe(oxyhydr)oxides, including goethite, hematite, ferrihydrite, and lepidocrocite, can absorb Hg in soil solution, and its reduction-oxidation processes drive Hg mobilization and immobilization. Fe(oxyhydr)oxides can immobilize Hg^{2+} and $MeHg^+$ by forming $\equiv$S-OHg$^+$, $\equiv$S-OMeHg, and $Hg(OH)_2$-$Fe(OH)_3$ complexes (Feyte et al., 2010; Tiffreau et al., 1995). Under anaerobic conditions, reductive dissolution of Fe(oxyhydr)oxides produces Fe^{2+} and liberates its associated Hg^{2+} and Hg_2^{2+} complexes (Gygax et al., 2019). The Hg^{2+} and Hg_2^{2+} can either serve as electron acceptors to be reduced to Hg^0 or be converted to bioavailable $Hg(SH)_2^0$(aq) and HgS^0(aq) or be converted to HgS. Under strong reducing conditions, sulfide produced from sulfate reduction can bind with Fe^{2+} to form a nano-FeS cluster, which is able to absorb Hg^{2+}, and promote Hg^{2+} reduction (Bone et al., 2014).

The Hg^0 in soil can be oxidized by hydroxyl radicals to form Hg^{2+}, or it can be absorbed by Fe(oxyhydr)oxides (Lin and Pehkonen, 1997; Richard et al., 2016). Under aerobic conditions, the oxidation of Fe^{2+} forms amorphous Fe(oxyhydr)oxides capable of adsorption of Hg^{2+}, $MeHg^+$, and Hg^0. However, the binding of reduced dissolved organic matter (DOM) to Fe^{2+} forms Fe^{2+}-DOM, by which Fe^{2+} oxidation is inhibited (Daugherty et al., 2017). In summary, the reduction and oxidation of Fe(oxyhydr)oxides affects Hg mobilization, reduction, and oxidation, which is coupled with S^{2-} and DOM.

Sulfur has a rather close geochemical association with Hg in the environment. In soils, sulfur speciation is dominated by organic sulfur compounds (C-O-SO$_3$, C-S, and SH$^-$), zero-valence sulfur, and inorganic sulfur (S^{6+} and S^{2-}). Most sulfur in soils cannot directly react with Hg, except for reduced sulfur compounds (Skyllberg, 2008). Under reducing conditions, SO_4^{2-} is microbially reduced to H_2S, which binds with Hg^{2+}, forming nano particulate HgS. However, excessive S^{2-} reacts with HgS to produce soluble Hg complexes such as $HgHS^{2-}$, $Hg(S_x)_2^{2-}$, and HgS_2^{2-}. In DOM-enriched sediment, S^{2-}/S^- binds with Hg^{2+} to form neutrally charged complexes such as $Hg(SH)_2^0(aq)$ and $HgS^0(aq)$, which are available for microbial-mediated methylation (Drott et al., 2007). It should be noted that the presence of Fe^{2+}, Cu^+, or Cu^{2+} can eliminate S^{2-} by producing nano-FeS and CuS clusters. The decrease in S^{2-} will affect the geochemical reaction between S^{2-} and Hg^{2+}.

Soils and sediments contain abundant DOM, especially reduced DOM. DOM plays an important role in the biogeochemical cycle of Fe, S, and Hg. The reduced DOM can not only induce Hg^0 oxidation but also promote Hg^{2+} reduction (Gu et al., 2011). Mercury has a close association with DOM and sulfide, and they are coupled as Hg-DOM-S clusters. The concentrations of DOM, sulfide, and Hg^{2+} determine the characteristic of Hg-DOM-S clusters. Under the low S^{2-} condition, Hg-DOM is prevalent in soils, in which the high molecular weight of Hg-DOM complexes makes for limited availability to microorganisms because they cannot pass through the cellular plasma membrane (Hammerschmidt et al., 2008). However, Zhao et al. (2017) reported that the ability of microorganisms to uptake Hg-DOM is dependent on microbial species. For instance, the ability of Desulfovibrio *desulfuricans* ND132 to methylate Hg-DOM is stronger than that of *Geobacter sulfurreducens* PCA. Under the high S^{2-} condition, the reaction between Hg^{2+} and S^{2-} forms HgS. The presence of DOM inhibits the aggregation and growth of HgS by forming disordered nano HgS-DOM clusters with a diameter of 10–100 nm. A certain group of nano-HgS-DOM clusters can be converted to MeHg by microorganisms (Graham et al., 2012; Moreau et al., 2015). Poulin et al. (2017) further studied the impact of a change of concentration of S^{2-} and composition of DOM on the formation of HgS. They found that the increasing of the concentration of S^{2-} is favorable for the formation of large nano-HgS clusters with ordered crystal structure; the presence of more aromatic functional groups in DOM favors the formation of small nano-HgS clusters with poorly crystallized structures. The oxidation of FeS and CuS_x produces SO_4^{2-} and subsequently releases Hg associated with FeS and CuS_x.

Although much progress has been achieved, several aspects of the biogeochemical transformation of Hg in paddy soils are unclear. For example, what's the hub species of microorganisms responsible for the methylation of Hg in paddy fields in Hg mining regions? How does Hg transformation couple with elements such as S, N, Fe, Cu, etc., in paddy soil? Which Hg species are bioavailable to Hg-methylation microorganisms? Also, it should be noted that the climatic change and enhanced anthropogenic activities due to the blooming of population do impact the biogeochemical cycle of elements in the terrestrial ecosystem. It is of great interest to explore the biogeochemical transformation of Hg in paddy soils under the scenario of climatic change and enhanced anthropogenic activities.

1.3 MERCURY ACCUMULATION IN RICE PLANTS AND HUMAN HEALTH RISKS ASSOCIATED WITH RICE CONSUMPTION

Rice plants can take up both methylmercury (MeHg) and inorganic mercury from the environment. The main source of MeHg in rice plants is soil. MeHg can cross the root barrier and enter the aboveground tissues of rice. Meng et al. (2011) studied the accumulation process of MeHg in rice plants. They found that MeHg from soil is stored in the leaf and stalk during rice growing stages, and it is further transported to rice grain in the rice ripening period. It has been supposed that MeHg is co-transported with nutrient and organic molecules during their filling into grain. Meng et al. (2014) studied the speciation of Hg in rice bran and found that Hg is dominated by about 77% Hg-cysteine and 23% MeHg-cysteine complexes. Thus, thiol molecules such as cysteine are proposed to be involved in Hg uptake and translocation in rice plants. Also, the presence of cysteine can facilitate the uptake of MeHg by roots and translocation to shoots of rice plants (Hao et al., 2022).

The ability of rice grain to accumulate inorganic Hg is weaker than its ability to accumulate MeHg. The bioaccumulation factor of MeHg (BAF_{MeHg}) of rice grain is several orders of magnitudes higher than that of inorganic Hg. Inorganic Hg in rice plants originates from both soil and the atmosphere. However, the contribution of soil Hg to plants is limited because most inorganic Hg in soil has limited bioavailability for plants and the root of the plant acts as a barrier for inorganic Hg (Figure 1.3). Atmospheric Hg^0 is an important Hg contributor to rice plants in Hg mining regions, where the atmospheric Hg^0 concentration is extremely high. The aboveground tissue of rice can accumulate Hg^0 and oxidize it to Hg(II), which can be transported to rice grain (Aslam et al., 2022) (Figure 1.3). Yin et al. (2013) used Hg-stable isotopes to trace Hg sources in the different tissues of rice plants and found that the fractional

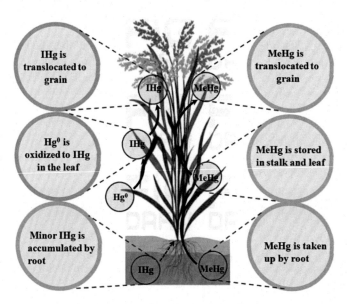

FIGURE 1.3 The accumulation process of Hg in rice.

amount of atmospheric Hg^0 in rice tissue (f) follows the trend $f_{leaf} > f_{stem} > f_{seed} > f_{root}$. Several studies showed that Hg is associated with thiol compounds in plants, and thus the detoxification and sequestration of Hg(II) with thiols has been proposed. Hg-thiol compounds are considered bioavailable to plants. By adopting Hg-stable isotope tracers, Wang et al. (2022) found that the cysteine-extractable Hg pool in soil is an important source of Hg to *Houttuynia cordata*. Also, Wang et al. (2022) proposed that amino acid transporters were responsible for transportation of Hg(cysteine)$_2$ in plants. The above studies point to a hypothesisthat cysteine and its transporters are critical for Hg uptake and transportation in plants. However, there is a lack of evidence to support this hypothesis. To fill this knowledge gap, a combination of physiological, genetic, and geochemical tools to explore gene clusters for Hg uptake and transportation in rice plants is needed in future studies.

Rice is the staple food for billions of people in the world, especially in Asian countries. Also, in the southwestern part of China, rice is the main staple food. In Hg mining regions in China, people have elevated concentrations of MeHg in their hair due to consumption of rice, as revealed by a significant linear correlation between hair MeHg concentration and MeHg intake from rice (Feng et al., 2008). The PDIs of THg and MeHg for people in Hg mining regions have been calculated, and results show that a certain number of people have PDI_{THg} and PDI_{MeHg} exceeding the maximum allowable PDI values defined by WHO and US EPA, respectively (Zhang et al., 2010b). The routes of human exposure to total Hg and MeHg have been further studied. Human exposure to MeHg is mainly through consumption of rice, while human exposure to total Hg is mainly through consumption of crops. Therefore, it is important to develop cost-effective methods to reduce the concentration of total Hg and MeHg in crops, thereby lowering human Hg exposure risks.

1.4 CONTENTS OF THIS BOOK AND FUTURE WORK TO MANAGE HG RISKS IN PADDY FIELDS

This book is divided into 12 chapters covering crucial aspects of Hg in soil-rice plant systems and their links to environmental and human health consequences, as well as technologies and strategies used for controlling Hg risks. This chapter provided a general view of Hg in the environment, Hg speciation transformation in soils, the Hg accumulation process in rice plants, and human health risks associated with rice consumption, highlighting priority areas for future research. A comprehensive review of Hg distribution in global surface soil and some major regional surface soils to trace the sources and driving factors is presented in Chapter 2. Mercury contamination in soils, plants, and waters is summarized in Chapter 3 to provide an overview of Hg levels in different environmental sectors in Hg mining regions. Human Hg exposure risks via rice consumption in Wanshan Hg mining regions are summarized in Chapter 4 to show the human MeHg exposure pathways, to present adults' and children's MeHg exposure levels via rice consumption, and to show the Wanshan children's Hg exposure and intelligence quotient losses and lifetime economic losses. The biogeochemical transformation process of Hg in soils and the microbial community responsible for Hg (de)methylation are summarized in Chapter 5, while Chapter 6 presents important biogeochemical processes and reactions controlling

Hg mobilization and MeHg production in soil. Mercury as a redox-sensitive element, underlying processes, and how redox changes affect Hg mobilization and (de)methylation are summarized in Chapter 7. Accurate determination of Hg concentration in soil pore water is a prerequisite to studying Hg transfer in the soil-rice plant system; the use of the DGT technique to study the bioavailability of Hg in soil is summarized in Chapter 8. Mercury accumulation in rice plants is described in Chapter 9 to explain the transfer process of Hg from soil to rice grain during the rice growing season. Mercury-stable isotope tracing is a powerful tool to trace the source of Hg and reveal the biogeochemical transformation processes in the environment. The use of Hg-stable isotope tracers to trace the Hg in soil paddy fields is summarized in Chapter 10. Reducing the bioavailability of Hg in soils to control the transfer of Hg from soil to rice is important to reduce Hg risks. The mechanism underlying application of sulfur-containing amendments, as well as carbon-based amendments, in reducing Hg mobility in soil is explained in Chapters 11 and 12.

The research on various geochemical, environmental, geological, and health aspects of Hg has made significant progress, although further understanding and programs are needed to meet this challenge faced by humanity. There is a dearth of information required to understand the Hg exposure risks via rice consumption. Taking into account the social-economic aspects and comprehensive Hg risk management, integrated risk management strategies should be implemented in Hg-polluted regions. The development of strict mitigation strategies, which may end up in unnecessarily high treatment costs, causes high Hg exposure risks to people. Therefore, those Hg mitigation and remediation programs may need research on the following aspects: (i) the optimization of land use types to avoid planting rice in Hg-polluted regions, (ii) the capacity of different rice cultivars to accumulate Hg from the environment, screening cultivars with low Hg accumulation capacity for Hg-polluted regions, and (iii) environment-friendly and low-cost amendments to immobilize Hg in soils. The implementation of the above remediation techniques and strategies should be based on the social-economic levels and the awareness of the local population and relevant stakeholders.

REFERENCES

Alina, K. P., 2011. Trace Elements in Soils and Plants (Fourth Edition). CRC Press, New York.
Aslam, M. W., Meng, B., Abdelhafiz, M. A., et al., 2022. Unravelling the interactive effect of soil and atmospheric mercury influencing mercury distribution and accumulation in the soil-rice system. Science of the Total Environment 803, 149967.
Bolaños-Álvarez, Y., Alonso-Hernández, C. M., Morabito, R., et al., 2016. Mercury contamination of riverine sediments in the vicinity of a mercury cell chlor-alkali plant in Sagua River, Cuba. Chemosphere 152, 376–382.
Bone, S. E., Bargar, J. R., Sposito, G., 2014. Mackinawite (FeS) reduces mercury(II) under sulfidic conditions. Environmental Science & Technology 48, 10681–10689.
Clarkson, T. W., 1993. Mercury: Major issues in environmental health. Environmental Health Perspectives 100, 31–38.
Daugherty, E. E., Gilbert, B., Nico, P. S., et al., 2017. Complexation and redox buffering of iron(II) by dissolved organic matter. Environmental Science & Technology 51, 11096–11104.

Drott, A., Lambertsson, L., Bjorn, E., et al., 2007. Importance of dissolved neutral mercury sulfides for methyl mercury production in contaminated sediments. Environmental Science & Technology 41, 2270–2276.

Feng, X., Li, P., Qiu, G., et al., 2008. Human exposure to methylmercury through rice intake in mercury mining areas, Guizhou province, China. Environmental Science & Technology 42, 326–332.

Feng, X., Qiu, G., 2008. Mercury pollution in Guizhou, Southwestern China — An overview. Science of the Total Environment 400, 227–237.

Feyte, S., Tessier, A., Gobeil, C., et al., 2010. In situ adsorption of mercury, methylmercury and other elements by iron oxyhydroxides and organic matter in lake sediments. Applied Geochemistry 25, 984–995.

Frohne, T., Rinklebe, J., Langer, U., et al., 2012. Biogeochemical factors affecting mercury methylation rate in two contaminated floodplain soils. Biogeosciences 9, 493–507.

Graham, A. M., Aiken, G. R., Gilmour, C. C., 2012. Dissolved organic matter enhances microbial mercury methylation under sulfidic conditions. Environmental Science & Technology 46, 2715–2723.

Gu, B., Bian, Y., Miller, C. L., et al., 2011. Mercury reduction and complexation by natural organic matter in anoxic environments. Proceedings of the National Academy of Sciences of the United States of America 108, 1479–1483.

Gygax, S., Gfeller, L., Wilcke, W., et al., 2019. Emerging investigator series: Mercury mobility and methylmercury formation in a contaminated agricultural flood plain: Influence of flooding and manure addition. Environmental Science: Processes & Impacts 21, 2008–2019.

Hammerschmidt, C. R., Fitzgerald, W. F., Balcom, P. H., et al., 2008. Organic matter and sulfide inhibit methylmercury production in sediments of New York/New Jersey Harbor. Marine Chemistry 109, 165–182.

Hao, Y., Zhu, Y., Yan, R., et al., 2022. Important roles of thiols in methylmercury uptake and translocation by rice plants. Environmental Science & Technology 56, 6765–6773.

Harada, M., 1995. Minamata disease: methylmercury poisoning in Japan caused by environmental pollution. Critical Reviews in Toxicology 25, 1–24.

Higueras, P., Oyarzun, R., Biester, H., et al., 2003. A first insight into mercury distribution and speciation in soils from the Almaden mining district, Spain. Journal of Geochemical Exploration 80, 95–104.

Hsu-Kim, H., Eckley, C. S., Achá, D., et al., 2018. Challenges and opportunities for managing aquatic mercury pollution in altered landscapes. Ambio 47, 141–169.

Huang, J. H., Shetaya, W. H., Osterwalder, S., 2020. Determination of (bio)-available mercury in soils: A review. Environmental Pollution 263, 114323.

Li, Y., Cai, Y., 2013. Progress in the study of mercury methylation and demethylation in aquatic environments. Chinese Science Bulletin 58, 177–185.

Lin, H., Lu, X., Liang, L., Gu, B., 2015. Cysteine inhibits mercury methylation by geobactersulfurreducens PCA mutant ΔomcBESTZ. Environmental Science & Technology Letters 2, 144–148.

Lin, C. J., Pehkonen, S. O., 1997. Aqueous free radical chemistry of mercury in the presence of iron oxides and ambient aerosol. Atmospheric Environment 31, 4125–4137.

Liu, Y., Johs, A., Bi, L., et al., 2018. Unraveling microbial communities associated with methylmercury production in paddy soils. Environmental Science & Technology 52, 13110–13118.

Mazrui, N., Seelen, E., King'ondu, C. K., et al., 2018. The precipitation, growth and stability of mercury sulfide nanoparticles formed in the presence of marine dissolved organic matter. Environmental Science: Processes & Impacts 20, 642–656.

Meng, B., Feng, X., Qiu, G., et al., 2011. The process of methylmercury accumulation in rice (Oryza sativa L.). Environmental Science & Technology 45, 2711–2717.

Meng, B., Feng, X., Qiu, G., et al., 2014. Localization and speciation of mercury in brown rice with implications for pan-Asian public health. Environmental Science & Technology 48, 7974–7981.

Moreau, J. W., Gionfriddo, C. M., Krabbenhoft, D. P., et al., 2015. The effect of natural organic matter on mercury methylation by desulfobulbus propionicus 1pr3. Frontiers in Microbiology 6, 1–15.

Parks, J. M., Johs, A., Podar, M., et al., 2013. The genetic basis for bacterial mercury methylation. Science 339, 1332–1335.

Poulin, B. A., Gerbig, C. A., Kim, C. S., et al., 2017. Effects of sulfide concentration and dissolved organic matter characteristics on the structure of nanocolloidal metacinnabar. Environmental Science & Technology 51, 13133–13142.

Qiu, G., Feng, X., Wang, S., et al., 2005. Mercury and methylmercury in riparian soil, sediments, mine-waste calcines, and moss from abandoned Hg mines in east Guizhou province, southwestern China. Applied Geochemistry 20, 627–638.

Renneberg, A. J., Dudas, M. J., 2001. Transformations of elemental mercury to inorganic and organic forms in mercury and hydrocarbon co-contaminated soils. Chemosphere 45, 1103–1109.

Richard, J. H., Bischoff, C., Ahrens, C. G. M., et al., 2016. Mercury (II) reduction and co-precipitation of metallic mercury on hydrous ferric oxide in contaminated groundwater. Science of the Total Environment 539, 36–44.

Schaefer, J. K., Morel, F. M. M., 2009. High methylation rates of mercury bound to cysteine by *Geobacter sulfurreducens*. Nature Geoscience 2, 123–126.

Schaefer, J. K., Rocks, S. S., Zheng, W., et al., 2011. Active transport, substrate specificity, and methylation of Hg(II) in anaerobic bacteria. Proceedings of the National Academy of Sciences 108, 8714–8719.

Skyllberg, U., 2008. Competition among thiols and inorganic sulfides and polysulfides for Hg and MeHg in wetland soils and sediments under suboxic conditions: Illumination of controversies and implications for MeHg net production. Journal of Geophysical Research-Biogeosciences, 113.

Tiffreau, C., Lützenkirchen, J., Behra, P., 1995. Modeling the adsorption of mercury(II) on (hydr)oxides: I. amorphous iron oxide and α-quartz. Journal of Colloid and Interface Science 172, 82–93.

Vishnivetskaya, T. A., Hu, H., Van Nostrand, et al., 2018. Microbial community structure with trends in methylation gene diversity and abundance in mercury-contaminated rice paddy soils in Guizhou, China. Environmental Science: Processes & Impacts 20, 673–685.

Wang, J., Feng, X., Anderson, C. W., et al., 2011. Ammonium thiosulphate enhanced phytoextraction from mercury contaminated soil – Results from a greenhouse study. Journal of Hazardous Materials 186, 119–127.

Wang, J. X., Feng, X. B., Anderson, C. W. N., et al., 2012. Remediation of mercury contaminated sites – A review. Journal of Hazardous Materials 221, 1–18.

Wang, J., Man, Y., Yin, R., et al., 2022. Isotopic and spectroscopic investigation of mercury accumulation in houttuynia cordata colonizing historically contaminated soil. Environmental Science & Technology 56, 7997–8007.

Wang, J., Shaheen, S. M., Jing, M., et al., 2021. Mobilization, methylation, and demethylation of mercury in a paddy soil under systematic redox changes. Environmental Science & Technology 55, 10133–10141.

Wu, Q., Hu, H., Meng, B., et al., 2020. Methanogenesis is an important process in controlling MeHg concentration in rice paddy soils affected by mining activities. Environmental Science & Technology 54, 13517–13526.

Yin, R., Feng, X., Meng, B., 2013. Stable mercury isotope variation in rice plants (*Oryza sativa* L.) from the Wanshan mercury mining district, SW China. Environmental Science & Technology 47, 2238–2245.

Yin, R., Gu, C., Feng, X., et al., 2016. Distribution and geochemical speciation of soil mercury in Wanshan Hg mine: Effects of cultivation. Geoderma 272, 32–38.

Zahir, F., Rizwi, S. J., Haq, S. K., et al., 2005. Low dose mercury toxicity and human health. Environmental Toxicology and Pharmacology 20, 351–360.

Zhang, H., Feng, X., Larssen, T., et al., 2010a. Bioaccumulation of methylmercury versus inorganic mercury in rice (*Oryza sativa* L.) grain. Environmental Science & Technology 44, 4499–4504.

Zhang, H., Feng, X.B., Larssen, T., et al., 2010b. In Inland China, rice, rather than fish, is the major pathway for methylmercury exposure. Environmental Health Perspectives 118, 1183–1188.

Zhao, L., Chen, H., Lu, X., et al., 2017. Contrasting effects of dissolved organic matter on mercury methylation by *Geobacter sulfurreducens* PCA and *Desulfovibrio desulfuricans* ND132. Environmental Science & Technology 51, 10468–10475.

2 Global Mercury Distribution in Surface Soil

Xun Wang, Wei Yuan, and Xinbin Feng

2.1 INTRODUCTION

As a global pollutant, Hg accumulating in remote regions poses an increasing concern worldwide (Fu et al., 2016; Wang et al., 2020; Obrist et al., 2021; Zhou et al., 2023). The ratification of the Minamata Convention on Mercury in 2017 is widely considered to have successfully protected human health and the environment from the detrimental effects of Hg (Selin et al., 2018). Assessment of the benefits of policies to reduce human and wildlife exposure to Hg should be based on a complete understanding of Hg cycling (Selin, 2018). Knowledge of the global spatial distribution of Hg concentrations in soils is critical for quantifying legacy Hg emissions from soil to the atmosphere (Selin, 2018), estimating Hg runoff from uplands to aquatic environments (Lindberg et al., 2007), and assessing the potential risks of human and wildlife Hg exposure globally (Li et al., 2015).

The concentrations, distribution, and reservoirs of soil Hg would be best estimated from representative soil samples collected in a global observational network. However, such an approach is challenging to accomplish due to sampling limitations and the costs associated with global research. Recently, Liu et al. (2023) investigated surface soil Hg concentrations and distributions based on samples from 17 countries. Regression modeling using a large geological database is an alternative approach for reliably reconstructing global Hg concentrations and distributions in soil. The coupling of Hg concentration and distribution data for China and the United States (e.g., Smith et al., 2014; Wang et al., 2015; Schuster et al., 2018) with global organic carbon, meteorological, and anthropogenic Hg emissions data, as well as other basic datasets, would allow us to gain insight into the contributing sources and pathways of Hg accumulation in soil on a global scale (Wang et al., 2019a).

Such a methodology has been applied in recent years to assess surface soil Hg concentrations and distributions on a global scale (Wang et al., 2019a), particularly for China (Wang et al., 2016a; Zhang et al., 2020), Europe (Panagos et al., 2021), and the United States (Olson et al., 2022). Precipitation, vegetation cover, organic matter, and extreme weather (e.g., droughts and forest fires) are regarded as the dominant factors forcing spatial Hg distribution in surface soil (Wang et al., 2019a; Yuan et al., 2022). Because these factors are controlled by global climate change, it is important to focus on the variation in soil Hg storage and global Hg cycling under climate change scenarios.

Surface soil constitutes some of the largest reservoirs of actively cycling Hg on Earth, accounting for three-fourths of the Hg budget in epigenetic systems (Mason

 DOI: 10.1201/9781003404941-2

et al., 2012; Sonke et al., 2023). Previous studies have shown that surface soils store approximately 235–1150 Gg of Hg globally (Smith-Downey et al., 2010; Amos et al., 2013; Wang et al., 2019a). Half of the Hg stored in surface soil is in South America (20%), North America (19%), East Asia (6%), and Southeast Asia (5%) (Wang et al., 2019a). Such data are critical for a complete understanding of Hg cycling. However, great uncertainties remain, limiting our understanding of global Hg cycling.

2.2   Hg DISTRIBUTION IN GLOBAL SURFACE SOILS

2.2.1   Hg IN GLOBAL SOILS

Field data from standardized global analyses are critical for reducing uncertainties when analyzing the environmental drivers of soil Hg accumulation and predicting global Hg distribution. Recently, Liu et al. (2023) investigated global surface soil Hg concentrations in 17 countries on six continents in different climate zones. They found that the Hg content of surface soil ranges from 3.8 to 618.2 (average 74.0) ng g^{-1} worldwide. Climate zones, biomes, and land-use types significantly influence the surface soil Hg content (Liu et al., 2023). Generally, soil Hg content was found to be high in temperate and continental areas at 80–100 ng g^{-1}, 2–5 times higher than in tropical, arid, and polar areas. The highest soil Hg content was measured in forest ecosystems, followed by moss-dominated open areas, grasslands, and shrublands (Liu et al., 2023). This pattern was attributed to the highest Hg biomass deposition in forest ecosystems into surface soil (Wang et al., 2019b). Soil Hg content was also higher in urban areas than in these natural ecosystems, likely due to soil contamination from human activities (Liu et al., 2023).

Liu et al. (2023) found that 38.0% of the soil Hg variation was explained by the environmental variables investigated. Soil properties and climate variables are the most important factors explaining soil Hg variation. Soil properties play important roles in soil retention via adsorption and reduction (Hararuk et al., 2013; Xue et al., 2019). Solar radiation, annual temperature, and precipitation were found to influence atmospheric Hg dry deposition patterns via the vegetation distribution and wet deposition patterns via rainfall amounts (Wang et al., 2019a).

Liu et al. (2023) used a machine learning-based random forest algorithm and global datasets of environmental drivers to predict the global Hg distribution (Figure 2.1). They identified hotspots of soil Hg accumulation in East Asia and Northern Hemispheric temperate and boreal regions, including central Europe and eastern United States, and tropical areas, including Southeast Asia, the Amazon basin, and central Africa (Liu et al., 2023). These hotspots are influenced by intensive human activities and climate–vegetation patterns. Human activities induce high anthropogenic emissions rates and cropland expansion, which may be responsible for hotspots in East Asia, central Europe, and eastern United States (Liu et al., 2023). Elevated vegetation biomass input and slower litterfall decomposition result in surface soil Hg accumulation in most Northern Hemispheric temperate and boreal regions (Liu et al., 2023). Although Hg accumulation hotspots are observed in tropical areas, soils in these regions have depleted Hg concentrations (Wang et al., 2016b;

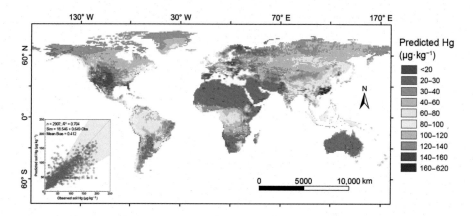

FIGURE 2.1 Predicted global Hg distribution in surface soils by a machine learning algorithm (random forest modeling). (Reprinted with permission from (Liu et al., 2023.)

Liu et al., 2023). A recent sample plot investigation showed that microbial reduction induced elevated emissions from the soil surface, reducing the soil Hg reservoir (Xia et al., 2022; Yuan et al., 2023).

A global standardized field survey by Liu et al. (2023) suggested that the global Hg distribution in surface soils is driven by multidimensional environmental variables via both direct and indirect effects and revealed three underlying mechanisms regarding sources and sinks of Hg in surface soils. Multidimensional environmental variables can be used to predict global Hg distribution in surface soils; however, uncertainties remain (Liu et al., 2023). For example, large uncertainties in Hg concentrations were found in India, the Indochina Peninsula, southern South America, South Africa, and the region between central and northern Africa, which were attributed to heterogeneity in sampling locations and the horizontal resolution of environmental variables (Liu et al., 2023). Further field measurements of soil Hg content in different regions and greater horizontal resolution of global data could reduce these uncertainties.

Wang et al. (2019a) also mapped global surface soil Hg distribution using stable-Hg isotopic analysis and geospatial data. They estimated that 1088 ± 379 Gg of Hg is stored in surface soil globally, of which 32% resides in tropical/subtropical forest regions; 23% in temperate/boreal forest regions; 28% in grasslands, steppes, and shrublands; 7% in tundra; and 10% in deserts and xeric shrublands (Figure 2.2). Although relatively high soil Hg concentrations were observed in temperate forests, the low forest coverage (ninth largest) led to an intermediate range of Hg storage among the 14 terrestrial ecoregions. The boreal ecoregion had the fourth largest forest coverage, where low soil density resulted in the fifth largest store of surface soil Hg (Wang et al., 2019a).

Interestingly, Wang et al. (2019a) found that Hg storage was greater in tropical/subtropical forest regions, which they attributed to higher litterfall driving greater Hg input to the forest soil. Global litterfall-induced Hg deposition is estimated at $1000-1200$ Mg yr^{-1}, of which ~70% occurs in tropical/subtropical forest ecosystems (Wang et al., 2016b; Zhou and Obrist, 2021a). These results are significantly different from the relatively low Hg concentrations and Hg pool estimated from field

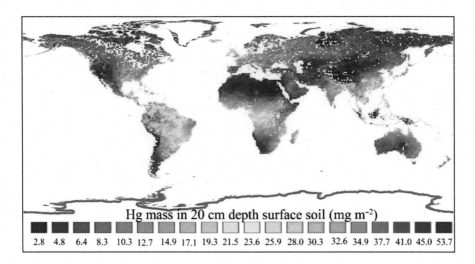

Hg mass in 20 cm depth surface soil (mg m⁻²)

2.8 4.8 6.4 8.3 10.3 12.7 14.9 17.1 19.3 21.5 23.6 25.9 28.0 30.3 32.6 34.9 37.7 41.0 45.0 53.7

FIGURE 2.2 Simulated Hg mass in top 20 cm of soils across the globe. (Reprinted with permission from Wang et al., 2019a.)

measurements by Liu et al. (2023), as mentioned above. The dominant cause of these differences is the uncertainties in Hg reemission occurring in tropical forest (Yuan et al., 2023). Currently, measurements of soil Hg deposition and reemission in tropical forests are limited, particularly air–soil Hg flux measurements. Future studies of soil Hg deposition and reemission in tropical forests are necessary to obtain more reasonable estimates of global soil Hg distribution patterns.

2.2.2 Hg in American Soil

Olson et al. (2022) analyzed soil Hg based on 4857 samples collected from sites across the United States. The Hg concentration in surface soil was 35 ± 5 ng g⁻¹, higher than that in C horizon soil (27 ± 4 ng g⁻¹) (Olson et al., 2022) (Figure 2.3). Regionally, northeastern and northwestern United States had significantly higher surface soil Hg contents than other regions, mainly measuring > 50 ng g⁻¹. This pattern may be attributed to development (i.e., urbanization), planted vegetation cover, and the presence of megacities,which typically release high levels of Hg through processes such as coal combustion and waste incineration (Olson et al., 2022). Forest soil had significantly higher Hg concentrations (43 ng g⁻¹) than all other ecosystems (Olson et al., 2022), which emphasizes the important role played by forest canopies in mediating Hg deposition through foliar uptake, litterfall, and throughfall (Wang et al., 2016b; Yuan et al., 2019a; Zhou et al., 2021b). In addition, extensive canopy shading in forest areas reduces solar radiation and temperature, limiting surface soil Hg reemission (Zhu et al., 2016; Yuan et al., 2019b).

Olson et al. (2022) used a generalized additive model to estimate the Hg concentrations of each soil layer (Figure 2.3), which ranged from 33 ng g⁻¹ in topsoil to 21 ng g⁻¹ in the deepest layers. Surface soil showed high spatial heterogeneity in Hg concentrations, whereas deeper soil showed low variability. This pattern suggests

FIGURE 2.3 Mercury concentration in the top 5 cm of soil of the conterminous United States. (Reprinted with permission from Olson et al., 2022.)

that although litterfall and throughfall are important determinants of the Hg concentrations of surface soils, soil characteristics are more important in deeper soil layers (Olson et al. 2022).

Based on data obtained from the Conterminous United States Soil Database, Olson et al. (2022) estimated that Hg mass was highest in surface soils, at 11.8 ± 0.2 Gg within the top 5 cm, 44 Gg in the top 20 cm, and 158.0 ± 1.8 Gg in the top 1 m (Figure 2.4). Generally, the eastern half of the United States has greater Hg mass than the western half, with the exception of the west coast (Olson et al., 2022). The soil Hg density pattern was significantly correlated with that of soil organic carbon,

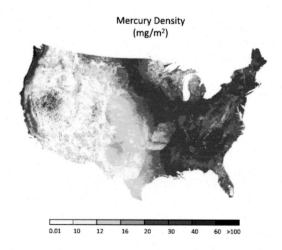

FIGURE 2.4 Mercury areal densities in the top 1 m of soil of the conterminous United States. (Reprinted with permission from Olson et al., 2022.)

suggesting that soil Hg is predominantly derived from exogenous inputs. Lower Hg/titanium ratios also suggested that 62–95% of soil Hg is derived from non-parental sources (Olson et al., 2022).

Variation in the physical characteristics of soils of different land cover types can lead to land cover effects on soil Hg concentrations and distribution patterns (Olson et al., 2022). Soil organic carbon and bedrock types have notable impacts on soil Hg pool calculations. Overall, Hg areal densities are highest in mixed and deciduous forests, pastures, croplands, and developed land and lowest in grasslands, shrublands, and barren land (Olson et al., 2022).

2.2.3 Hg in European Soil

Ballabio et al. (2021) determined Hg concentrations in European topsoil based on 21,591 samples from 26 European Union countries, using deep neural network learning models (Figure 2.5). The overall average topsoil Hg concentration was 55.4 ± 4.9 (range: 0.054–49,200) ng g^{-1}. The median topsoil Hg concentration was 23.3 ng g^{-1}, and the 99th percentile level was 429 ng g^{-1}. Given that the highest soil

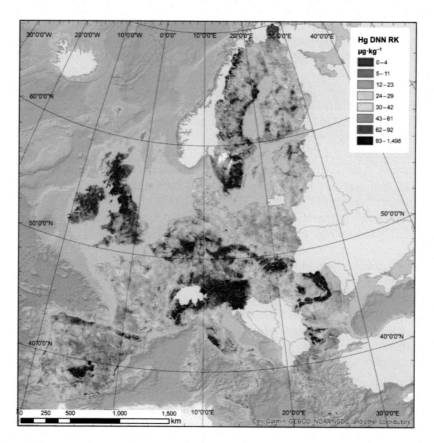

FIGURE 2.5 Top soil Hg concentrations (μg kg^{-1} or ng g^{-1}) across 26 EU countries, estimated by deep neural network–regression kriging. (Reprinted with permission from Ballabio et al., 2021.)

concentration (49 µg g^{-1}) was determined for soils collected near the Almadén Hg mine, the median value is thought to represent European soil Hg levels (Ballabio et al., 2021).

Climate appears to have a strong influence on the distribution of Hg on a continental scale (Wang et al., 2019a, 2019b). Elevated soil Hg concentrations prevail in cold climate regions such as high-latitude and high-altitude areas (Ballabio et al., 2021), likely due to the large proportion of atmospheric Hg bound to soil organic matter (Obrist et al., 2011; Jiskra et al., 2015). Although wet atmospheric deposition (rain and snowfall) is high in southern Europe, topsoil Hg concentrations in Sweden (60 ± 53 ng g^{-1}) were higher than those in Italy (49 ± 45 ng g^{-1}) (Ballabio et al., 2021). In regions where woodlands are the prevalent land cover type and humus-rich topsoil dominates, Hg concentrations are elevated despite lower inputs by wet atmospheric deposition, suggesting that forest ecosystem soils act as Hg reservoirs (Fu et al., 2010; Ballabio et al., 2021). Additionally, mountainous areas of Europe (above 600 m a.s.l.) had significantly higher (70 ± 62 ng g^{-1}) topsoil Hg concentrations than lowlands (32 ± 29 ng g^{-1}), implying increased atmospheric Hg uptake by vegetation with altitude (Wang et al., 2019b).

Soil properties can also determine the topsoil Hg distribution (Wu et al., 2023). The increase in topsoil Hg concentrations with latitude and elevation may be at least partly explained by increased organic carbon concentrations (Ballabio et al., 2021). Ballabio et al. (2021) suggested that iron oxides and clay minerals act as sorption sites for Hg. Furthermore, the positive relationship between the topsoil Hg content and soil pH indicates that Hg accumulation increases with pH in European soil (Ballabio et al., 2021). The pH may influence the soil Hg reservoir by reducing soil reemissions. Moreover, bedrock condition also affects soil Hg concentrations, such that the highest Hg contents are found in mineralized regions characterized by subduction zones and volcanic deposits (Schlüter, 2000).

Panagos et al. (2021) estimated the Hg distribution in topsoil in Europe using a machine learning model based on previous work by Ballabio et al. (2021); they further modeled the topsoil Hg pool, which was found to total approximately 44.8 Gg, with an average density of 103 g ha^{-1} (Figure 2.6). The soil Hg pool is determined by the soil Hg concentration and soil bulk density. For example, the high bulk density (>1.25 t m^{-3}) in the Baltic states and Denmark results in higher Hg stocks compared to their concentrations. Slovakia, which is almost three times smaller than Greece, has higher Hg stocks due to much the higher Hg density (152 vs. 50 g ha^{-1}). Similarly, Slovenia is more than three times smaller than Lithuania and has a higher total Hg stock due to its Hg density (226 vs. 68 g ha^{-1}) (Panagos et al., 2021). Except for the bulk density effect, the Hg pool distribution pattern is comparable to the soil Hg concentration. Elevated soil Hg concentrations and a larger Hg pool were observed in mountain areas (Panagos et al., 2021; Ballabio et al., 2021), perhaps due to active mining in Europe, which leads to mining waste, metal extraction and refinement residues, and increased atmospheric deposition (Ferrara et al., 1997). The highest Hg deposit was found in the Almadén district of Spain, which contributes almost one-third of total global Hg production (Hylander and Meili, 2003). Chlor-alkali plants and coal combustion also cause soil Hg contamination, depending on past or present local pollution activities (Panagos et al., 2021).

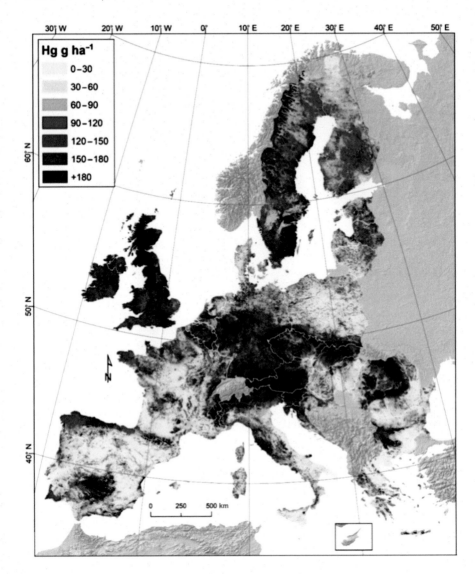

FIGURE 2.6 Map of Hg stock (g ha⁻¹) in European topsoil. (Reprinted with permission from Panagos et al., 2021.)

2.2.4 Hg in Chinese Soil

Wang et al. (2016a) investigated the Hg concentration distribution (ng g⁻¹) in surface soil (0–20 cm) in China (Figure 2.7). The Hg content in 0–20 cm of surface soil was found to vary according to land use type, with forests, shrublands, savannas/grasslands, croplands, and other land use types containing mean concentrations of 119–211, 61–197, 80–82, 80–82, and 31–162 ng g⁻¹ of Hg, respectively (Wang et al., 2016a). The surface soil Hg concentration was higher in southeast China, where the annual precipitation exceeds 800 mm and there is greater litterfall deposition (Wang et al., 2016a).

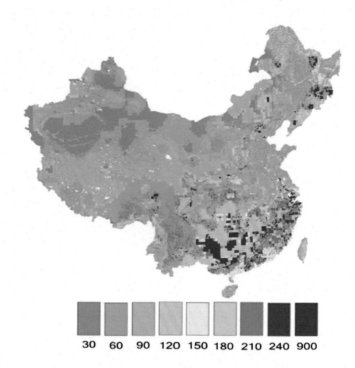

30   60   90   120   150   180   210   240   900

FIGURE 2.7 Updated Hg concentrations (ng g^{-1}) in surface soil (0–20 cm) of China. (Reprinted with permission from Wang et al., 2016a.)

Atmospheric Hg deposition fluxes in western China, such as those on the Tibetan plateau and in Xinjiang Province, ranged from 0.74 to 7.89 µg m^{-2}yr^{-1} and were at least one order of magnitude (71.2 µg m^{-2} yr^{-1}) lower than in East Asia (forest cover) (Zhang et al., 2012; Luo et al., 2016; Wang et al., 2017). Zhang et al. (2012) highlighted that vegetation cover types were associated with the soil Hg distribution in China. This pattern can be attributed to atmospheric Hg^0 deposited in terrestrial ecosystems, which occurs predominantly via foliage assimilation (Zhou and Obrist, 2021a). The desert region in northwestern China had the lowest soil Hg concentrations because of the barren soils (Zhang et al.. 2020).

The presence of any soil cover decreases the atmospheric Hg emission flux compared to bare soil, which leads to greater Hg sequestration in surface soil. Wang et al. (2016a) estimated the spatial distribution of the annual air–soil fluxes in China and identified three high-emission flux regions: croplands/grasslands in southern and southwestern China, croplands in northern China, and grasslands in northern China (Wang et al., 2016a). Given the high canopy shading and low Hg emission fluxes in forest ecosystems, these regions represented the dominant Hg reservoir in China.

2.3 Hg DISTRIBUTION IN RICE ECOLOGICAL SYSTEMS OF CHINA

The mean surface soil Hg concentration in rice ecosystems in China was 67.5 ± 51.3 ng g^{-1}, with a median value of 52.8 ng g^{-1} (Table 2.1). The soil Hg concentration showed distinct spatial heterogeneity. Soils in southern China had the highest Hg

TABLE 2.1

Soil Hg Concentration (ng g⁻¹) in Rice System of China

Province	Mean Soil THg Concentration (ng g⁻¹)	Median Soil Hg Concentration (ng g⁻¹)	N
Guizhou	135.0 ± 86.6	115.6	88
Hunan	115.2 ± 28.8	111.5	33
Jiangxi	106.8 ± 71.7	79.6	39
Guangdong	96.3 ± 42.6	88.3	79
Zhejiang	89.7 ± 58.4	67.4	58
Fujian	85.1 ± 48.8	76.2	34
Anhui	84.1 ± 65.0	57.5	43
Hubei	63.7 ± 35.9	51.5	41
Guangxi	62.9 ± 46.2	46	30
Chongqing	51.3 ± 29.6	51	17
Sichuan	48.7 ± 20.4	43	37
Jiangsu	38.5 ± 31.9	26.7	49
Jilin	27.8 ± 7.8	29.1	15
Heilongjiang	27.0 ± 8.2	25.7	90
Xinjiang	25.8 ± 19.4	16.6	26
Total	67.5 ± 51.3	52.8	679

concentrations, particularly in Guizhou, Hunan, and Jiangxi Provinces (>100 ng g⁻¹). The rice yield in these three provinces is >20% of the total rice yield of China. Currently, only <3% of this rice carries a potential health risk due to high Hg concentrations (Zhao et al., 2019). Elevated soil Hg concentrations in southern China promote Hg emissions to the atmosphere and into rice grains, increasing future potential risks (Liu et al., 2019). The mining of nonferrous metals such as Hg, lead, and zinc in Guizhou, Hunan, and Jiangxi Provinces has led to extraordinarily high soil Hg concentrations in rice ecosystems (>10 µg g⁻¹) (Xia et al., 2020; Xu et al., 2020). Rice Hg and methylmercury (MeHg) concentrations in these areas also exceed the Hg limits for food (Xia et al., 2020; Xu et al., 2020). Future studies should evaluate the potential risks of high rice Hg concentrations caused by elevated soil Hg levels in mining areas.

The soil Hg concentrations in the rice ecosystems of central China, including Anhui, Hubei, and Jiangsu Provinces, was 38–85 ng g⁻¹,which is comparable to the background surface soil Hg concentration in China (Wang et al., 2019a), suggesting a limited ecological risk of Hg pollution. Additionally, northeastern (Jilin and Heilongjiang) and northwestern (Xinjiang) China had extremely low soil Hg concentrations in rice ecosystems (<30 ng g⁻¹). The tillage method, climate, and soil parent materials are regarded as the dominant factors inducing soil Hg differences in the rice ecosystems of China (Zhao et al., 2019).

Future studies should investigate the soil Hg and MeHg concentrations in rice ecosystems. Soil legacy Hg emissions into the atmosphere and migration to grain could influence the risk of consuming rice contaminated with Hg. Studies of rice Hg pollution should focus not only on grain Hg and MeHg concentrations but also on the Hg concentration and form in soil.

REFERENCES

Amos, H. M., Jacob, D. J., Streets, D. G., et al., 2013. Legacy impacts of all-time anthropogenic emissions on the global mercury cycle. Global Biogeochemical Cycles 27, 410–421.

Ballabio, C., Jiskra, M., Osterwalder, S., et al., 2021. A spatial assessment of mercury content in the European Union topsoil. Science of the Total Environment 769, 144755.

Ferrara, R., Maserti, B. E., Andersson, M., et al., 1997. Mercury degassing rate from mineralized areas in the Mediterranean basin. Water Air and Soil Pollution 93, 59–66.

Fu, X., Feng, X., Zhu, W., et al., 2010. Elevated atmospheric deposition and dynamics of mercury in a remote upland forest of southwestern China. Environmental Pollution 158, 2324–33.

Fu, X., Zhu, W., Zhang, H., et al., 2016. Depletion of atmospheric gaseous elemental mercury by plant uptake at Mt. Changbai, Northeast China. Atmospheric Chemistry Physics 16, 12861–12873.

Hararuk, O., Obrist, D., Luo, Y., 2013. Modelling the sensitivity of soil mercury storage to climate-induced changes in soil carbon pools. Biogeosciences 10, 2393–2407.

Hylander, L. D., Meili, M., 2003. 500 years of mercury production: global annual inventory by region until 2000 and associated emissions. Science of the Total Environment 304, 13–27.

Jiskra, M., Wiederhold, J. G., Skyllberg, U., et al., 2015. Mercury deposition and re-emission pathways in boreal forest soils investigated with Hg isotope signatures. Environmental Science & Technology 49, 7188–96.

Li, P., Du, B., Chan, H., et al., 2015. Human inorganic mercury exposure, renal effects and possible pathways in Wanshan mercury mining area, China. Environmental Research 140, 198–204.

Lindberg, S., Bullock, R., Ebinghaus, R., et al., 2007. A synthesis of progress and uncertainties in attributing the sources of mercury in deposition. Ambio 36, 19–32.

Liu, Y., Guo, L., Yang, Z., et al., 2023. Multidimensional drivers of mercury distribution in global surface soils: Insights from a global standardized field survey. Environmental Science & Technology 57, 12442–12452.

Liu, M., Zhang, Q., Cheng, M., et al., 2019. Rice life cycle-based global mercury biotransport and human methylmercury exposure. Nature Communications 10, 5164.

Luo, Y., Duan, L., Driscoll, C. T., et al., 2016. Foliage/atmosphere exchange of mercury in a subtropical coniferous forest in south China. Journal of Geophysical Research-Biogeosciences 121, 2006–2016.

Mason, R. P., Choi, A. L., Fitzgerald, W. F., et al., 2012. Mercury biogeochemical cycling in the ocean and policy implications. Environmental Research 119, 101–117.

Obrist, D., Johnson, D. W., Lindberg, S. E., et al., 2011. Mercury distribution across 14 US forests. Part I: Spatial patterns of concentrations in biomass, litter, and soils. Environmental Science & Technology 45, 3974–3981.

Obrist, D., Roy, E. M., Harrison, J. L., et al., 2021. Previously unaccounted atmospheric mercury deposition in a midlatitude deciduous forest. Proceedings of the National Academy of Sciences of the United States of America 118, e2105477118.

Olson, C. I., Geyman, B. M., Thackray, C. P., et al., 2022. Mercury in soils of the conterminous United States: Patterns and pools. Environmental Research Letters 17, 074030.

Panagos, P., Jiskra, M., Borrelli, P., et al., 2021. Mercury in European topsoils: Anthropogenic sources, stocks and fluxes. Environmental Research 201, 111556.

Schlüter, K., 2000. Review: Evaporation of mercury from soils. An integration and synthesis of current knowledge. Environmental Geology 39, 249–271.

Schuster, P. F., Schaefer, K. M., Aiken, G.R., et al., 2018. Permafrost stores a globally significant amount of mercury. Geophysical Research Letters 45, 1463–1471.

Selin, N. E., 2018. A proposed global metric to aid mercury pollution policy. Science 360, 607–609.

Selin, H., Keane, S. E., Wang, S., et al., 2018. Linking science and policy to support the implementation of the Minamata Convention on Mercury. Ambio 47, 198–215.

Smith, D. B., Cannon, W. F., Woodruff, L. G., et al., 2014. Geochemical and mineralogical maps for soils of the conterminous United States, in Open-File Report. Reston, VA, 399.

Smith-Downey, N. V., Sunderland, E. M., Jacob, D. J., 2010. Anthropogenic impacts on global storage and emissions of mercury from terrestrial soils: Insights from a new global model. Journal of Geophysical Research-Biogeosciences 115, G03008.

Sonke, J. E., Angot, H., Zhang, Y., et al., 2023. Global change effects on biogeochemical mercury cycling. Ambio 52, 853–876.

Wang, X., Lin, C. J., Yuan, W., et al., 2016a. Emission-dominated gas exchange of elemental mercury vapor over natural surfaces in China. Atmospheric Chemistry and Physics 16, 11125–11143.

Wang, X., Bao, Z., Lin, C. J., et al., 2016b. Assessment of global mercury deposition through litterfall. Environmental Science & Technology 50, 8548–57.

Wang, X., Liu, X., Han, Z., et al., 2015. Concentration and distribution of mercury in drainage catchment sediment and alluvial soil of China. Journal of Geochemical Exploration 154, 32–48.

Wang, X., Luo, J., Yin, R., et al., 2017. Using mercury isotopes to understand mercury accumulation in the montane forest floor of the eastern Tibetan plateau. Environmental Science & Technology 51, 801–809.

Wang, X., Luo, J., Yuan, W., et al., 2020. Global warming accelerates uptake of atmospheric mercury in regions experiencing glacier retreat. Proceedings of the National Academy of Sciences of the United States of America 117, 2049–2055.

Wang, X., Yuan, W., Lin, C. J., et al., 2019a. Climate and vegetation as primary drivers for global mercury storage in surface soil. Environmental Science & Technology 53, 10665–10675.

Wang, X., Yuan, W., Lu, Z. Y., et al., 2019b. Effects of precipitation on mercury accumulation on subtropical montane forest floor: Implications on climate forcing. Journal of Geophysical Research-Biogeosciences 124, 959–972.

Wu, X., Fu, X., Zhang, H., et al., 2023. Changes in atmospheric gaseous elemental mercury concentrations and isotopic compositions at Mt. Changbai during 2015–2021 and Mt. Ailao during 2017–2021 in China. Journal of Geophysical Research-Atmospheres 128, e2022JD037749.

Xia, J., Wang, J., Zhang, L., et al., 2020. Screening of native low mercury accumulation crops in a mercury-polluted mining region: Agricultural planning to manage mercury risk in farming communities. Journal of Cleaner Production 262, 121324.

Xia, S., Yuan, W., Lin, L., et al., 2022. Latitudinal gradient for mercury accumulation and isotopic evidence for post-depositional processes among three tropical forests in Southwest China. J Hazard Mater 429, 128295.

Xue, W., Kwon, S. Y., Grasby, S. E., et al., 2019. Anthropogenic influences on mercury in Chinese soil and sediment revealed by relationships with total organic carbon. Environmental Pollution 255, 113186.

Xu, X., Han, J., Pang, J., et al., 2020. Methylmercury and inorganic mercury in Chinese commercial rice: Implications for overestimated human exposure and health risk. Environmental Pollution 258, 113706.

Yuan, W., Sommar, J., Lin, C. J., et al., 2019a. Stable isotope evidence shows re-emission of elemental mercury vapor occurring after reductive loss from foliage. Environmental Science & Technology 53, 651–660.

Yuan, W., Wang, X., Lin, C. J., et al., 2019b. Process factors driving dynamic exchange of elemental mercury vapor over soil in broadleaf forest ecosystems. Atmospheric Environment 219, 117047.

Yuan, W., Wang, X., Lin, C. J., et al., 2022. Impacts of extreme weather on mercury uptake and storage in subtropical forest ecosystems. Journal of Geophysical Research-Biogeosciences 127, e2021JG006681.

Yuan, W., Wang, X., Lin, C. J., et al., 2023. Deposition and re-emission of atmospheric elemental mercury over the tropical forest floor. Environmental Science & Technology 57, 10686–10695.

Zhang, Q., Huang, J., Wang, F., et al., 2012. Mercury distribution and deposition in glacier snow over western China. Environmental Science & Technology 46, 5404–5413.

Zhang, Z., Li, G., Yang, L., et al., 2020. Mercury distribution in the surface soil of China is potentially driven by precipitation, vegetation cover and organic matter. Environmental Sciences Europe 32, 89.

Zhao, H., Yan, H., Zhang, L., et al., 2019. Mercury contents in rice and potential health risks across China. Environment International 126, 406–412.

Zhou, J., Bollen, S. W., Roy, E. M., et al., 2023. Comparing ecosystem gaseous elemental mercury fluxes over a deciduous and coniferous forest. Nature Communications 14, 2722.

Zhou, J., Obrist, D., 2021a. Global mercury assimilation by vegetation. Environmental Science & Technology 55, 14245–14257.

Zhou, J., Obrist, D., Dastoor, A., et al., 2021b. Vegetation uptake of mercury and impacts on global cycling. Nature Reviews Earth & Environment 2, 269–284.

Zhu, W., Lin, C. J., Wang, X., et al., 2016. Global observations and modeling of atmosphere-surface exchange of elemental mercury: A critical review. Atmospheric Chemistry and Physics 16, 4451–4480.

3 Mercury Contamination in Mercury Mining Area in China

Xiaohang Xu, Jicheng Xia, Jianxu Wang, and Xinbin Feng

3.1 INTRODUCTION

Mercury (Hg) is a heavy metal pollutant of global concern. One of the major anthropogenic Hg contamination sources is Hg mining and retorting activities (Essa et al., 2002; Fernández-Martínez et al., 2015). There are three mercuriferous belts distributed along global plate boundaries. Many large and super-large Hg mines are located at those mercuriferous belts, such as Almadén Hg mine in Spain, Mt. Amiata Hg mine in Italy, Wanshan Hg mine in China, and California and Nevada Hg mines in the United States. China is enriched with Hg mineral resources, and its reserve ranks third in the world. The exploration of Hg resources in China dates back to 2000 BC. At that time, cinnabar was used as a kind of medicine. Today, cinnabar is still used as an important component in Tibetan medicine, red pigment, and preservatives (Jiang et al., 2006).

Mercury mining and retorting activities produce a huge amount of Hg waste (e.g., calcine) which is abandoned to the environment (Figure 3.1) (Gamboa-Herrera et al., 2021). Meantime, those activities also release Hg and its compounds into the

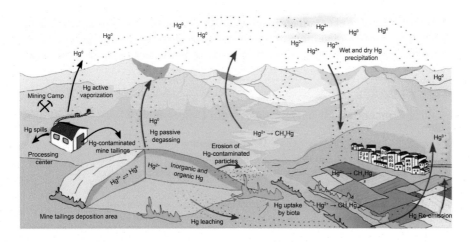

FIGURE 3.1 The impact of Hg mining on the local environment. (Reprinted with permission from Gamboa-Herrera et al., 2021.)

DOI: 10.1201/9781003404941-3

atmosphere and water bodies (Gray et al., 2004). Therefore, Hg contamination in soils, water, and atmosphere is heavy in Hg mining regions (Feng and Qiu, 2008). In addition to Hg mines, there are over 15 million artisanal and small-scale gold mines spread across more than 70 countries, leading to Hg contamination in nearby soil, sediments, and water bodies (Opiso et al. 2018).

Crops cultivated for food production in Hg-contaminated areas have varying capacities to bioaccumulate Hg from the environment (Lima et al., 2019), and consumption of such crops can have detrimental effects on human health (Arvay et al., 2017). Previous studies have shown that rice intake is the main pathway of MeHg exposure for residents living in the Wanshan Hg mining area of Guizhou Povince (Du et al., 2018; Xing et al., 2019). Also, it is reported that the consumption of local agricultural products contributed about 77% of the inorganic Hg exposure of the residents of the Wanshan Hg mining region (Li et al., 2015). Despite the extensive record of health risks, a certain amount of contaminated farmland is still used for production of food due to the limited land resources across the Hg mining region (Peng et al., 2011; Qiu et al., 2008).

3.2 Hg CONTAMINATION IN TAILING AND CALCINE

As the largest mine in China, Wanshan Hg mine produced approximately 125.8 million tons of calcines from 1949 to the 1990s (Feng and Qiu, 2008; Zhang et al., 2004). Mercury waste (i.e., tailing and calcine) is piled up near the Hg mining and retorting sites without appropriate treatment. Due to the inefficient Hg retorting activities, Hg wastes have a high concentration of Hg. The concentration of total Hg in calcines is highly elevated, ranging from 5.7 to 4450 mg kg^{-1} (Li et al., 2008b; Qiu et al., 2005). The concentration of total Hg in Hg wastes from different Hg mines in the world is shown in Table 3.1.

Mercury in Hg wastes is dominated by α-HgS, β-HgS, elemental Hg (Hg^0), and secondary Hg phases (Hg^{2+}) (Li et al., 2013). The concentration of Hg^0 in calcine ranges from 0.22 to 79 mg kg^{-1} with an average of 16 mg kg^{-1} and in Hg wastes ranges from 0.14 to 15 mg kg^{-1} with an average of 6.2 mg kg^{-1}. The retorting of Hg ores converts most HgS to Hg^0 which is subsequently recovered. Meantime, Hg^0 can be absorbed by calcine, remaining in the solid phases. The Hg^0 can be emitted to the atmosphere under natural conditions, thereby acting as a source of Hg contamination.

TABLE 3.1

Total Hg Concentrationr in Hg Wastes from Different Hg Mines in the World

Hg Mine	Location	THg Concentration Range (mg kg^{-1})	Reference
Palawan Quicksilver Mine	Philippines	43–660	Gray et al., 2003
Abbadia S. Salvatore Hg mine	Italy	25–1500	Rimondi et al., 2012
Wuchuan Hg mine	China	3.3–810	Li et al., 2012; Qiu et al., 2006
Wanshan Hg mine	China	5.7–4450	Feng et al., 2003; Qiu et al., 2009; Zhang et al., 2010b

The concentration of Hg^{2+} in calcine ranges from 0.002 to ~3.81 mg kg^{-1}, accounting for 1.8% of total Hg, and that in Hg wastes ranges from 0.003 to ~8.33 mg kg^{-1}, accounting for 0.4% of total Hg (Li et al., 2013). It has been found that there is a significant linear correlation between Hg^{2+} and total Hg in Hg wastes, showing that Hg^{2+} increases as a function of total Hg. Kim et al. (2000) used a synchrotron-based technique to analyze Hg speciation in Hg wastes, and they found that Hg is dominated by $HgCl_2$ and $HgSO_4$. This case study confirms the presence of Hg^{2+} in Hg wastes. Although Hg^{2+} accounts for a small fractional amount of total Hg, it has a high mobility and leaching risk. Mobile Hg can leach from Hg wastes by way of rain, resulting in contamination of the soil and body of water. For example, the concentration of total Hg in soil near an Hg waste pile reached 170 mg kg^{-1} (Zhang et al., 2004), which is far beyond the maximum allowable Hg concentration of 3.4 mg kg^{-1} defined by the Chinese government. Further, Hg^{2+} can be converted to more toxic MeHg by microorganisms in soil under anaerobic conditions. In addition to leaching, Hg in wastes can also enter the atmosphere through volatilization driven by solar radiation. Therefore, Hg wastes act as the dominant Hg contamination source to the environment after the closure of an Hg mine (Qiu et al., 2013; Wang et al., 2005).

At Wanshan Hg mine, MeHg in Hg wastes represents a small fraction of the total Hg, and it is at ppb levels (Qiu et al. 2005). Such levels are within the values recorded in calcine from Palawan Quicksilver Mine in the Philippines (0.13–3.2 ng g^{-1}) and in calcine from Nevada Hg mine in America (31 ng g^{-1}) (Gray et al., 2000). Although the MeHg concentration is orders of magnitude lower than that of other Hg forms in Hg wastes, it is of the greatest concern due to its high neurotoxicity. Yin et al. (2016) analyzed the concentration of MeHg in a profile of calcine at Wanshan Hg mining region (Figure 3.2),

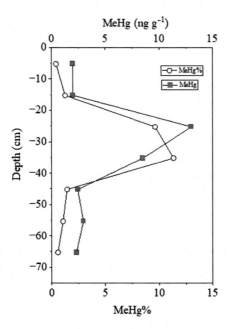

FIGURE 3.2 MeHg concentration and MeHg% (MeHg/THg × 100%) in the profile of the Wukeng pile. (Reprinted with permission from Yin et al., 2016.)

and they found that the MeHg concentration ranged from 0.3 to 11.3 ng g⁻¹. It is worth mentioning that cementation occurred near the surface of the calcine piles, and MeHg production was also present near this cementation layer. The presence of MeHg in this layer is attributed to the anaerobic conditions that favor its formation.

3.3   Hg CONTAMINATION IN WATER

After the closure of an Hg mine, Hg wastes act as an important Hg source to the local environment. Most Hg waste is piled up in close proximity to the upstream sections of rivers, and it releases both Hg-bearing particles and dissolved Hg into the river due to external forces such as rainwater leaching, wind erosion, and surface runoff (Figure 3.3) (Jin et al., 2023; Xu et al., 2019). Therefore, water samples close to Hg wastes are heavily contaminated with Hg (Xu et al., 2019).

In the Wanshan Hg mine, the concentrations of total Hg and MeHg in river water can be up to 12,000 ng L⁻¹ and 11 ng L⁻¹, respectively (Zhang et al., 2010a, 2010b). In the Lanmuchang Hg mine, the total Hg in the water can reach 7020 ng L⁻¹(Qiu et al., 2006). In the Yanwuping Hg mine, the average concentration of total Hg in drainage from the Hg slagheap is 127 ng L⁻¹ (Qiu et al., 2013). In the Xiushan Hg mine, the mean concentration of total Hg in surface waters is 180 ng L⁻¹, with a range from 13 to 1004 ng L⁻¹ (Xu et al., 2018). All those values exceed the maximum allowable Hg concentration in surface water (50 ng L⁻¹) recommended by the Chinese government. Worse still, Hg concentrations in some surface water samples close to Hg tailings exceeded the maximum allowable levels of Hg (2000 ng L⁻¹) in drinking water and the recommended limits of the aquatic life criteria (1400 ng L⁻¹, acute exposure) and (770 ng L⁻¹, chronic exposure) (US EPA, 2011).

In the Wanshan Hg mining region, during the high water flow period, higher total Hg concentrations (≥50 ng L⁻¹) are typically observed within 100–500 meters downstream of the Hg waste piles, while lower total Hg concentrations (<50 ng L⁻¹)

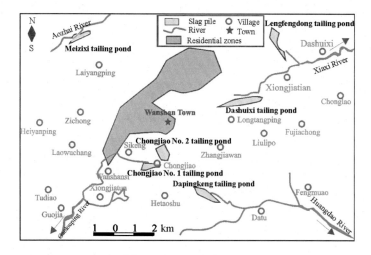

FIGURE 3.3   The locations of Hg tailing ponds in Wanshan Hg mining areas.

are found further downstream of the Hg waste piles (Zhang et al., 2010). A similar phenomenon is also observed in the surface water of the river in the Wuchuan Hg mining region, where the concentration of Hg is higher in surface water close to Hg waste piles (2000 ng L^{-1}) but is lower downstream of Hg waste piles (28 ng L^{-1}) (Li et al., 2012). The decrease in total Hg concentration in surface water as a function of distance from the Hg waste pile is associated with the fraction of Hg. The fraction of total Hg in surface water can be divided into particulate Hg and dissolved Hg, and the former can deposit in the riverbed depending on the hydrodynamic condition of river. In the Wuchuan Hg mining region, particulate Hg accounts for 65–96% of the total Hg in river water (Li et al., 2012), particularly in upstream river water close to the mine waste deposits, where particulate Hg comprises 80–99.6% of the total Hg (Xu et al., 2019; Zhang et al., 2010b). As the water velocity slows down in the downstream area, particulates tend to deposit, leading to the removal of particulate Hg from the water column.

With regard to MeHg in river water, the concentration of MeHg decreases in river water as a function of distance from the calcine deposits, indicating a significant impact of the calcine on MeHg in the river. In the Wanshan Hg mining areas, the concentration of MeHg accounts for up to 12% of the total Hg in water samples (Zhang et al., 2010a). Furthermore, the concentration of MeHg in surface water during the dry season is 0.43 ng L^{-1}, ranging from 0.035 to 11 ng L^{-1}, while in the normal season it is 0.21 ng L^{-1} with a range of 0.035–3.4 ng L^{-1}. The concentration of MeHg is higher in the dry season than in the normal season (Zhang et al., 2010a). Further, there is a positive correlation between MeHg concentration and total Hg concentration ($R^2 = 0.2–0.58$, $P < 0.001$) in river water (Zhang et al., 2010a). This correlation suggests that desorption of MeHg from particles to water plays a crucial role in controlling the transportation of MeHg in rivers.

In Wuchuan Hg mining areas, the concentration of MeHg represents less than 1% of the total Hg in river water (Li et al., 2012). Furthermore, the concentrations of total MeHg and dissolved MeHg range from 0.31 to 1.1 ng L^{-1} and 0.26 to 1.0 ng L^{-1}, respectively, with dissolved MeHg accounting for 67.4–97.8% of the total MeHg. The concentrations of MeHg are significantly higher during the dry season than during the normal season, likely due to less dilution of the seepage enriched in MeHg from the calcines during the dry season (Qiu et al., 2013).

In summary, erosion and particle transportation are the primary mechanisms that control the distribution and transportation of Hg in rivers in Hg mining areas. Additionally, the transportation of MeHg is primarily governed by desorption from particles into the dissolved phase. Evidence from Hg isotopes indicates a significant difference in δ^{202}Hg values (1.24%) between dissolved Hg and particulate Hg in surface water, further supporting the importance of particle desorption in controlling MeHg transportation in rivers (Yan et al., 2023).

Drawing upon our understanding of the process of Hg transportation in rivers, a pilot study was conducted to investigate the effectiveness of building weirs across rivers at the Wanshan Hg mining areas to control Hg transportation. The results indicate that waterflow plays a critical role in controlling the mobilization and transportation of Hg in rivers (Figure 3.4) (Xu et al., 2019); approximately 40.4% of the

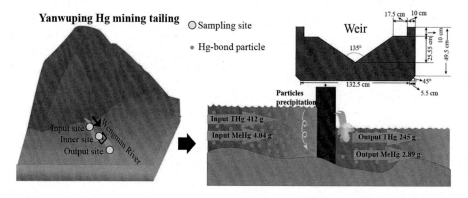

FIGURE 3.4   The Hg removal mechanism of weir building. (Reprinted with permission from Xu et al., 2019.)

total Hg (167 g) and 38.4% of the total MeHg (1.15 g) are retained by the weir each year. Therefore, the construction of weirs across rivers represents a cost-effective method for removing Hg from river water.

Furthermore, paddy fields can also act as an MeHg source to river waters. When inorganic Hg in surface water enters a paddy field, it can be converted into MeHg. Before harvest, water from the paddy fields is discharged into nearby rivers, leading to MeHg contamination. Precipitation is also an important source of Hg contamination for water bodies. For instance, the concentration of unfiltered total Hg and MeHg in precipitation is 159 ng L^{-1} and 0.75 ng L^{-1} at artisanal Hg smelting areas, respectively, while it is 513 ng L^{-1} and 1.7 ng L^{-1} at abandoned Hg mine sites, respectively (Zhao et al. 2016).

3.4   Hg CONTAMINATION IN AIR

The atmospheric Hg contamination is of utmost concern, as inhalation of Hg^0 exceeding a certain amount can have adverse effects on human health, affecting the kidneys and central nervous system. The majority of Hg in the atmosphere exists in the elemental gaseous form, with a residence time in the atmosphere ranging from approximately 0.5 to 2 years (Beckers and Rinklebe, 2017).

Mercury mining and retorting activities are one of the most important anthropogenic emission sources that lead to the contamination of the atmosphere. The Hg artisanal smelting workshop, which has been closed for 15 years, was previously a significant source of Hg^0 contamination in Hg mining regions. It has been reported that the concentration of total gaseous Hg at Hg artisanal smelting workshops in the Wuchuan Hg mine area can reach approximately 30,000–40,000 ng m^{-3}. Additionally, both mercuriferous belts and Hg waste materials (e.g., calcine) can serve as Hg^0 sources to the atmosphere (Gustin et al., 2002). In the Lanmuchang Hg-Tl mining areas, the emission of Hg^0 from calcine leads to the rising of atmospheric Hg^0 concentration 7.9 to 353.8 ng m^{-3} in the cold season and 12.7 to 468 ng m^{-3} in the warm season (Wang et al., 2005). In summary, Hg mining and retorting activities, Hg wastes, and artisanal Hg mining activities are the main Hg^0 contamination sources to the atmosphere in Hg mining regions (Dai et al., 2012).

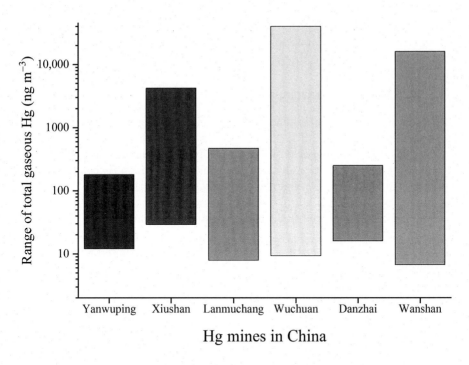

FIGURE 3.5   Atmospheric Hg in different Hg mining areas.

The atmospheric Hg^0 concentration is exceptionally high in Hg mining regions (Figure 3.5). In the Xiushan Hg mining area, the concentration of total gaseous Hg ranges from 29 to 4209 ng m^{-3}, with an average concentration of 498 ng m^{-3} (Xu et al., 2018). In the Wanshan Hg mining areas, the concentration of total gaseous Hg exhibits a wide range of 17.8–1101.8 ng m^{-3}. In the Yanwuping Hg mine, the concentration of total gaseous Hg during the warm season ranges from 43.3 to 700 ng m^{-3}, with an average concentration of 153 ng m^{-3} (Jin et al., 2023; Qiu et al., 2013). There is a significant health risk associated with inhalation of Hg^0 in Hg mining regions, as indicated by a strong correlation between atmospheric Hg^0 and hair Hg concentration (Li et al., 2008a).

The total gaseous Hg (TGM) in the atmosphere can deposit onto land surface via dry and wet deposition (Lynam et al., 2014). This newly deposited Hg in soil is readily converted into MeHg by microorganisms, which enhances the risk of Hg given the high bioavailability of MeHg to biota (Ao et al., 2017; Xu et al., 2017). It is estimated that the annual Hg^0 emission from Lanmuchang Hg-Tl mining areas (around 2.9 km^2) to the ambient air is about 3.54 kg Hg (Wang et al., 2005). Further, in order to understand the regional budget of atmospheric Hg in Hg mining areas, Hg in both precipitation and throughfall samples has been investigated in Wanshan Hg mining areas (Dai et al., 2012). The mean total Hg concentrations in throughfall and precipitation are 9641.5 and 7490.1 ng L^{-1} at the village of Supeng, 3392.1 and 814.1 ng L^{-1} at the village of Dashuixi, and 977.8 ng L^{-1} and 502.6 ng L^{-1} at the village of Shenchong, respectively. The annual dry Hg deposition fluxes are 6178, 2613.6, and

378.9 μg m^{-2} yr^{-1} at Supeng, Dashuixi, and Shenchong, which are two magnitudes higher than those for wet deposition (Dai et al., 2012), suggesting a dominant role of dry deposition in leading to Hg contamination of land surface.

3.5 Hg CONTAMINATION IN SOIL

In Wanshan Hg mining regions, the concentration of total Hg in soil ranges from 5.1 to 790 mg kg^{-1} (Qiu et al., 2005) (Figure 3.6). Hg waste, atmospheric Hg deposition, and irrigation with contaminated water are the primary sources of Hg contamination in soil. Soils contaminated by Hg waste typically have high Hg concentrations. For instance, the total Hg concentration in paddy soil near a slag heap at the Meizixi Hg mining site can reach up to 790 mg kg^{-1}, while that at the Dashuixi mining site is 130 mg kg^{-1}. Most paddy fields in the Wanshan Hg mining area are situated alongside rivers, making them vulnerable to contamination through irrigation with river water. In the Wanshan Hg mining area, the total Hg concentration in paddy soil downstream of the Aozhai River is 16 mg kg^{-1} and downstream of the Dashuixi River is 89 mg kg^{-1}. Atmospheric Hg deposition is another significant source of soil contamination, particularly in the vicinity of Hg smelting plants. For example, soil near one smelting plant has a total Hg content of 740 mg kg^{-1} due to atmospheric Hg deposition (Qiu et al., 2005). In addition to those in Hg mining sites, soils in mercuriferous belts have a concentration of Hg higher than the global background value, as parent rock is enriched with Hg (Senesil et al., 1999).

Mercury can be converted to MeHg in paddy fields. The content of MeHg in soils in the Wanshan Hg mining area ranges from 0.13 to 15 μg kg^{-1}, which is significantly higher than the MeHg levels in soils from the background area (0.10–0.28 μg kg^{-1}). The content of MeHg is 15 μg kg^{-1} in soil contaminated by calcine. It should be noted that Hg methylation depends on the availability of Hg forms. Mercury in the leachate

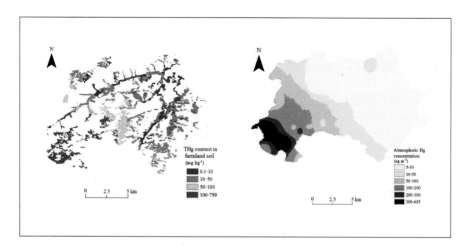

FIGURE 3.6 Map of total Hg (THg) concentration in the soils and the elemental Hg concentration in the atmosphere at the Wanshan mining area. (Reprinted with permission from Xia et al., 2020.)

from calcine is bioavailable for methylation, and thus soils that receive more Hg from calcine tend to have a high MeHg concentration. The content of MeHg in soils in Hg mining areas tends to increase in proportion to the total Hg content.

The deposition of atmospheric Hg^0 causes Hg contamination in soils. The deposited Hg^0 is converted to nanoparticulate metacinnabar, the availability of which depends on the crystal structure of the mineral. The newly deposited atmospheric Hg in soil is preferentially methylated by bacteria because its mineral facet has more binding sites for Hg-methylation bacteria (Gray et al., 2000). The demethylation of MeHg occurs in soil, which inhibits the accumulation of MeHg in soil (Hines et al., 2012).

Mercury in soils can be operationally divided into different fractions according to their solubility in different extracting agents. For example, Hg fractions include soluble and exchangeable Hg, specifically sorbed Hg, Fe/Mn oxide bound Hg, organic bound Hg, and residual Hg. The amount of each Hg fraction in soil often is in the order residual Hg > organic bound Hg > Fe/Mn oxide bound Hg > specifically sorbed Hg > soluble and exchangeable Hg. Among them, soluble and exchangeable Hg and specifically sorbed Hg are considered as bioavailable, Fe/Mn oxide bound Hg is potentially bioavailable, and residual Hg and organic bound Hg are less bioavailable. The amount of bioavailable Hg fractions in soils from different Hg-contaminated sites is different. For example, in the Yunchangping Hg mining area, most soils have a bioavailable Hg concentration of about 0.024 mg kg^{-1}, while in other regions soils have a bioavailable Hg concentration of 1.24 mg kg^{-1}. This difference is because the spatial distribution of Hg in soil is highly heterogeneous in Hg mining regions.

3.6 Hg CONTAMINATION IN WILD PLANTS

Plants can directly absorb Hg from soil through their roots or absorb atmospheric Hg through their leaves. Plants colonized in Hg mining areas often have a high concentration of Hg. Previous studies have investigated the concentration of Hg in different wild plants collected from the Wanshan Hg mining region (Qian et al., 2018). The results showed that the concentration of Hg in the root of plants ranges from 0.08 to 163 mg kg^{-1}. The average total Hg content in the roots of some plants such as *Artemisia frigida*, *Paeonia suffruticosa*, *Viola odorata*, and *Artemisia annua* exceeds 10 mg kg^{-1} (Table 3.2); most plants have a low concentration of Hg in their roots.

The accumulation of Hg by plants is affected by various factors (Fay and Gustin, 2007). The bioavailability of Hg in soil is the main factor affecting total Hg content in the roots of plants. Although the total Hg content in soils in the Wanshan Hg mining area is high, the bioavailable Hg concentration only accounts for less than 0.25% of the total Hg (Wang et al., 2011). The low bioavailable Hg concentration can limit the accumulation of Hg by plants. In addition, soil pH, organic matter content, soil carbon exchange capacity, and redox potential can affect the accumulation of Hg by the roots of plants (Frohne et al., 2012). The acidification of soil can enhance the bioavailability of Hg in soils. Thus, plants growing in acidic soil are likely to have a higher Hg concentration than those grown in alkaline soil. Soils have a high pH in the Wanshan Hg mining regions due to the dominance of carbonate rocks. Also, soils contaminated by calcine are alkaline, as calcine has a high pH. The high pH

TABLE 3.2

THg and MeHg Concentrations in Plants across the Wanshan Mining Area (mg kg⁻¹ for THg, ng g⁻¹ for MeHg)

	THg		MeHg	
Plant Species	**Root (mg kg⁻¹)**	**Aboveground (mg kg⁻¹)**	**Root (µg kg⁻¹)**	**Aboveground (µg kg⁻¹)**
Allium tuberosum	2.2 ± 0.063	0.40 ± 0.004	1.8 ± 0.09	6.0 ± 0.11
Arthraxonhispidus	130 ± 9.4	70 ± 39	85 ± 3.2	25 ± 0.81
Aster ageratoides	1.8 ± 1.7	6.3 ± 6.7	1.1 ± 0.76	3.2 ± 1.1
Aster subulatus	1.5 ± 0.10	0.42 ± 0.01	14 ± 0.85	11 ± 0.55
Brassica ampestris	0.10 ± 0.006	2.2 ± 0.43	0.79 ± 0.18	0.50 ± 0.11
Buddlejalindleyana	8.5 ± 19	5.3 ± 9.3	2.8 ± 2.2	2.0 ± 1.1
Buddlejaofficinalis	0.52 ± 0.25	1.4 ± 1.1	1.2 ± 0.52	2.8 ± 0.20
Cassia nomame	0.66 ± 0.19	0.50 ± 0.18	2.2 ± 0.48	0.99 ± 1.0
Chenopodiumglaucum	0.44 ± 0.058	0.43 ± 0.009	0.82 ± 0.011	0.28 ± 0.017
Chromolaeneodorata	1.5 ± 1.9	1.2 ± 0.50	1.8 ± 1.6	1.7 ± 1.1
Cibotiumbarometz	1.7 ± 0.044	3.6 ± 0.075	0.24 ± 0.02	0.65 ± 0.05
Cirsiumjaponicum	5.0 ± 0.24	3.8 ± 0.01	4.1 ± 0.18	0.44 ± 0.02
Clerodendrumbunge	22 ± 34	3.0 ± 4.2	1.6 ± 1.3	1.1 ± 0.66
Conyzacanadensis	1.5 ± 1.3	1.2 ± 0.60	2.9 ± 3.5	2.1 ± 1.5
Coriarianepalensis	3.4 ± 1.0	1.8 ± 0.19	0.34 ± 0.13	0.43 ± 0.11
Corydalisedulis maxim	0.27 ± 0.008	0.87 ± 0.012	6.5 ± 0.68	5.1 ± 0.01
Cyclosorusacuminatus	1.3 ± 0.06	3.4 ± 0.77	1.4 ± 0.15	1.5 ± 0.13
Desmodiumsequax	3.5 ± 4.2	3.2 ± 2.1	0.36 ± 0.13	0.33 ± 0.09
Equisetum ramosissimum	7.0 ± 11	1.7 ± 0.82	2.4 ± 0.33	5.0 ± 0.09
Eremochloaciliaris	8.6 ± 14	12 ± 26	6.4 ± 7.4	3.8 ± 5.5
Euphorbia esula	0.89 ± 0.62	0.66 ± 0.48	2.2 ± 1.7	1.4 ± 1.1
Fallopiamultiflora	7.8 ± 14	14 ± 17	0.92 ± 0.33	0.39 ± 0.15
Herbabidentis	3.1 ± 2.0	1.1 ± 0.56	0.91 ± 0.71	0.39 ± 0.33
Macleayacordata	0.68 ± 0.063	0.98 ± 1.1	1.3 ± 0.96	0.79 ± 0.23
Neyraudiareynaudiana	1.2 ± 0.81	0.76 ± 0.38	2.5 ± 3.1	0.97 ± 0.40
Primulasikkimensis	2.5 ± 0.11	6.3 ± 0.23	2.1 ± 0.22	1.4 ± 0.08
Sonchusoleraceus	3.1 ± 6.3	2.4 ± 3.8	5.7 ± 8.4	2.8 ± 2.2
Telosmacordata	1.0 ± 0.76	1.7 ± 0.12	0.58 ± 0.01	0.54 ± 0.02

Source: From Qian et al., 2018.

leads to the low bioavailability of Hg in soils. The organic matter, particularly thiol-containing molecules, has a high binding affinity to Hg. A high content of organic matter is favorable for the accumulation of Hg in soils, while a low content may lead to limited ability of the soil to retain Hg. Thus, Hg in soils with little organic matter tends to be mobilized under changing environmental conditions, increasing the bioavailability of the Hg. An increase in organic matter content can inhibit the accumulation of Hg by plants (Beckers and Rinklebe, 2017).

The leaves of plants can absorb atmospheric Hg^0 (Egler et al., 2006; Wang et al., 2011). Therefore, in areas with high atmospheric Hg^0 concentration, atmospheric Hg is the major source of Hg to the leaves of plants (Fay and Gustin, 2007). Indeed, the behavior of Hg^0 at the air-leaf interface is a bi-directional process in which leaves can either accumulate Hg^0 or emit Hg^0 depending on environmental conditions, such as atmospheric Hg^0 concentration, soil Hg concentration, and leaf stomata (Obrist et al., 2018; Zhu et al., 2016). The emission of Hg^0 from leaves is related to the following aspects: the re-emission of Hg previously deposited in the epidermis of leaves through photo-reduction and the release of Hg previously fixed in the tissue of leaves after being reduced to Hg in the cell fluid (Wang et al., 2017; Yuan et al., 2019). Leaves are able to oxidize Hg^0 to Hg(II) via forming Hg-thiolate complexes (Manceau et al., 2018). This Hg^0 oxidation leads to the accumulation of Hg in the leaf. It is generally believed that Hg in leaves is sourced from the atmosphere, as the translocation of Hg from root to leaf is limited because the loading of Hg into xylem is difficult (Yuan et al., 2022).

3.7 Hg CONTAMINATION IN CROPS

The edible sections of most crops have a total Hg concentration exceeding the maximum allowable Hg concentration (10 µg kg^{-1} for vegetables or 20 µg kg^{-1} for rice grain) defined by the Chinese government (GB 2762-2017). A comprehensive investigation of Hg contamination of crops in Hg mining regions showed that the concentrations of Hg in the edible parts of crops range from 2.4 to 1075 µg kg^{-1} in the Wanshan Hg mining area (Figure 3.7) (Xia et al., 2020).

Among those crops studied, the concentrations of total Hg in radishes, strawberries, corn, and potatoes were lower than the maximum allowable Hg concentrations for vegetables and fruits (10 µg kg^{-1}) and grains (20 µg kg^{-1}) defined by the Chinese government (GB 2762-2017); the red amaranth, cabbage, shallots, lettuce, peas, taro, celery, carrots, broad beans, and garlic had Hg concentrations exceeding the standard by 2–5 times (GB 2762-2017); the Chinese cabbage, spinach, ginger, chives, parsley, pumpkins, bitter gourds, tomatoes, sponge gourds, cucumbers, beans, eggplants, and chilies had Hg concentrations exceeding the governmental reference values by 5–20 times (GB 2762-2017); and the *Herbahouttuyniae* accumulated the highest concentration in its edible section, with the value of 57.8–1075 µg kg^{-1}.

The blueberries, walnuts, peaches, oranges, and grapes had Hg concentrations exceeding the standard by 2–5 times (GB 2762-2017), and the melons, watermelons, jujubes, pears, and plums had Hg concentrations exceeding the standard by 5–8 times (GB 2762-2017). The average concentration of Hg in green bean, peanut, sorghum, rice, soybean, and sweet potato samples was 2–7 times above the standard (20 µg kg^{-1} for grain crops, and 10 µg kg^{-1} for vegetables).

Despite the cessation of Hg mining and smelting activities 16 years ago, Hg concentrations in the edible sections of most agricultural products still exceeded the standards (<20 µg kg^{-1}) at the time of sampling. A similar phenomenon has also been observed in other Hg mining regions both in China and around the world. For example, Hg concentrations in beans, cabbage, chilies, cucumbers, eggplants, scallions, and tomatoes collected from an active Hg mine in central China ranged from

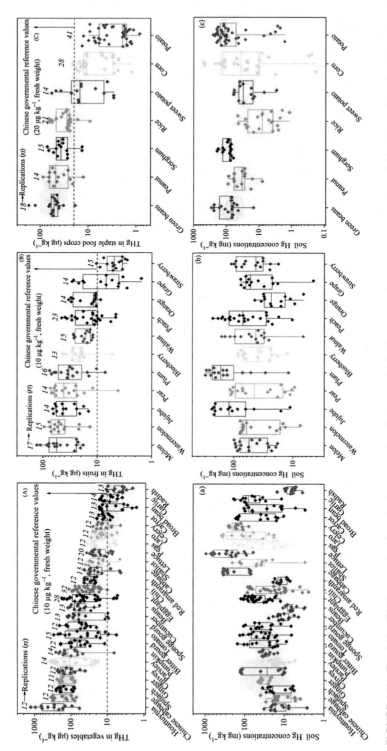

FIGURE 3.7 Total Hg (THg) concentrations in the vegetables, fruits, staple food crops, and corresponding soils collected from Wanshan Hg mine. The y-axis in graph (A) is THg in the vegetables (mg kg⁻¹); the y-axis in graph (a) is THg in the corresponding rhizosphere soil (mg kg⁻¹) for vegetables. The y-axis in graph (B) is THg in the fruits (mg kg⁻¹); the y-axis in graph (b) is THg in the corresponding rhizosphere soil (mg kg⁻¹) for fruits. The y-axis in graph (C) is THg in the staple food crops (mg kg⁻¹); the y-axis in graph (c) is THg in the corresponding rhizosphere soil (mg kg⁻¹) for the staple food crops. (Reprinted with permission from Xia et al., 2020.)

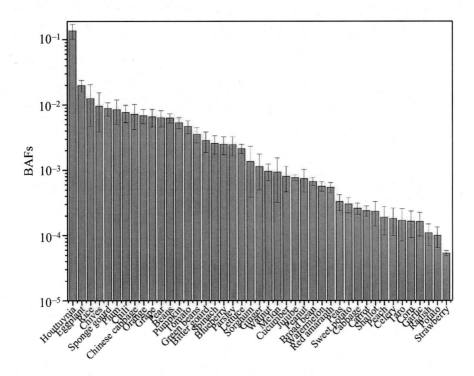

FIGURE 3.8 Bioaccumulation factors (BAFs) for THg in the edible portion of crops across the Wanshan mining area. (Reprinted with permission from Xia et al., 2020.)

24.8 to 781 µg kg^{-1} (Jia et al., 2018). Also, Hg concentrations in eggplants, chilies, and chicory root collected at Idrija Hg mining area in Slovenia ranged from 215 to 5680 µg kg^{-1} after the cessation of mining activities (Miklavcic et al., 2013).

The bioaccumulation factors (BAFs), defined as the ratio of the Hg concentration of the edible parts of crops to that of the corresponding soil, are shown in Figure 3.8. BAFs varied by four orders of magnitude, implying great variability in the capacity for Hg accumulation among the crops. The corn, radishes, strawberries, potatoes, and garlic showed smaller BAF values than the other crops (Xia et al., 2020).

The MeHg concentration in crops in the Hg mining region has been studied. Results showed that, except rice, most crops have a low concentration of MeHg (Qiu et al., 2008). Thus, rice contamination with MeHg is the primary concern for food safety in Hg mining regions.

3.8   SUMMARY

After the closure of Hg mines, mercury waste represents the primary source of Hg contamination of the environment. Soils, air, surface waters, wild plants, and crops are all susceptible to Hg pollution in Hg mining regions, particularly those located near mercury waste disposal sites. The primary concern for food safety in these regions is MeHg contamination in rice.

REFERENCES

Ao M., Meng B., Sapkota A., et al., 2017. The influence of atmospheric Hg on Hg contaminations in rice and paddy soil in the Xunyang Hg mining district, China. Acta Geochimica 36, 181–189.

Arvay J., Demkova L., Hauptvogl M., et al. 2017. Assessment of environmental and health risks in former polymetallic ore mining and smelting area, Slovakia: Spatial distribution and accumulation of mercury in four different ecosystems. Ecotoxicology and Environmental Safety 144, 236–244.

Beckers F., Rinklebe J., 2017. Cycling of mercury in the environment: Sources, fate, and human health implications: A review. Critical Reviews in Environmental Science & Technology 47, 693–794.

Dai Z., Feng X., Sommar J., et al., 2012. Spatial distribution of mercury deposition fluxes in Wanshan hg mining area, Guizhou province, China. Atmospheric Chemistry and Physics 12, 6207–6218.

Du B., Feng X., Li P., et al., 2018. Use of mercury isotopes to quantify mercury exposure sources in inland populations, China. Environmental Science & Technology 52, 5407–5416.

Egler S. G., Rodrigues-Filho S., Villas-Boas R. C., et al., 2006. Evaluation of mercury pollution in cultivated and wild plants from two small communities of the Tapajos gold mining reserve, Para state, Brazil. Science of the Total Environment 368, 424–433.

Essa A. M., Macaskie L. E., Brown N.L., 2002. Mechanisms of mercury bioremediation. Biochemical Society Transactions 30, 672–674.

Fay L., Gustin M. S., 2007. Investigation of mercury accumulation in cattails growing in constructed wetland Mesocosms. Wetlands 27, 1056–1065.

Feng, X., Tang, S., Shang, L., et al., 2003. Total gaseous mercury in the atmosphere of Guiyang, PR China. Science of the Total Environment 304(1-3), 61–72.

Feng X., Qiu G., 2008. Mercury pollution in Guizhou, southwestern China - An overview. Science of the Total Environment 400, 227–237.

Fernández-Martínez R., Larios R., Gómez-Pinilla I., et al., 2015. Mercury accumulation and speciation in plants and soils from abandoned cinnabar mines. Geoderma 253–254, 30–38.

Frohne T., Rinklebe J., Langer U., et al., 2012. Biogeochemical factors affecting mercury methylation rate in two contaminated floodplain soils. Biogeosciences 9, 493–507.

Gamboa-Herrera J. A., Rios-Reyes C. A., Vargas-Fiallo L. Y., 2021. Mercury speciation in mine tailings amended with Biochar: Effects on mercury bioavailability, methylation potential and mobility. Science of the Total Environment 760, 143959.

Gray, J. E., Greaves, I. A., Bustos, D. M., et al., 2003. Mercury and methylmercury contents in mine-waste calcine, water, and sediment collected from the Palawan Quicksilver Mine, Philippines. Environmental Geology 43(3), 298–307.

Gray J., Hines M., Higueras P., et al., 2004. Mercury speciation and microbial transformations in mine wastes, stream sediments, and surface waters at the Almaden mining district, Spain. Environmental Science & Technology 38, 4285–4292.

Gray J., Theodorakos P. M., Bailey E. A., 2000. Distribution, speciation, and transport of mercury in stream-sediment, stream-water, and fish collected near abandoned mercury mines in southwestern Alaska, USA. Science of the Total Environment 260, 21–33.

Gustin M. S., Biester H., Kim C. S. 2002. Investigation of the light-enhanced emission of mercury from naturally enriched substrates. Atmospheric Environment 36, 3241–3254.

Hines M. E., Poitras E. N., Covelli S., et al., 2012. Mercury methylation and demethylation in Hg-contaminated lagoon sediments (Marano and Grado Lagoon, Italy). Estuarine, Coastal and Shelf Science 113, 85–95.

Jia Q., Zhu X., Hao Y., et al., 2018. Mercury in soil, vegetable and human hair in a typical mining area in China: Implication for human exposure. Journal of Environmental Sciences 68, 73–82.

Jiang G., Shi J., Feng X., 2006. Mercury pollution in China. Environmental Science & Technology 40, 3672–3678.

Jin X., Yan J., Ali M., et al., 2023. Mercury biogeochemical cycle in Yanwuping Hg mine and source apportionment by Hg isotopes. Toxics 11.

Kim, C. S., Brown, G. E. and Rytuba, J. J. 2000. Characterization and speciation of mercury-bearing mine wastes using X-ray absorption spectroscopy. Science of The Total Environment 261(1), 157–168.

Li P., Du B., Chan H., et al., 2015. Human inorganic mercury exposure, renal effects and possible pathways in Wanshan mercury mining area, China. Environmental Research 140, 198–204.

Li P., Feng X., Qiu G., et al., 2008a. Mercury exposures and symptoms in smelting workers of artisanal mercury mines in Wuchuan, Guizhou, China. Environmental Research 107, 108–114.

Li P., Feng X., Qiu G., et al., 2012. Mercury pollution in Wuchuan mercury mining area, Guizhou, southwestern China: The impacts from large scale and artisanal mercury mining. Environment International 42, 59–66.

Li P., Feng X., Qiu G., et al., 2013. Mercury speciation and mobility in mine wastes from mercury mines in China. Environmental Science & Pollution Research 20, 8374–8381.

Li P., Feng X., Shang L., et al., 2008b. Mercury pollution from artisanal mercury mining in Tongren, Guizhou, China. Applied Geochemistry 23, 2055–2064.

Lima F. R. D., Martins G. C., Silva A. O., et al., 2019. Critical mercury concentration in tropical soils: Impact on plants and soil biological attributes. Science of the Total Environment 666, 472–479.

Lynam M. M., Dvonch J. T., Hall N. L., et al., 2014. Spatial patterns in wet and dry deposition of atmospheric mercury and trace elements in central Illinois, USA. Environmental Science and Pollution Research International 21, 4032–4043.

Manceau A., Wang J., Rovezzi M., et al., 2018. Biogenesis of mercury-sulfur nanoparticles in plant leaves from atmospheric gaseous mercury. Environmental Science & Technology 52, 3935–3948.

Miklavcic A., Mazej D., Jacimovic R., et al., 2013. Mercury in food items from the Idrija mercury mine area. Environmental Research 125, 61–68.

Obrist D., Kirk J. L., Zhang L., Sunderland E. M., et al., 2018. A review of global environmental mercury processes in response to human and natural perturbations: Changes of emissions, climate, and land use. Ambio 47, 116–140.

Opiso E. M., Aseneiro J. P. J., Banda M. H. T., et al., 2018. Solid-phase partitioning of mercury in artisanal gold mine tailings from selected key areas in Mindanao, Philippines, and its implications for mercury detoxification. Waste Management & Research 36, 269–276.

Peng J., Xu Y., Cai Y., et al., 2011. The role of policies in land use/cover change since the 1970s in ecologically fragile karst areas of southwest China: A case study on the Maotiaohe watershed. Environmental Science & Policy 14, 408–418.

Qian X., Wu Y., Zhou H., et al., 2018. Total mercury and methylmercury accumulation in wild plants grown at wastelands composed of mine tailings: Insights into potential candidates for phytoremediation. Environmental Pollution 239, 757–767.

Qiu G., Feng X., Li P., et al., 2008. Methylmercury accumulation in rice (*Oryza sativa* L.) grown at abandoned mercury mines in Guizhou, China. Journal of Agricultural and Food Chemistry 56, 2465–2468.

Qiu G., Feng X., Meng B., et al., 2013. Environmental geochemistry of an abandoned mercury mine in Yanwuping, Guizhou province, China. Environmental Research 125, 124–130.

Qiu G., Feng X., Wang S., et al., 2005. Mercury and methylmercury in riparian soil, sediments, mine-waste calcines, and moss from abandoned hg mines in east Guizhou province, southwestern China. Applied Geochemistry 20, 627–638.

Qiu G., Feng X., Wang S., et al., 2006. Mercury contaminations from historic mining to water, soil and vegetation in Lanmuchang, Guizhou, southwestern China. Science of the Total Environment 368, 56–68.

Qiu, G., Feng, X., Wang, S., et al., 2009. Mercury distribution and speciation in water and fish from abandoned Hg mines in Wanshan, Guizhou province, China. Science of the Total Environment 407(18), 5162–5168.

Rimondi, V., Gray, J. E., Costagliola, P., et al., 2012. Concentration, distribution, and translocation of mercury and methylmercury in mine-waste, sediment, soil, water, and fish collected near the Abbadia San Salvatore mercury mine, Monte Amiata district, Italy. Science of The Total Environment 414, 318–327.

Senesil G. S., Baldassarre G., Senesi N., et al., 1999. Trace element inputs into soils by anthropogenic activities and implications for human health. Chemosphere 39, 343–377.

US EPA. 2011. Mercury: Human Exposure. https://www.epa.gov/sites/default/files/2018-12/documents/national-recommended-hh-criteria-2002.pdf .

Wang J., Feng X., Anderson C. W., et al., 2011. Mercury distribution in the soil-plant-air system at the Wanshan mercury mining district in Guizhou, southwest China. Environmental Toxicology and Chemistry 30, 2725–2731.

Wang S., Feng X., Qiu G., et al., 2005. Mercury emission to atmosphere from Lanmuchang Hg–Tl mining area, southwestern Guizhou, China. Atmospheric Environment 39: 7459–7473.

Wang X., Yuan W., Feng X., 2017. Global review of mercury biogeochemical processes in forest ecosystems. Progress in Chemistry 29, 970–980.

Xia J., Wang J., Zhang L., et al., 2020. Screening of native low mercury accumulation crops in a mercury-polluted mining region: Agricultural planning to manage mercury risk in farming communities. Journal of Cleaner Production 262,121324.

Xing Y., Wang J., Xia J., et al., 2019. A pilot study on using biochars as sustainable amendments to inhibit rice uptake of Hg from a historically polluted soil in a karst region of China. Ecotoxicology and Environmental Safety 170, 18–24.

Xu X., Gu C., Feng X., et al., 2019. Weir building: A potential cost-effective method for reducing mercury leaching from abandoned mining tailings. Science of the Total Environment 651, 171–178.

Xu X., Lin Y., Meng B., et al. 2018. The impact of an abandoned mercury mine on the environment in the Xiushan region, Chongqing, southwestern China. Applied Geochemistry 88, 267–275.

Xu X., Meng B., Zhang C., et al., 2017. The local impact of a coal-fired power plant on inorganic mercury and methyl-mercury distribution in rice (*Oryza sativa* L.). Environmental Pollution 223, 11–18.

Yan J., Li R., Ali M., et al. 2023. Mercury migration to surface water from remediated mine waste and impacts of rainfall in a karst area - Evidence from Hg isotopes. Water Research 230, 119592.

Yin R., Gu C., Feng X., et al., 2016. Transportation and transformation of mercury in a calcine profile in the Wanshan mercury mine, SW China. Environmental Pollution 219, 976–981.

Yuan W., Sommar J., Lin C. J., et al., 2019. Stable isotope evidence shows re-emission of elemental mercury vapor occurring after reductive loss from foliage. Environmental Science & Technology 53, 651–660.

Yuan W., Wang X., Lin C. J., et al., 2022. Mercury uptake, accumulation, and translocation in roots of subtropical forest: Implications of global mercury budget. Environmental Science & Technology 56, 14154–14165.

Zhang H., Feng X., Larssen T., et al., 2010a. Fractionation, distribution and transport of mercury in rivers and tributaries around Wanshan Hg mining district, Guizhou province, southwestern China: Part 2 – methylmercury. Applied Geochemistry 25, 642–649.

Zhang H., Feng X., Larssen T., et al., 2010b. Fractionation, distribution and transport of mercury in rivers and tributaries around Wanshan Hg mining district, Guizhou province, southwestern China: Part 1 – total mercury. Applied Geochemistry 25, 633–641.

Zhang G., Liu C., Wu P., et al., 2004. The geochemical characteristics of mine-waste calcines and runoff from the Wanshan mercury mine, Guizhou, China. Applied Geochemistry 19, 1735–1744.

Zhao L., Qiu G., Anderson C. W. N., et al., 2016. Mercury methylation in rice paddies and its possible controlling factors in the Hg mining area, Guizhou province, southwest China. Environmental Pollution 215, 1–9.

Zhu W., Lin C., Wang X., et al., 2016. Global observations and modeling of atmosphere–surface exchange of elemental mercury: A critical review. Atmospheric Chemistry and Physics 16, 4451–4480.

4 Human Health Risks Associated with Rice Consumption

Ping Li, Buyun Du, Lin Feng, and Xinbin Feng

4.1 HUMAN METHYLMERCURY EXPOSURE VIA RICE CONSUMPTION

4.1.1 INTRODUCTION

Methylmercury (MeHg) is a toxic substance for humans (Basu et al., 2018; Ha et al., 2017). It can cross the blood-brain and placental barriers to the human brain and the human fetus (Clarkson, 1993). Generally, the main pathway of human exposure is consumption of fish, fish products, and marine mammals (Mergler et al., 2007). Many studies have found that MeHg concentrations in human hair show a positive correlation with fish consumption (Al-Majed and Preston, 2000; Holsbeek et al., 1996; Santos et al., 2002). The long-range transport of atmospheric mercury (Hg), as well as the effects of acid rain and water impoundment, has led to Hg elevation in fish in North America and northern Europe (Lindqvist et al., 1991; Lucotte et al., 1999). Tremendous efforts have been devoted to understanding the relationship of the Hg deposition rate and MeHg concentrations in fish in those areas.

China is rich in Hg resources, and the most important Hg production center is Guizhou Province. So far, 12 large or super-large Hg deposits have been discovered in Guizhou Province (Qiu et al., 2005). A long history of Hg mining activities has resulted in serious Hg contamination of soil in Hg mining areas (Horvat et al., 2003; Qiu et al., 2005, 2006a, 2006b). Relatively high concentrations of both total Hg (THg, up to 569 ng/g) and MeHg (up to 144 ng/g) have been reported in rice samples collected from Wanshan Hg mining areas in Guizhou (Horvat et al., 2003). Rice is the staple food for local residents and, therefore, may constitute an important source of MeHg exposure. In this study, we used the dietary calculation method to quantify the relative contribution of human MeHg exposure via rice consumption.

Use of mercury-stable isotopes has been demonstrated as a useful approach to unravel sources and biogeochemical processes of Hg in the environment (Blum et al., 2014; Yin et al., 2014). Mercury has seven stable isotopes (196–204 amu), which can undergo mass-dependent isotope fractionation (MDF, reported as δ values) and mass-independent fractionation (MIF, reported as Δ values) during various biogeochemical processes (Blum et al., 2014). MDF occurs under both kinetic and equilibrium conditions, while MIF for odd mass number isotopes ($\Delta^{199}Hg$ and $\Delta^{201}Hg$) is affected by the magnetic isotope effect and nuclear volume effect (Buchachenko, 2001; Schauble, 2007) and for even mass number isotopes ($\Delta^{200}Hg$ and $\Delta^{204}Hg$) is likely a result of gas

 DOI: 10.1201/9781003404941-4

phase reactions in the atmosphere (Sun et al., 2016). Combining the "MDF-MIF" of Hg isotopes can provide multidimensional information about sources and geochemical fates of Hg in the environment. Hg isotopes have been used as tracers to understand exposure sources and bioaccumulation processes in food chains (Bergquist and Blum, 2007; Kwon et al., 2012, 2013; Tsui et al., 2012) and humans (Laffont et al., 2009, 2011; Li et al., 2014, 2016; Rothenberg et al., 2017; Sherman et al., 2013). No significant MDF or MIF of Hg isotopes has been observed during consumption of dietary MeHg by fish (Kwon et al., 2012, 2013; Tsui et al., 2012). However, an offset of ~2‰ in δ^{202}Hg was observed between fish and the hair of fish consumers such as humans and whales, indicating that MDF of Hg isotopes may occur during metabolic processes in mammals (Laffont et al., 2009, 2011; Li et al., 2014, 2016; Sherman et al., 2013). Significant MIF signatures have also been reported in fish and fish consumers; however, the MIF was mainly explained by Hg photo-degradation in ecosystems prior to trophic transfer, not by metabolic and trophic transfer processes (Bergquist and Blum, 2007; Gehrke et al., 2011; Kritee et al., 2007, 2009; Perrot et al., 2012). The absence of MIF during metabolic and trophic transfer processes suggests that MIF can be a robust tracer to identify Hg sources in food webs.

In previous studies, Hg isotopes in hair were successfully used to identify exposure sources of Hg for gold miners (Laffont et al., 2009; Sherman et al., 2015) and fish consumers (Laffont et al., 2011; Li et al., 2014, 2016; Sherman et al., 2013). Recently, the isotopic composition of Hg in rice from the Wanshan Hg mine in China was investigated, and the rice showed more negative δ^{202}Hg and Δ^{199}Hg than fish (Feng et al., 2015; Li et al., 2017; Rothenberg et al., 2017; Yin et al., 2013). We hypothesized that populations from Guizhou may have distinct hair isotopic signatures compared to previous results, since rice consumption is the most important pathway for human Hg exposure in Guizhou (Feng et al., 2008; Zhang et al., 2010a). To test this hypothesis, we investigated the Hg isotopic composition of human hair samples from three areas of Guizhou: a mining, an urban, and a rural area. The isotopic composition of potential dietary Hg sources (e.g., rice, fish, and vegetables consumed by the study populations) was investigated as well.

4.1.2 MATERIALS AND METHODS

4.1.2.1 Study Area

The Wanshan Hg mining area and one control site (Changshun) were selected for our study. The Wanshan Hg deposit was located in the eastern part of Guizhou Province, southwestern China (Figure 4.1), which ranked as the largest Hg mine in China. Large-scale mining activities officially ceased in 2001 (Qiu et al., 2005), but they resulted in serious Hg contamination of the local environment, including contamination of air, water, soil, sediment, and organisms (Horvat et al., 2003; Qiu et al., 2005; Zhang et al., 2004). All Hg adits and historical retorts are situated upstream of rivers in the region, as shown in Figure 4.1. The rice paddies are located immediately downstream of the calcine pile. Our previous study had demonstrated that the paddy soil has been seriously contaminated with Hg and the THg concentrations varied from 5.1 to 790 μg/g (Qiu et al., 2005). Residents from the villages of Dashuixi (DSX), Xiachangxi (XCX), and Baoxi (BX), which are situated about 1.5, 3, and 5 km

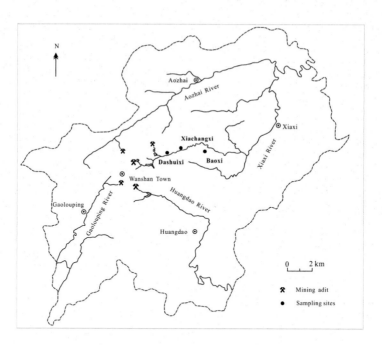

FIGURE 4.1 Locations of the study areas in Guizhou Province. (From Feng et al., 2008. with permission for reuse.)

downstream of the calcine pile shown in Figure 4.1, respectively, were chosen for the study. For comparison, residents in Changshun (CS) village were selected as a control group because there were no obvious Hg contamination sources in that area. CS is located in the south of Guizhou Province and is about 90 km away from Guiyang, the capital of Guizhou Province. Local residents in the study areas seldom eat fish, and rice is the staple food, which provides more calories than any other single food.

For Hg isotope study, three primary schools in Guiyang (GY), Changshun (CS), and Wanshan (WS) in Guizhou Province were selected. GY primary school is located in Guiyang, the capital of Guizhou. WS primary school is located in a small village in the Wanshan area, the largest Hg mine in China. CS primary school is located in a rural area, in a small residential community, 70 km from Guiyang.

Pupils and their supervisors were selected for investigation. Sampling work was conducted from November 2013 to October 2014. Regarding human sampling, 26, 21, and 9 participants in WS, GY, and CS, respectively, were randomly selected for hair sample collection. People from GY consume more fish than WS and CS residents. Every participant signed a consent agreement before starting the survey. The study obtained ethics approval from the Institute of Geochemistry, Chinese Academy of Sciences.

4.1.2.2 Sample Collection

The sampling campaign in Wanshan area was conducted in December 2006. We selected 30, 25, and 43 participants in DSX, XCX, and BX villages, respectively. The numbers of participants in the villages constituted 15%, 21%, and 22% of the total populations of DSX, XCX, and BX, respectively. Basically, they were farmers, and we asked all participants to fill in a questionnaire including information on age, weight, profession, history of involvement in artisanal Hg smelting activity, dental fillings, smoking and alcohol drinking habits, illnesses, and food consumption such as average daily intakes of rice, vegetables, meat, and fish. The food consumption information (g/d) was provided by the housewives based on monthly and/or annual food consumption by the whole family. We used the daily water consumption of average Chinese people of 2 L to estimate MeHg exposure through drinking water.

Hair samples were cut with stainless steel scissors from the occipital region of the scalp of each participant, bundled together with scrip, and placed in polyethylene bags, which were then sealed, properly identified, and taken to the laboratory for analysis. Raw rice and vegetable samples were collected from each participating family. All rice and vegetables consumed by local residents were cultivated from their own land. The commonly consumed vegetables in Wanshan Hg mining area are Chinese mustard (*B. chinensis* L.), radish leaves (*Raphanus sativus* L.), Chinese cabbage (*B. campestris* L.), and carrots (*Daucus carota* L.). Raw samples of Chinese mustard, radish leaves, Chinese cabbage, and carrots were collected from the family of each participant. Three to four replicate drinking water samples were collected from the public well in each village to assess possible MeHg exposure from drinking water. Water samples were filled into pre-cleaned borosilicate glass bottles, and 0.4% (v/v) of sub-boiling distilled ultrapure HCl acid was added within 24 h. Since local residents do not often eat meat, we managed to collect only a few raw (pork) meat samples from each village. The sampling campaign in CS was carried out in June 2005. We selected 24 participants from CS as the control group. The study obtained ethics approval from the Institute of Geochemistry, Chinese Academy of Sciences. All participants were required to sign a consent form.

For the Hg isotope study, hair samples (0.2–0.5 g) were cut with stainless steel scissors from the occipital region of the scalp, bundled together by stapler, and placed in polythene bags, which were then sealed. Fillet fish (15–20 g), rice (15–20 g), and vegetables (10–25 g) were collected from the kitchen of each participant. According to our investigation, rice and vegetables collected from WS and CS were grown and harvested locally, but food samples collected from GY were bought from the market. The fish samples were collected directly from the participant's house to ensure that these species were consumed regularly by local residents. The fish species were not identified but Guizhou Province is an inland area and most of fish obtained at the market are caught from freshwater aquaculture. All the hair and food samples were kept in a cooler before being delivered to the laboratory. The samples were washed with distilled water. The filleted fish and vegetable samples were freeze-dried, and the rice samples were air-dried. The dried samples were then powdered and stored in polyethylene bags at room temperature until chemical analyses.

4.1.2.3 Analytical Methods

The portion of hair within 1–3 cm from the scalp was selected for Hg analysis. Hair samples were washed with nonionic detergent, distilled water, and acetone and dried in an oven at 60°C overnight. Rice and vegetable samples were air-dried, crushed, and sieved to 150-mesh size. Hair, vegetable, meat, and rice samples were digested in a water bath (95°C) with a fresh mixture of HNO_3/H_2SO_4 (v/v 4:1) for THg analysis (US EPA, 2002). THg concentrations in these samples were determined by BrCl oxidation, $SnCl_2$ reduction, purge, gold trap, and cold vapor atomic fluorescence spectrometry (CVAFS). For MeHg analysis, prepared hair, rice, meat, and vegetable samples were digested using the KOH-methanol/solvent extraction technique (Liang et al., 1994, 1996). MeHg contents in these samples were measured using aqueous ethylation, purge, trap, and GC-CVAFS detection. THg concentrations in water samples were analyzed within 28 days after sampling using the dual-stage gold amalgamation method and CVAFS detection according to Method 1631 (US EPA, 2002). MeHg in water was analyzed using distillation and ethylation processes and GC-CVAFS detection following Method 1630 (US EPA, 2001). The daily average MeHg exposures for the participants in the Wanshan Hg mining area through food and water consumption were simply computed by multiplying the average MeHg concentration in foods or water by the daily average consumption of the corresponding foods or water. The relative contribution of MeHg exposure from each food category was calculated by dividing the MeHg exposure from each food category by the total MeHg exposure.

4.1.2.4 Mercury Isotope Measurement

Mercury isotopes were measured by a Nu-Plasma II multicollector inductively coupled plasma mass spectrometer (MC-ICP-MS) following a previous method (Yin et al., 2010). For all hair and filleted fish samples, and for vegetable and rice samples from WS, approximately 0.1–0.5 g of the sample was digested in a water bath (95°C, 3 h) using 5 mL of a fresh mixture of HNO_3/H_2SO_4 (v/v, 4:1). After complete digestion, the sample solutions were diluted to Hg concentrations of 1 ng/mL and acid concentrations of 10–20%, prior to isotopic ratio analysis. Certificated reference materials BCR482 (lichen) and sample duplicates were prepared. Instrumental mass bias was corrected using an internal Tl standard (NIST SRM 997, 20 ng/mL) and sample-standard bracketing. Mercury concentrations and acid matrices of the bracketing standard (NIST 3133) were systematically matched to the neighboring samples. Mercury concentration in sample solutions was determined by MC-ICP-MS using ^{202}Hg signals, the results of which were matched within 10% by Lumex RA915+ or CVAFS.

Hg-MDF is expressed in $\delta^{202}Hg$ notation in units of permil (‰) referenced to the neighboring NIST-3133 Hg standard (Eq. 4.1):

$$\delta^{xxx}Hg = [(^{xxx}Hg/^{198}Hg_{sample})/(^{xxx}Hg/^{198}Hg_{NIST3133}) - 1] \times 1000 \qquad (4.1)$$

where *xxx* refers to the mass of each isotope between 199 and 202 amu.

MIF is expressed as the difference between the measured $\delta^{xxx}Hg$ values, the value predicted based on MDF, and the $\delta^{202}Hg$ value (Eqs. 4.2, 4.3, and 4.4).

$$\Delta^{199}Hg = \delta^{199}Hg - 0.252 \times \delta^{202}Hg \qquad (4.2)$$

$$\Delta^{200}Hg = \delta^{200}Hg - 0.502 \times \delta^{202}Hg \qquad (4,3)$$

$$\Delta^{201}Hg = \delta^{201}Hg - 0.752 \times \delta^{201}Hg \qquad (4.4)$$

4.2.2 Materials and Methods

4.2.2.1 Study Area

The Wanshan Hg mining area, located in the eastern part of Guizhou Province, held the largest Hg mine in China. Large-scale Hg mining activities operated in the area for over 50 years, leading to serious Hg contamination of the local environment. The Hg adits and historical retorts are situated upstream of four rivers in the region, and significant quantities of mine wastes are the primary Hg contamination source for rivers. Rice is widely cultured throughout the valleys in this region and the river water is the main source for irrigation. Wanshan County covers an area of approximately 338 km². The population in 2012 was 68,000, and the rural population constituted about 80%. The local economy is undeveloped, and the per capita gross domestic product was 14,914 RMB (US$2400) in 2011 (GBS, 2012), which was about half of the national average in China.

For the adults' Hg exposure study, seven sites in the towns of Xiaxi and Aozhai were selected for survey, as they were distributed along the Aozhai and Xiaxi Rivers with different gradients from the Hg pollution source. For the children's Hg exposure study, four regions named Xiaxi, Aozhai, Huangdao, and Gaolouping (regions A, B, C and D, respectively, in Figure 4.6) were selected. There are 4202 primary school students (5 to 14 years old) living in this area, among which 45% are female and 55% are male. For the children's IQ study, primary schools at sites A, B, and C were selected (Figure 4.7).

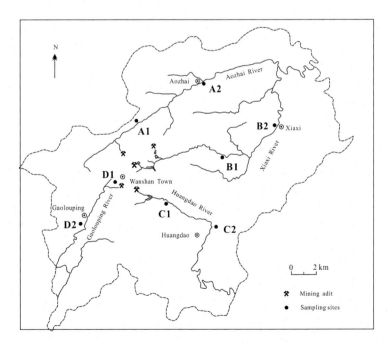

FIGURE 4.6 Locations of the study area and sampling sites. (From Du et al., 2016 with permission for reuse.)

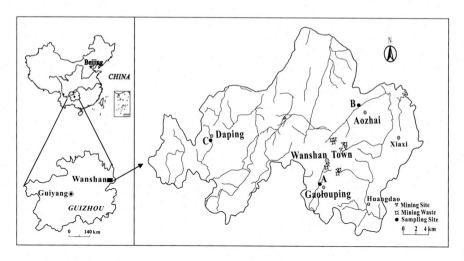

FIGURE 4.7 Spatial locations of the study sites in the Wanshan area. Schools A, B, and C were 3 km, 7 km, and 24 km away from the Hg mine, respectively. (From Feng et al., 2020 with permission for reuse.)

4.2.2.2 Sample Collection

Sampling of adult Hg exposure was conducted in December 2012. Participants were recruited with the criteria of being a local resident living in the area for over three months. A questionnaire was used to obtain basic information on age, body weight, profession, history of involvement in artisanal Hg mining activity, dental fillings, smoking and alcohol drinking habits, illnesses, and amount of daily rice consumption. Daily rice intake (g/day) was quantified by participants according to eating habits and whole family monthly and/or annual rice consumption figures reported by housewives. Residents in the Wanshan area seldom eat fish, and fish consumption is similar to the average daily fish intake of 1.2 g/day for Guizhou rural residents (GBS, 2012). Our previous study has shown that the MeHg concentrations in fish samples collected from Wanshan Hg mine were relatively low, with a mean of 0.060 µg/g (Qiu et al., 2009). Fish samples were not collected in this study since fish is not a significant dietary source of MeHg in the local population (Zhang et al., 2010a). Hair samples were cut with stainless steel scissors from the occipital region of the scalp of each participant, bundled together in polyethylene bags, and then transferred to the laboratory. Venous blood samples (5 mL) were collected from each participant in prepared EDTA vacuum tubes. Blood samples were stored on ice during the field-work and transferred to –20°C upon receipt at the laboratory. Raw rice samples were collected from each participating household.

For children's Hg exposure, two primary schools within each region were selected. Inside regions A, B, and C, the selected two schools were (1) distributed along the respective rivers of Hg catchment, which makes it easier to compare results with the results for adults in formal studies, and (2) within varying distances from the sources. A1 was located upstream of A2 in region A, along the Xiaxi River; B1 was located upstream of B2 in region B, along the Aozhai River; and C1 was located upstream of C2 in region C, along the Huangdao River. In region D, only one primary school was located downstream. As a result, D1 was located in the center of the town of Wanshan, upstream of all of the mining sites, while D2 was located downstream of the Gaolouping River. The spatial distribution of the sampling sites is shown in Figure 4.6. Sampling was conducted in March 2013. All the students at schools A1 and C1 (100%) were invited to participate. For the other six sampling sites, a class in grade three was chosen randomly in each school, and all the students in the class were invited to participate. In total, 237 primary school children were sampled. After the children who did not complete hair and urine samples and questionnaires were eliminated, 217 children were included in this study. All the participants lived in villages near the schools, and none had left the area in the last three months. Hair samples were cut with stainless steel scissors from the occipital region of the scalp, bundled together with strips of scrip, and placed in polyethene bags, which were sealed, properly identified, and brought to the laboratory. Hair samples were washed with nonionic detergent, distilled water, and acetone and then dried in an oven at 60°C overnight. Each child was required to fill out a questionnaire which included information on age, gender, home location, amalgam use by his or her family, illnesses, food consumption habits, and frequency of eating at the school cafeteria. The teachers explained the questionnaire and helped the children to fill out the questionnaire. All children and their guardians gave their informed consent before participating in the study.

The children's IQ study was granted ethics approval from the Affiliated Hospital of Guizhou Medical University. The guardians of the participants in this study all signed informed consent forms. Wanshan has six township-level primary schools. Hair sample collection, administration of IQ tests, and completion of questionnaires were carried out for pupils 8–10 years old in these three schools between September 2018 and March 2019. The criteria to select the participants included (1) being a local student who had not left home during the previous three months; (2) having the ability to complete an IQ test (no communication impairment, hand disability, etc.); and (3) having parents with no history of mental illness. In total, 322 volunteer participants were recruited into this study. After excluding children who could not complete the IQ test, 314 children were analyzed in this study. Among them, 11.1%, 67.2%, and 21.7% are the proportions of 8-, 9-, and 10-year-olds in the study population, respectively. A total of 314 hair samples were collected.

The children's guardians completed the questionnaire. The questionnaires provided information about potential confounding factors (Gustin et al., 2018; Pan et al., 2018; Sun et al., 2015; Taylor et al., 2017) and included children's basic information (gender, age, ethnicity, primary school grade, and school); socioeconomic and lifestyle factors of the family (parents' education, parents' marriage, number of siblings, annual per capita income in RMB, whether the parents were migrant workers, passive smoke at home, maternal drinking, and house decoration within the past year); newborn situation of children (breastfeeding and birth weight); child's diet (frequency of consuming fish); presence of any child social adaptability disorder; and summer school attendance. Among these, the question on social adaptability disorder was adopted from the mental health rating scale for primary school students (Chinese version; MHRSP) (Chen et al., 2000).

4.2.2.3 Analytical Methods

The portion of hair within 3 cm from the scalp was selected for THg and MeHg analysis. Hair samples were washed with nonionic detergent, distilled water, and acetone and dried in an oven at 60 °C overnight. Rice samples were air-dried, crushed, and sieved to 150-mesh size. The THg concentrations in the hair and rice samples were analyzed by the RA-915+ Hg analyzer coupled with the PYRO-915+ attachment (Lumex, Russia). THg concentrations in whole blood samples (0.1 mL) were acid digested and detected by CVAFS. MeHg concentrations in hair, rice, and blood samples were digested using the KOH-methanol/solvent extraction technique and measured by GC-CVAFS (Brooks Rand MERX).

4.2.2.4 Calculation of Probable Daily Intake (PDI)

To estimate daily MeHg intake from rice consumption, we calculated a PDI value for each participant at the seven sites using Eq. 4.9:

$$PDI = (C \times IR \times 10^{-3})/bw \qquad (4.9)$$

where PDI is given in micrograms per kilogram of body weight per day (µg/kg/d); bw is body weight (kg); C is the MeHg concentration in rice (ng/g); and IR is daily intake rate of rice (g/d), which was obtained from the questionnaire of each participant.

4.2.2.5 Cognitive Assessment

The IQ test was the Wechsler Intelligence Scale for Children–Fourth Edition, Chinese version (WISC-IV). The Wechsler Intelligence Scale is internationally recognized as the most reliable and widely applicable diagnostic intelligence test (Whitaker., 2008; Nuovo et al., 2012). The WISC-IV is composed of 10 subtests, from which children's total IQ scores and four ability scores (verbal comprehension, perceptual reasoning, working memory, and processing speed) can be obtained. All testers were trained by a professional before the test. We provided separate rooms for one-to-one, face-to-face interviews for the IQ test. A total IQ score of 80 is considered as the upper bound cut-off for borderline intellectual disability (Jacobson et al., 2015), and a total IQ score of 100 is the average level of Chinese children (Wechsler and Zhang, 2008).

4.2.2.6 Economic Loss Calculation

The economic loss calculation model was adopted from Trasande et al. (2005). The calculated approach was initially developed by the Institute of Medicine (IOM, 1981) to assess the costs of environmental and occupational disease. It was also used to estimate the environmental costs of lead poisoning and neurodevelopmental disabilities in American children (Landrigan et al., 2002; Trasande et al., 2005). We used hair Hg concentrations in children for the calculation in Eq. 4.10:

$$Costs = EAF \times population\ size \times cost\ per\ case \qquad (4.10)$$

where Costs refer to the cost of Hg exposure in every year's birth cohort; population size refers to the number of births in a year; cost per case refers to each person's loss of money in their lifetime under Hg exposure; and EAF refers to the environmentally attributable fraction. As this study concerned estimation of the costs caused by anthropogenic sources of Hg, EAF means the portion of Hg that can be attributed to human activities. The anthropogenic sources of Hg were set at 70% of the total global Hg pool (Mason and Sheu, 2002).

Trasande et al. (2005) used the method described by Salkever (1995) to assess the economic cost of Hg exposure based on IQ scores. When the IQ fell by one point, a person's lifetime earnings were reduced by 1.9% for men and 3.2% for women, respectively. The US EPA (2000) used a participation-weighted average of 2.379% per IQ point for the combined lifetime earnings, which was adopted in this study. Therefore, cost per case can be calculated as in Eq. 4.11:

$$\text{Cost per case} = 2.379\% \times \sum \$ \times (1 + n\%)^k \tag{4.11}$$

where $\$$ refers to annual income; $n\%$ refers to the annual growth rate of income; and k refers to the average number of years of work in a person's life.

4.2.2.7 Statistical Analysis

SPSS 24.0 was used for statistical analysis. The normal distribution of the data was determined using the Kolmogorov–Smirnov test. Since the hair Hg data were not normally distributed, a non-parametric test was used in the following analysis. Arithmetic means were used to describe the hair Hg concentrations and IQ scores. The correlation between hair Hg and IQ was tested by Spearman's correlation, and the mean value was compared for different sites using the Kruskal–Wallis H rank-sum test. Binary logistic regression was used to assess the relationship between hair Hg and IQ < 80 (IQ < 80 regarded as $y = 1$). Children's age was considered as a qualitative variable. Initially, univariable logistic regression analysis was performed. Then, the confounders were added into the model to adjust the logistic regression analysis. Multiple linear regression analysis was used to assess the relationship between IQ and hair Hg. To make sure of the regression coefficient (B value) range, the multivariable-adjusted linear regressions of models 5 and 6 were analyzed. The confounders were used in the model due to the model R-squared value and previous relevant research (Gustin et al., 2018; Pan et al., 2018; Sun et al., 2015; Taylor et al., 2017). If $p < 0.05$, the statistical test results were considered as significantly different.

4.2.3 MeHg Exposure in Wanshan Adults

4.2.3.1 Rice Hg and PDIs of MeHg

The THg and MeHg concentrations in the rice samples collected from the seven sites are shown in Figure 4.8. The average of the THg concentrations in all rice samples was 42.4 ± 52.7 ng/g, and 53% of samples exceeded the national limit (20 ng/g). The MeHg concentrations in all rice samples averaged 11.7 ± 8.84 ng/g, and MeHg constituted 44.8 ± 23.9% of the THg on average. The average percentages of THg that were MeHg in rice samples from sites D and E were relatively low (23.0 ± 16.7% and 19.1 ± 8.44%, respectively). A significant correlation between THg and MeHg concentrations was found in all rice samples ($r = 0.44$, $p < 0.001$). The PDIs

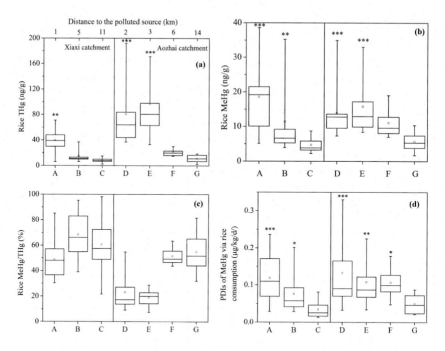

FIGURE 4.8 Comparison of rice Hg and PDIs of MeHg via rice consumption at seven sites. *$p < 0.05$; **$p < 0.01$; ***$p < 0.001$. A and B compared with C; D, E, and F, compared with G. Each box represents an interquartile range (25th and 75th percentile), the band near the middle of the box is the 50th percentile (the median), the whiskers represent the 5th and 95th percentile, and the dot under the box is the mean. (From Li et al., 2015 with permission for reuse.)

of MeHg through rice consumption for the residents at the seven sites are presented in Figure 4.8d. The average PDI of MeHg from rice consumption ranged from 0.050 to 0.132 μg/kg/d.

4.2.3.2 Hair and Blood Hg

The distribution of THg and MeHg concentrations in hair samples from the seven sites is shown in Figure 4.9. The averages of hair THg concentrations ranged from 1.33 to 5.07 μg/g, and those for MeHg ranged from 0.79 to 3.67 μg/g. MeHg constituted $71.7 \pm 18.2\%$ of the THg in all hair samples on average, and it was the main form of Hg in hair. A significant correlation ($r = 0.84$, $p < 0.001$) between hair THg and MeHg concentrations was observed. In the total population, the overall average blood THg concentration was 12.2 ± 15.0 μg/L (2.15–30.8, 95%CI). The average blood MeHg concentration at different sites ranged from 2.20 to 9.36 μg/L. MeHg constituted $52.8 \pm 17.5\%$ of the THg in all blood samples on average.

In this study, a significant positive correlation ($r^2 = 0.83$, $p < 0.001$) was observed between human blood MeHg concentration and the PDI of MeHg via rice consumption (Figure 4.10a). A significant positive correlation ($r^2 = 0.74$, $p < 0.001$) was also observed between human hair MeHg concentration and the PDI of MeHg via rice consumption (Figure 4.10b).

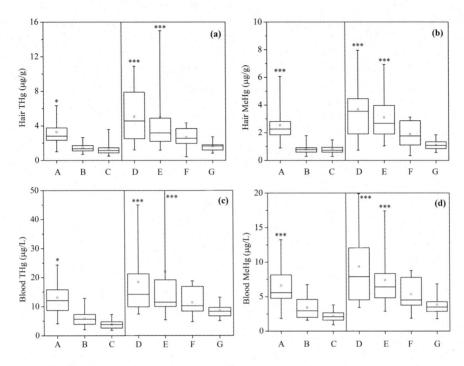

FIGURE 4.9 Comparison of hair and blood Hg in the population at different sites. *$p < 0.05$; **$p < 0.01$; ***$p < 0.001$. A and B compared with C; D, E, and F, compared with G. (From Li et al., 2015 with permission for reuse.)

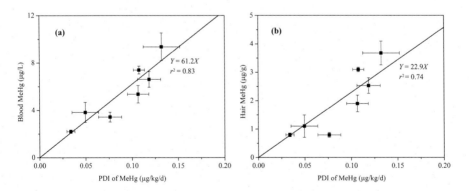

FIGURE 4.10 Relationship between human blood/hair MeHg and PDIs of MeHg via rice consumption at different sites. (From Li et al., 2015 with permission for reuse.)

4.2.3.3 Geographical Difference

The THg and MeHg concentrations in rice samples reduced within the two catchments as a function of distance from the pollution source (Figure 4.8). Both THg and MeHg concentrations in rice samples were elevated in the upstream region (sites A, D, and E), where people were seriously impacted by the mine wastes downstream

(Zhang et al., 2010c, d). The Hg in the paddy soil could serve as a source of Hg in rice both for IHg and for MeHg (Zhang et al., 2010b). Average values for the PDI at each site showed a similar trend of reduction with increasing distance from the point source of Hg contamination within the two catchments (Figure 4.8d).

Almost 73% (122/168) of blood THg concentrations exceeded 5.8 μg/L, which is the blood Hg level equivalent to the RfD set by the US EPA. Individuals from sites close to the mine waste heaps (A, D, and E) showed significantly higher hair and blood THg and MeHg levels than those at sites C and G, who recorded values in agreement with the regional background (Figure 4.9c).

4.2.3.4   Hair-to-Blood Ratio

A "normal" hair:blood Hg concentration ratio of 250:1 is frequently cited in the literature (US EPA, 1997); however, uncertainty over the accuracy of this ratio exists in many reports. In one study, the median ratios in Faroese children were 370 at 7 years of age and 264 at 14 years of age (Budtz-Jørgensen et al., 2004). The median ratio in a Swedish population was 373 (Berglund et al., 2005), and the mean ratio after adjustment of time lag was 344 ± 54 (with a range of 263–478) in Japan (Yaginuma-Sakurai et al., 2012). In risk assessment for MeHg, both NAS/NRC and JECFA adopted an uncertainty factor of 3.2 on the toxicokinetic variability (JECFA, 2003; NRC, 2000).

The mean ratio of hair-to-blood MeHg concentration in this study (expressed as μg MeHg/g hair to μg MeHg/L blood) was 361 ± 105, and the 5th and 95th percentiles were 178 and 538, respectively. As well, the ratios of hair-to-blood THg concentrations were calculated for comparison; the mean ratio was 268 ± 112, and the 5th and 95th percentiles were 127 and 493, respectively. The percentage of THg that was MeHg in hair was much higher than that in blood (average of 72% to 52%), which resulted in an elevation of hair-to-blood ratios for MeHg relative to THg. Significant correlations were found between the hair/blood MeHg and THg concentration in the study population. The results from this study (361 ± 105) were 44% higher than the average value of 250, which indicates that the reported average may underestimate the MeHg distribution between human hair and blood in the study population.

4.2.3.5   PDI and Body Burden

The one compartment model calculated the steady-state Hg concentration in blood (C) in μg/L from the average daily dietary intake (in μg Hg per kg body weight per day), as shown in Eq. 4.12:

$$C = \frac{d \times A \times f \times bw}{b \times V} \qquad (4.12)$$

where d represents the PDI of MeHg in μg/kg/d; A is the absorption factor, which is assumed to be 0.95 (US EPA, 1997); f is the absorbed dose found in blood, and the value is 0.05 (US EPA, 1997); bw is the body weight (kg); b is the elimination constant (0.014/d; US EPA, 1997); and V is the blood volume (L, 8% of bw; Yiengst and Shock, 1962).

TABLE 4.5

Simulation Runs for Blood and Hair MeHg at the Seven Sites

Site	PDI of MeHg (μg/kg/d)	Blood MeHg (μg/L)			Hair MeHg (μg/g)		
		Modeled	Measured	Variability (%)	Modeled	Measured	Variability (%)
A	0.119 ± 0.068	5.03	6.60	76	1.26	2.53	50
B	0.076 ± 0.051	3.23	3.44	94	0.81	0.79	103
C	0.034 ± 0.025	1.44	2.20	65	0.36	0.80	45
D	0.132 ± 0.105	5.61	9.36	60	1.40	3.67	38
E	0.108 ± 0.076	4.57	7.40	62	1.14	3.09	37
F	0.107 ± 0.037	4.52	5.36	84	1.13	1.90	59
G	0.050 ± 0.030	2.10	3.83	55	0.53	1.10	48

Source: From Li et al., (2015) with permission for reuse.

Using Eq. 4.12, modeled MeHg concentrations in blood can be obtained from the PDI values. Considering the hair-to-blood ratio as the average of 250:1, modeled hair MeHg concentrations (H) also can be obtained from the PDI values for individuals. Table 4.5 presents the calculated MeHg PDIs at the seven sites and a comparison of the simulated value with the measured blood and hair MeHg concentrations. There was good agreement between the measured blood and hair MeHg levels and the estimated value at site B. However, the modeled blood and hair MeHg levels for other sites were significantly lower than the measured concentrations.

A significant positive correlation was obtained between human hair MeHg concentrations (H) and PDIs of MeHg via rice consumption (d) at the different sites (Figure 4.10b), with the regression equation quantified as $H = 22.9d$. The corresponding reported model for the fish-eating population is $H = 10d$ (US EPA, 1997). In practical terms, this means that an RfD of 0.1 μg/kg/d corresponds to a hair MeHg concentration of 1 μg/g. The regression coefficient for the model derived from our study was 2.3 times greater than that for the fish model, indicating that hair MeHg levels are highly elevated at the same exposure dose for the population consuming MeHg-contaminated rice relative to the fish consumers. The MeHg toxicokinetics model based on fish consumption is therefore not suitable for risk assessment of MeHg exposure via rice consumption.

Compared with fish, rice is of poor nutritional quality and lacks specific micronutrients identified as having health benefits (e.g., n-3 LCPUFA, Se, essential amino acids; Li et al., 2010). A wide variety of foods and nutrients may impact the absorption, distribution, and elimination of MeHg in the human body, and the inconsistency of the MeHg toxicity observed in different populations is commonly attributed to possible effects of dietary modulation (Chapman and Chan, 2000). Our results indicate that the RfD and PTWI based on fish consumption may underestimate the risks caused by MeHg exposure via rice consumption.

4.2.3.6 Implication for Public Health

The hair MeHg concentrations obtained in this study (2.07 ± 1.79 µg/g) were comparable with those previously reported for residents at the Wanshan Hg mine (1.85 ± 1.16 µg/g; Feng et al., 2008) and Wuchuan Hg mine (1.25 ± 0.74 µg/g; Li et al., 2008), but were lower than those for residents at the Tongren Hg mines (5.24 ± 2.80 and 3.76 ± 1.73 µg/g for workers and residents, respectively; Li et al., 2011) and that for fishermen on Zhoushan Island (3.8 µg/g; Cheng et al., 2009). The blood THg concentrations in this study (12.2 ± 15.0 µg/L) were comparable with the mean of blood THg in residents from Chatian Hg mine (6.09 ± 3.26 µg/L; Li et al., 2013) and lower than serum Hg in residents also from Wanshan Hg mine (with a mean of 38.5 µg/L; Chen et al., 2006).

In this study, hair MeHg levels are highly elevated at the same exposure dose for the population consuming Hg-contaminated rice relative to those consuming fish. We propose that hair MeHg concentrations should be used as a more accurate measure of human exposure to Hg in the study population. The equivalent hair MeHg levels of 1.0 and 2.3 µg/g recommended by US EPA and JECFA have been adopted for risk assessment of MeHg exposure on a developing fetus. The total population in the Wanshan area is 68,000. For women of child-bearing age (15–44 years), the distribution of hair MeHg concentration within the population was calculated: >1 µg/g, 5600 inhabitants (8.2% of total population); >2.3 µg/g, 1400 inhabitants (2.1% of total population). In addition to Wanshan, there are 11 other Hg mining and smelting areas in Guizhou, with a population totaling approximately 320,000. Considering women of child-bearing age (15–44 years), there are 26,240 inhabitants with hair MeHg concentrations higher than 1 µg/g and 6720 inhabitants with hair MeHg concentrations higher than 2.3 µg/g.

Rice is the staple food of more than half the world's population. MeHg accumulation in rice and related health risks should be a concern in Hg-polluted areas (e.g., Hg mines, abandoned chlor-alkali facilities, artisanal and small-scale gold mines) where rice is served as a staple food. The findings obtained in this study can advise human MeHg exposure and risk assessment via rice consumption in these areas.

4.2.4 MERCURY EXPOSURE IN WANSHAN CHILDREN

4.2.4.1 Basic Information

A total of 18 children in A1 and 29 children in C1 (100% of students at the schools), from grade one to grade three, were investigated in this study. As for the other six sampling sites, 88% of all students at the school in B1 and 6.3–14% of those in A2, B2, C2, D1, and D2 were investigated in this study. The pupils were distributed with 51% girls and 49% boys. The average age of the children was 9.8 ± 1.3 (6–13) years old, and the average body weight (bw) and height were 28 ± 7.3 (17–70) kg and 133 ± 9.0 (110–160) cm, respectively.

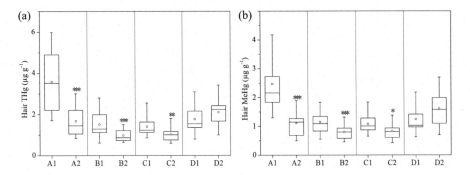

FIGURE 4.11 Hair THg (a) and hair MeHg (b) of the children in the Wanshan Hg mining areas. compared with the those at the sampling site in the same region. $*p < 0.05$; $**p < 0.01$; $***p < 0.00$. (From Du et al., 2016 with permission for reuse.)

4.2.4.2 Hair Hg

THg and MeHg concentrations in the hair samples of the children at different sites are shown in Figure 4.11. The mean THg concentration in all hair samples was 1.4 µg/g (with a range of 0.50 to 6.0 µg/g), but significant differences were shown among the eight sites. Site A1 showed significantly higher ($p < 0.05$) hair THg concentrations (with a mean of 3.3 µg/g) than the seven other sites (0.96–1.9 µg/g). In addition, 75% (163/217) of hair THg concentrations exceeded the reference value of 1 µg/g suggested by the United States Environmental Protection Agency (US EPA, 1997), while 18% (40/217) exceeded the reference value of 2.3 µg/g suggested by the Joint Expert Committee on Food Additives (JECFA, 2003). Remarkably, in A1, 100% of the hair THg samples surpassed the US EPA reference value, and 80% surpassed that of the JECFA.

The mean hair MeHg concentration in all the children was 1.1 µg/g (with a range of 0.35 to 4.2 µg/g). The average values across the eight sites ranged from 0.75 to 2.6 µg/g, with the highest in A1 and the lowest in C2. MeHg concentrations in hair accounted for $78 \pm 15\%$ of the THg for all the children (ranging from 39% to 99%), with no obvious difference found between the different sites ($p > 0.05$). Significant correlations were found between hair THg and MeHg concentrations at the eight sites (R^2 values were between 0.74 and 0.94, $p < 0.01$ for all pairs). No differences in hair Hg concentrations between different genders or different ages have been observed ($p > 0.05$).

4.2.4.3 Geographical Differences

Compared with those at sampling sites downstream, hair Hg concentrations upstream were higher in regions A, B, and C ($p < 0.001$ for A1 and A2; $p < 0.001$ for B1 and B2; $p < 0.01$ for C1 and C2, independent t-test) (Figure 4.11). The same tendency was also observed in soil, river sediment, and rice cultivated in this area (Dai et al., 2012; Feng and Qiu, 2008). The THg concentrations of the samples were inversely proportional to the distance from the mine waste. Indeed, Hg levels in the samples matched the background concentrations in the area (Feng and Qiu, 2008). Finally, the distance-related concentrations of Hg in rice resulted in distance-related concentrations of hair Hg.

4.2.4.4   Comparison with Adults

Four sampling sites were identified that matched the location of a study previously undertaken on adults in the same geographic area by Li et al. (2015). No significant difference has been observed between rice Hg concentrations from students' homes and adults' homes ($p > 0.05$). Hair Hg concentrations of children were slightly lower than those of adults within A1 and A2 zones ($p < 0.05$ for THg in A1, while $p < 0.01$ for THg in A2 and MeHg in both A1 and A2). This may be explained by two reasons: (1) the ingestion of the less-Hg-contaminated rice at school cafeterias than at home may reduce the exposure levels of children below those of adults and (2) the specific metabolic reactions of children may affect the behavior of Hg in children's bodies. For instance, the mean breathing rate over the first 12 years of life is almost twice as fast as adult breathing rates (452 vs. 232 L/kg/day; Layton, 1993), showing that the metabolic reactions of children are more active than those of adults, which can affect the Hg transfer and speciation in children's bodies. Additionally, the enzymatic activity of children may modify different reactions kinetics such as absorption, methylation/demethylation, distribution, and excretion compared with those of adults. More studies are needed to understand the details of Hg metabolic reactions of children's bodies (Caurant et al., 1996; Smith et al., 2009).

4.2.4.5   Worldwide Comparison

Hair Hg concentrations in children in this study were compared with those in other studies conducted over the past 10 years in mining sites throughout the world. Brazilian children living in a gold-mining region showed the highest hair THg concentrations, with average values of 2.3 to 17 µg/g (Barbosa et al., 2001; Dorea et al., 2005; Grandjean et al., 1999; Malm et al., 2010; Marinho et al., 2014; Murata and Dakeishi, 2002; Rocha et al., 2014). The results in this study were comparable with THg concentrations in children's hair from Ghana and Portugal (Adimado and Baah, 2002; Murata et al., 1999). Children located in the Philippines, Thailand, and Bolivia showed relatively low hair THg concentrations (with average values ranging from 0.49 to 0.99 µg/g) (Akagi et al., 2000; Barbieri et al., 2011; Umbangtalad et al., 2007).

4.2.4.6   Implication for Health of Children

Hair THg concentration is considered a good biomarker for human MeHg exposure. The hair THg levels of 1.0 and 2.3 µg/g recommended by US EPA and JECFA, respectively, were adopted for risk assessment of MeHg exposure. In total, 61% (2556/4202) of hair THg concentrations in primary school children exceeded 1.0 µg/g, while 8% (327/4202) exceeded 2.3 µg/g. These proportions were 75% (348/464) and 18% (84/464) in region A and 74% (1740/2348) and 10% (243/2348) in region D.

Children's Hg exposure levels were the highest in region A, 2 km downstream of the Hg mine sites, which was seriously contaminated by mining activities. Hair THg and MeHg concentrations in the children were high at upstream sites, especially in mining site A1. Hair THg concentrations were much lower in the children than in the adults in the same region, which resulted from lower rice Hg levels in school cafeterias. In the future, more research is needed to understand the metabolic processes influencing

Hg bioaccumulation and excretion in children. Moreover, pertinent policies should be adopted to reduce the Hg exposure level of the children living in this area.

4.2.5 CHILDREN'S Hg EXPOSURE AND INTELLIGENCE QUOTIENT (IQ) LOSS

4.2.5.1 Characteristics of Participants

The basic information on primary school students in Wanshan is shown in Table 4.6. A total of 314 (97.5%, 314/322) children were analyzed; 51.9% of the participants were boys, and 86.6% of the participants were the Dong minority. Less than 15% of parents attended senior high school. Of all the households, 26.7% had a per capita

TABLE 4.6

Characteristics of Primary School Students in the Wanshan Area

Variable		*n*	%
Total		314	100
Gender			
	Boys	163	51.9
Age			
	8	35	11.1
	9	211	67.1
	10	68	21.6
Ethnicity			
	Han	19	6.00
	Dong	272	86.6
	Others	22	6.80
School			
	A	218	69.4
	B	47	14.9
	C	49	15.6
Number of siblings			
	0	35	11.1
Father's education			
	≤Junior school	257	81.7
	≥Senior high school	33	10.4
Mother's education			
	≤Junior school	244	77.6
	≥Senior high school	35	11.0
Parents' marriage			
	cohabiting or married	252	80.1
	others	41	12.9
Annual per capital income (RMB)			
	<3900	84	26.7
	3900–29,999	135	42.5
	≥30,000	37	11.7

(Continued)

TABLE 4.6 *(Continued)*

Characteristics of Primary School Students in the Wanshan Area

Variable		*n*	%
Passive smoking at home			
	Yes	191	60.8
Maternal drinking			
	Yes	30	9.30
Frequency of consuming fish			
	< 1/week	240	76.4
	≥1/week	44	13.9
Breastfeeding			
	< 4 months	94	29.8
	4–6 months	36	11.4
	≥6 months	132	42.0
House decoration within 1 year			
	Yes	82	26.1
Summer school attendance			
	Yes	27	8.50
IQ score			
	<80	42	13.4
	80–99	198	67.8
	≥100	74	18.8
Hair Hg concentration (µg/g)			
	<1	108	34.4
	1–1.99	149	47.5
	2–5.99	53	16.9
	≥6	4	1.27

Source: From Feng et al., (2020) with permission for reuse.

annual income lower than 4,080 RMB (about $US574), which was the minimum standard of living allowance for rural residents in Guizhou in 2019. Most students (76.4%) ate fish less than once a week.

4.2.5.2 Hair Hg Level

Hair Hg concentrations of the participants are shown in Figure 4.12. The mean hair Hg concentration was 1.53 µg/g (range: 0.21–12.6 µg/g), and 65.6% (206/314) exceeded the reference value of 1 µg/g set by the US EPA, while 12.4% (39/314) exceeded the reference value of 2.3 µg/g suggested by JECFA (2003). Significant differences were found for the children's hair Hg concentrations between different schools ($p < 0.05$). School A was closest to the Wanshan Hg mine and showed the highest hair Hg concentrations in children. Hair Hg concentrations in students from school A averaged 1.73 µg/g; 77.6% exceeded the US EPA reference value, and 16.0% exceeded the JECFA reference value.

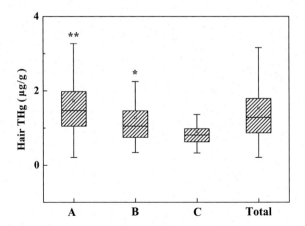

FIGURE 4.12 Hair THg in children of the Wanshan Hg mining area. *$p < 0.05$, compared with C; **$p < 0.05$, compared with B and C, Kruskal–Wallis *H* test. Each box represents an interquartile range (25th and 75th percentile), the band near the middle of the box is the 50th percentile (the median), the whiskers represent the 5th and 95th percentiles, and the squares in the box represent the mean value. (From Feng et al., 2020 with permission for reuse.)

4.2.5.3 Cognitive Test Results

The mean value of the total IQ scores for the children was 91.0 (range: 51–122), which is much lower than the average intelligence level (100) of Chinese children (Figure 4.13). Of note, 13.4% (42/314) of the children's IQ values were lower than 80, which is the upper bound cut-off for borderline intellectual disability. The means of the IQ scores of children from schools A, B, and C were 91.65, 88.85, and

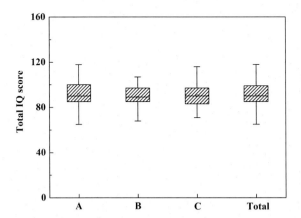

FIGURE 4.13 Total IQ of children of the Wanshan area. Total IQ = 100 is the average IQ level of Chinese children. Each box represents an interquartile range (25th and 75th percentile), the band near the middle of the box is the 50th percentile (the median), the whiskers represent the 5th and 95th percentiles, and the squares in the box represent the mean value. (From Feng et al., 2020 with permission for reuse.)

90.29 points, respectively. There was no significant difference in the total IQ scores between the students from the three schools.

4.2.5.4　Hair Hg and IQ

The correlation between hair Hg and IQ was negative but not significant ($r = -0.054$, $p > 0.05$). In logistic regression analysis, there was no significant association between hair Hg and IQ (< 80 or ≥ 80) without adjusting for confounders in model 1 ($R^2 = 0.002$, $p > 0.05$; Table 4.7a). However, after adjusting for confounders in models 3 and 4, statistically significant associations were found between hair Hg and IQ < 80. The odds of children having IQ < 80 increased by 1.58 times when the hair Hg increased by 1 µg/g in model 4 ($R^2 = 0.20$, $p = 0.03$).

As more confounders were adjusted, the regression coefficients between IQ and hair Hg were stable between −0.9 and −1.1 in multiple linear regression analysis, but there was no significant association between hair Hg and IQ (Table 4.7b). Attending summer school, parents' marriage, and the age of the child were the most important confounders affecting IQ in multiple linear regression model 4 (Table 4.8).

4.2.5.5　Economic Costs of IQ Loss

Based on the multiple linear analysis, the regression coefficients between IQ and hair Hg were stable between −0.9 and −1.1. Therefore, we propose that an increase in hair Hg of 1 µg/g would result in a one-point decrease in the child population's IQ on average. According to the US EPA reference value of 1 µg/g and our previous study also carried out in this area (Du et al., 2016), we chose the towns of Wanshan, Gaolouping, Aozhai, Xiaxi, and Huangdao to calculate the economic cost of Hg exposure. We studied the Hg exposure of 237 children at eight primary schools in the Wanshan Hg mining area in 2013 (Du et al., 2016). The schools A and B in this study were primary schools A2 and D2 studied in Du et al. (2016), but the children involved in this study are not the same group of children as in Du et al. (2016).

Wanshan area had serious environmental Hg pollution in previous studies (Li et al., 2015). Combining the results obtained in this study and previous results from Du et al. (2016), we set 1.64 µg/g ($n = 482$) as the mean hair Hg concentration of children in the Wanshan area. The total population of the Wanshan area was 84,624

TABLE 4.7

(a) Logistic Regression Analysis of Hair Hg and the Children's Total IQ

			IQ < 80		
Model	n	OR	95% CI	R^2	p
Model 1	314	1.106	(0.883, 1.385)	0.002	0.379
Model 2	314	1.116	(0.891, 1.397)	0.018	0.341
Model 3	297	1.421	(1.012, 1.995)	0.139	0.043
Model 4	295	1.580	(1.043, 2.394)	0.195	0.031

Source:　From Feng et al. (2020) with permission for reuse.

TABLE 4.7 *(Continued)*

(b) Linear Regression Analyses of Hair Mercury and the Children's Total IQ Scores

Model	n	B	95% CI	R^2	p
Model 1	314	−0.294	(−1.226, 0.637)	0.001	0.535
Model 2	314	−0.254	(−1.182, 0.675)	0.019	0.591
Model 3	296	−0.957	(−2.057, 0.144)	0.077	0.088
Model 4	295	−1.035	(−2.121, 0.050)	0.106	0.062
Model 5	297	−0.999	(−2.114, 0.115)	0.045	0.079
Model 6	297	−1.041	(−2.156, 0.740)	0.066	0.067

Source: From Feng et al. (2020) with permission for reuse

Model 2: Adjusted for child gender and age.

Model 3: Adjusted for child gender, age, ethnicity, school, father's education, mother's education, parents' marriage, annual per capita income (RMB), number of siblings, breastfeeding, frequency of consuming fish, and house decoration within 1 year.

Model 4: Adjusted for child gender, age, ethnicity, school, father's education, mother's education, parents' marriage, annual per capita income (RMB), number of siblings, breastfeeding, frequency of consuming fish, house decoration within 1 year, passive smoking at home, maternal drinking, and summer school attendance.

Model 5: Adjusted for child gender, age, ethnicity, school, father's education, mother's education, annual per capita income (RMB), frequency of consuming fish, house decoration within 1 year, and whether parents were migrant workers (more than half year).

Model 6: Adjusted for child gender, age, ethnicity, school, father's education, mother's education, annual per capita income (RMB), frequency of consuming fish, house decoration within 1 year, whether parents were migrant workers (more than half year), primary school grade, passive smoking at home, maternal drinking, and child social adaptability disorder.

TABLE 4.8

The Contribution of Each Factor to IQ in Multiple Linear Regression Model 4

Factor	R^2	Adjusted R^2
Father's education	0	−0.003
Passive smoking at home	0	−0.003
Mother's education	0.001	−0.003
Hair Hg	0.001	−0.002
Maternal drinking	0.004	0.001
Ethnicity	0.004	0.001
House decoration within 1 year	0.005	0.001
Frequency of consuming fish	0.005	0.002
Per capita income	0.006	0.002
Child gender	0.005	0.002
Number of siblings	0.006	0.004
School	0.009	0.005
Breastfeeding	0.010	0.006
Age	0.013	0.010
Parents' marriage	0.016	0.013
Summer school attendance	0.021	0.018

Source: From Feng et al., (2020) with permission for reuse.

TABLE 4.9

Economic Costs of IQ Loss in the Wanshan Area

Variable	Wanshan Hg Mining Area
Population	84,624
Birth rate (%)	10.7
Number of births in a year	905
Per capita GDP ($)	5843
Growth rate of per capita GDP (%)	10.7
Per capita lifetime income ($)	2,822,852.7
Costs of hair Hg of 1.64 µg/g ($)	69,770,707.6
Costs of hair Hg of 0.1 µg/g ($)	4,254,311.4

Source: From Feng et al. (2020) with permission for reuse.

in 2012. According to the local birth rate of 10.7%, there were 905 newborns in the Wanshan area annually. The GDP and the per capita GDP of the town of Wanshan were 5.06 billion RMB (US$0.74 billion) and 40,183 RMB (US$5843) in 2018, respectively. We assumed that the average number of years of work in a person's life was 39 years, because the ages of 16, 50, and 60 are the legal minimum working age, female retirement age, and male retirement age in China, respectively.

We estimated that the total cost of IQ loss due to Hg exposure was US$69.8 million per year in the Wanshan area. If human hair Hg in the Wanshan area was reduced 0.1 µg/g by pollution control and remediation actions, the economic benefit was estimated to be US$4.25 million per year in the Wanshan area (Table 4.9).

4.2.5.6 Discussion

Hair Hg concentrations in Wanshan children averaged 1.53 µg/g. This is consistent with the THg concentration (1.4 µg/g) in children's hair in our previous study (Du et al., 2016). A comparison of hair Hg concentrations in children from different studies is shown in Table 4.10. For comparison of Hg levels between different biological materials, we assumed a ratio of 250:1 for Hg in hair to that in blood and we assumed that cord blood Hg is equivalent to blood Hg of children (WHO, 1990). Notably, hair Hg concentrations in Wanshan children were much higher than those in Zhoushan, China, who ate 32.19 kg fish per person in 2013 (Gao et al., 2007). Furthermore, the hair Hg concentrations of Wanshan children were higher than those of children from the United States (0.22 µg/g) and Canada (1.43 µg/g) (McDowell et al., 2004; Tian et al., 2011). However, the hair Hg concentrations of Wanshan children were much lower than those of children of the Faroe Islands (2.99 µg/g), the Seychelles (6.50 µg/g), and Hong Kong (Davidson et al., 1998; Grandjean et al., 1997; Lam et al., 2013). The median of cord blood Hg in Hong Kong ($n = 608$) was 9.18 µg/L, which is equivalent to 2.30 µg/g for hair Hg (Lam et al., 2013). Fok et al. (2007) thought that the high consumption of fish during pregnancy caused high hair Hg concentrations in Hong Kong people. In summary, the hair Hg concentrations of Wanshan children were at a low or medium level.

TABLE 4.10

Comparison of Hair/Blood and Cord Blood Hg Levels in Children from Different Study Areas

Reference	Study Area	Exposure Source	n	Age	Hair ($\mu g/g$)	Cord Blood ($\mu g/L$)	Blood ($\mu g/L$)
This study	Wanshan	Rice	314	8–10	1.53		
McDowell et al. (2004)	USA	Fish	838	1–5	0.22		
Yan et al. (2017)	Shanghai	Fish	1982		0.30		
Gao et al. (2018)	China	Fish	14,202	0–6			1.39
Ou et al. (2015)	North China	Fish	42	0	0.62	2.93	
Gao et al. (2007)*	Zhoushan	Marine fish	408	0		5.58	
Tian et al. (2011)	Canada	Fish, whale meat, seal meat	361	3–5	1.43		
Lam et al. (2013)#	Hong Kong	Marine fish	608	6–10		9.18	
Grandjean et al. (1997)*	Faroe Island	Whale meat	903	7	2.99	22.9	
Davidson et al. (1998)	Seychelles	Fish	708	5	6.50		

Source: From Feng et al., (2020) with permission for reuse.
* The average of the data was the geometric mean. #The average of the data was the median. For the rest of the studies, the average was the mean value.

The mean of the total IQ scores (91.0 points) of Wanshan children, obtained by the WISC-IV method, was much lower than that of general children in China (100 points). The mean total IQ of children in the ALSPAC study (n = 2217), using the WISC-III method, in the UK was 104.0 points (Golding et al., 2017). The means of the IQ values determined by the WISC-IV test for Italian and Canadian children were 106.0 (n = 299) and 101.2 (n = 259), respectively (Lucchini et al., 2019; Tian et al., 2011). The IQ points of children living in the Wanshan area were much lower than those of these populations, which may be due to socioeconomic factors, such as low family income and undeveloped school education level. Wanshan County is an undeveloped district, and the studied schools were township-level schools. In comparison, the effects of Hg exposure on IQ scores may be relatively low. This may be the main reason that we found no significant associations between IQ score and hair Hg in the multiple linear regression analysis (p = 0.062). In addition, low IQ score in children will not only affect the level of education and personal income but also affect the speed of technological progress and productivity. Many studies have found that small decreases in IQ will result in lower income (US EPA, 1985; Bellanger et al., 2013; Salkever, 1995). Generally, a lower average IQ value in the population will increase the number of people who have low IQ (IQ < 80 or 70) and who may be considered as intellectually challenged. It also reduces the number of talented and highly gifted people with high IQ (IQ > 130), who may contribute to the development of society (Muir and Zegarac, 2001).

We found that the odds of children having an IQ < 80 increased 1.58 times when hair Hg increased by 1 μg/g. The regression coefficients between IQ and hair Hg were stable from −0.9 to −1.1 in multiple linear regression analyses. This means that children's IQ scores will drop by about one point when hair Hg increases by 1 μg/g. We compared this relationship with that reported by Axelrad et al. (2007), who estimated that children's IQ would decrease by 0.18 point with each increase of 1 μg/g in maternal hair Hg from fish consumption. Previous studies showed that rice consumption is the main pathway of MeHg exposure (>95%) for our studied populations living in the Hg mining area (Feng et al., 2008; Zhang et al., 2010a). Our results suggest that the effects of Hg exposure via rice consumption on children's IQ development may be much higher than those via fish consumption.

In this study, we found that attending summer school, parents' marriage, and child's age were the most important contributing factors to IQ scores in model 4. This may be part of the reason that children's average IQ in the Wanshan area is lower than the average of Chinese children. We found that 9.8% and 8.5% of the students had attended cram schools and summer schools, respectively. Attending summer school is a factor that reflects the family's economy condition and the guardians' attention to education. Family economics, parents' attitudes toward education, and family harmony are important factors in IQ (Ali et al., 2013; Buckley et al., 2019; Hanson et al., 2015). The average total IQ score of children whose parents were married or cohabiting was 91.25 points, while the total IQ score of children whose parents were divorced or widowed was 90.30 points, but without significant difference. Several large longitudinal studies found that children whose parents were divorced had symptoms such as conduct disorders, antisocial behavior, difficulty with peers and authority figures, depression, and academic and achievement problems (Cherlin et al., 1991; Elliott and Richards, 1991; Kelly et al., 2000). Parents' divorce has been associated with lower academic performance and achievement test scores (Kelly et al., 2000). To get rid of age's impact on the IQ score, we selected the children with an age of 9 years for study, as this age group was the majority (67.1%) of the studied population. The 8-year-old students ($n = 36$) came from the third grade of primary school, and 97.1% of the 10-year-old students (66/68) came from the fourth grade. The averages of IQ scores of children with ages of 8, 9, and 10 were 93.0±9.94, 91.4±10.2, and 88.8±9.99 points, respectively, but without significant difference.

Based on the multiple linear analysis, we assumed that a hair Hg increase of 1 μg/g would result in a one-point decrease in IQ. According to this result, the economic losses caused by Hg exposure in the Wanshan area were US$69.8 million in 2018, which accounted for 9.43% of the Wanshan total GDP in 2018. This cost will occur each year with every new birth cohort without Hg pollution control. We also found that when hair Hg drops by 0.1 μg/g, the economic loss will decline by US$4.25 million per year in 2018 dollars. These results can provide a theoretical basis for Hg pollution control and remediation for local government.

The average hair THg concentration in Wanshan children was 1.53 μg/g, which indicated health risks to children from Hg exposure in this area. The mean value of the total IQ scores was 91.0 (range: 51–122) for Wanshan children, which is much lower than the average (100) of Chinese children. We found that the odds of children having an IQ < 80 increased by 1.58 times when hair Hg increased by 1 µg/g. The total cost of IQ loss due to Hg exposure was estimated to be US$69.8 million per year in the Wanshan area in 2018 dollars. The results obtained in this study indicated that Hg pollution control actions (such as soil remediation) are urgently needed to reduce Hg bioaccumulation in rice and health risks of human Hg exposure in the Wanshan area.

REFERENCES

Adimado, A. A., Baah, D. A. 2002. Mercury in human blood, urine, hair, nail, and fish from the Ankobra and Tano river basins in Southwestern Ghana. Bulletin of Environmental Contamination and Toxicology 68, 339–46.

Akagi, H., Castillo, E. S., Corles-Maramba, N., et al. 2000. Health assessment for mercury exposure among schoolchildren residing near a gold processing and refining plant in Apokon, Tagum, Davao del Norte, Philippines. Science of the Total Environment 259, 31–43.

Ali, A., Ambler, G., Strydom, A., et al. 2013. The relationship between happiness and intelligent quotient: The contribution of socio-economic and clinical factors. Psychological Medicine 43, 1303–12.

Al-Majed, N. B., Preston, M. R. 2000. Factors influencing the total mercury and methyl mercury in the hair of the fishermen of Kuwait. Environmental Pollution 109, 239–50.

Axelrad, A. D., Bellinger, C. D., Ryan, M. L., et al. 2007. Dose-response relationship of prenatal mercury exposure and IQ: An integrative analysis of epidemiologic data. Environmental Health Perspectives 115, 609–15.

Barbieri, F. L., Cournil, A., Sarkis, J. E. S., et al. 2011. Hair trace elements concentration to describe polymetallic mining waste exposure in Bolivian Altiplano. Biological Trace Element Research 139, 10–23.

Barbosa, A. C., Jardim, W., Dorea, J. G., et al. 2001. Hair mercury speciation as a function of gender, age, and body mass index in inhabitants of the Negro River basin, Amazon, Brazil. Archives of Environmental Contamination and Toxicology 40, 439–44.

Bartell, S. M., Ponce, R. A., Sanga, R. N., et al. 2000. Human variability in mercury toxicokinetics and steady state biomarker ratios. Environmental Research 84, 127–32.

Basu, N., Horvat, M., Evers, D. C., et al. 2018. A state-of-the-science review of mercury biomarkers in human populations worldwide between 2000 and 2018. Environmental Health Perspectives 126, 1–14.

Bellanger, M., Pichery, C., Aerts, D., et al. 2013. Economic benefits of methylmercury exposure control in Europe: Monetary value of neurotoxicity prevention. Environmental Health 12, 1–10.

Bellinger, D. C. 2011. A strategy for comparing the contributions of environmental chemicals and other risk factors to neurodevelopment of children. Environmental Health Perspectives 120, 501–7.

Berglund, M., Lind, B., Bjornberg, K.A., et al. 2005. Inter-individual variations of human mercury exposure biomarkers: A cross-sectional assessment. Environmental Health 4, 20.

Bergquist, B. A., Blum, J. D. 2007. Mass-dependent and mass-independent fractionation of Hg isotopes by photo-reduction in aquatic systems. Science 318, 417–20.

Blum, J. D., Bergquist, B. A. 2007. Reporting of variations in the natural isotopic composition of mercury. Analytical and Bioanalytical Chemistry 388(2), 353–9.

Blum, J. D., Popp, B. N., Drazen, J. C. 2013. Methylmercury production below the mixed layer in the North Pacific Ocean. Nature Geosciences 6 (10), 879–84.

Blum, J. D., Sherman, L. S., Johnson, M. W. 2014. Mercury isotopes in earth and environmental sciences. Annual Review of Earth and Planetary Sciences 42(1), 249–69.

Buchachenko, A. L. 2001. Magnetic isotope effect: Nuclear spin control of chemical reactions. Journal of Physical Chemistry A 105(44), 9995–10011.

Buckley, L., Broadley, M., Cascio, C. N. 2019. Socio-economic status and the developing brain in adolescence: A systematic review. Child Neuropsychology 25, 859–84.

Budtz-Jørgensen, E., Grandjean, P., Jørgensen, P. J., et al. 2004. Association between mercury concentrations in blood and hair in methylmercury-exposed subjects at different ages. Environmental Research 95, 385–93.

Canuel, R., de Grosbois, S. B., Atikessé, L., et al. 2006. New evidence on variations of human body burden of methylmercury from fish consumption. Environmental Health Perspectives 114, 302–6.

Caurant, F., Navarro, M., Amiard, J. C. 1996. Mercury in pilot whales: Possible limits to the detoxification process. Science of the Total Environment 186, 95–104.

Chapman, L., Chan, H. M. 2000. The influence of nutrition on methylmercury intoxication. Environmental Health Perspectives 108(S1), 29–56.

Chen, C. Y., Yu, H. W., Zhao, J. J., et al. 2006. The roles of serum selenium and selenoproteins on mercury toxicity in environmental and occupational exposure. Environmental Health Perspectives 114, 297–301.

Cheng, J., Gao, L., Zhao, W., et al. 2009. Mercury levels in fisherman and their household members in Zhoushan, China: Impact of public health. Science of the Total Environment 407, 2625–30.

Cherlin, A. J., Furstenberg, F. F. J., Chase-Linsdale, P. L., et al. 1991. Longitudinal studies of effects of divorce on children in Great Britain and the United States. Science 252, 1386–9.

Clarkson, T. W., 1993. Mercury - major issues in environmental-health. Environmental Health Perspectives 100, 31–8.

Clarkson, T. W., Magos, L. 2006. The toxicology of mercury and its chemical compounds. Critical Reviews in Toxicology 36, 609–62.

Clewell, H. J., Gearhart, J. M., Gentry, P. R., et al. 1999. Evaluation of the uncertainty in an oral reference dose for methylmercury due to interindividual variability in pharmacokinetics. Risk Analysis 19, 547–58.

Crump, K., Kjellstrom, T., Shipp, A. M., et al. 1998. Influence of prenatal mercury exposure upon scholastic and psychological test performance: Benchmark analysis of a New Zealand cohort. Risk Analysis 18, 701–13.

Dai, Z. H., Feng, X. B., Sommar, J., et al. 2012. Spatial distribution of mercury deposition fluxes in Wanshan Hg mining area, Guizhou province, China. Atmospheric Chemistry and Physics 12, 6207–18.

Davidson, P. W., Myers, G. J., Cox, C., et al. 1998. Effects of prenatal and postnatal methylmercury exposure from fish consumption on neurodevelopment: Outcomes at 66 months of age in the Seychelles Child Development Study. JAMA 280, 701–7.

Demers, J. D., Blum, J. D., Zak, D. R. 2013. Mercury isotopes in a forested ecosystem: Implications for air-surface exchange dynamics and the global mercury cycle. Global Biogeochemical Cycle 27(1), 222–38.

Dorea, J. G., Barbosa, A. C., Ferrari, I., et al. 2005. Fish consumption (hair mercury) and nutritional status of Amazonian Amer-Indian children. American Journal of Human Biology 17, 507–14.

Dorea, J. G., Bezerra, V. L. V. A., Fajon, V., et al. 2011. Speciation of methyl- and ethylmercury in hair of breastfed infants acutely exposed to thimerosal-containing vaccines. Clinica Chimica Acta 412, 1563–6.

Driscoll, C., Mason, R., Chan, H. M., et al. 2013. Mercury as a global pollutant: Sources, pathways, and effects. Environmental Science & Technology 47, 4967–83.

Du, B., Feng, X., Li, P., et al. 2018. Use of mercury isotopes to quantify mercury exposure sources in inland populations, China. Environmental Science & Technology 52(9), 5407–16.

Du, B. Y., Li, P., Feng, X. B., et al. 2016. Mercury exposure in children of the Wanshan mercury mining area, Guizhou, China. International Journal of Environmental Research and Public Health 13, 3–16.

Elliott, B. J., Richards, M. P. M., 1991. Children and divorce: Educational performance and behavior before and after parental separation. International Journal of Law, Policy and the Family 5, 258–76.

Enrico, M., Roux, G. L., Marusczak, N., et al. 2016. Atmospheric mercury transfer to peat bogs dominated by gaseous elemental mercury dry deposition. Environmental Science & Technology 50(5), 2405–12.

Estrade, N., Carignan, J., Sonke, J. E., et al. 2010. Measuring Hg isotopes in bio-geo-environmental reference materials. Geostandards and Geoanalytical Research 34(1), 79–93.

Feng, C., Pedrero, Z., Li, P., et al. 2015. Investigation of Hg uptake and transport between paddy soil and rice seeds combining Hg isotopic composition and speciation. Elementa: Science of the Anthropocene 4, 000087.

Feng, L., Zhang, C., Liu, H., et al. 2020. Impact of low-level mercury exposure on intelligence quotient in children via rice consumption. Ecotoxicology and Environmental Safety 202, 110870.

Feng, X., Qiu, G. 2008. Mercury pollution in Guizhou, Southwestern China—An overview. Science of the Total Environment 400, 227–37.

Feng, X. B., Li, P., Qiu, G. L., et al. 2008. Human exposure to methylmercury through rice intake in mercury mining areas, Guizhou Province, China. Environmental Science & Technology 42, 326–32.

Fok, T. F., Lam, H. S., Ng, P. C., et al. 2007. Fetal methylmercury exposure as measured by cord blood mercury concentrations in a mother–infant cohort in Hong Kong. Environment International 33, 84–92.

Fu, X., Feng, X., Qiu, G., et al. 2011. Speciated atmospheric mercury and its potential source in Guiyang, China. Atmospheric Environment 45(25), 4205–12.

Gao, Y., Yan, C. H., Tian, Y., et al. 2007. Prenatal exposure to mercury and neurobehavioral development of neonates in Zhoushan City, China. Environmental Research 105, 390–9.

GBS, 2012. Guizhou Statistical Yearbook. China Statistics Press. Guizhou Bureau of Statistics, Beijing.

Gehrke, G. E., Blum, J. D., Slotton, D. G., et al. 2011. Mercury isotopes link mercury in San Francisco Bay forage fish to surface sediments. Environmental Science & Technology 45(4), 1264–70.

Ginsberg, G., Toal, B., 2009. Quantitative approach for incorporating methylmercury risks and omega-3 fatty acid benefits in developing species-specific fish consumption advice. Environmental Health Perspectives 117, 267–75.

Golding, J., Hibbeln, J. R., Gregory, S. M., et al. 2017. Maternal prenatal blood mercury is not adversely associated with offspring IQ at 8 years provided the mother eats fish: A British prebirth cohort study. International Journal of Hygiene and Environmental Health 220, 1161–7.

Goodrich, J. M., Wang, Y., Gillespie, B., et al. 2011. Glutathione enzyme and selenoprotein polymorphisms associate with mercury biomarker levels in Michigan dental professionals. Toxicology and Applied Pharmacology 257, 301–8.

Grandjean, P., Budtzjørgensen, E., White, R. F., et al. 1999. Methylmercury exposure biomarkers as indicators of neurotoxicity in children aged 7 years. American Journal of Epidemiology 150, 301–5.

Grandjean, P., Budtzjørgensen, E., White, R. F., et al. 1999. Methylmercury exposure bio-markers as indicators of neurotoxicity in children aged 7 years. American Journal of Epidemiology 150, 301–5.

Grandjean, P., Weihe, P., White, R., et al. 1997. Cognitive deficit in 7-year-old children with prenatal exposure to methylmercury. Neurotoxicology and Teratology 19, 417–28.

Gustin, K., Tofail, F., Vahter, M., et al. 2018. Cadmium exposure and cognitive abilities and behavior at 10 years of age: A prospective cohort study. Environmental International 113, 259–68.

Ha, E., Basu, N., Bose-O'Reilly, S., et al. 2017. Current progress on understanding the impact of mercury on human health. Environmental Research 152, 419–33.

Hanson, J. L., Hair, N., Shen, D. G., et al. 2015. Family poverty affects the rate of human infant brain growth. PLoS One. 10, 1–9.

Harris, H. H., Pickering, I. J., George, G. N. 2003. The chemical form of mercury in fish. Science 301, 1203.

Holsbeek, L., Das, H. K., Joiris, C. R. 1996. Mercury in human hair and relation to fish con-sumption in Bangladesh. Science of the Total Environment 186, 181–8.

Horvat, M., Nolde, N., Fajon, V., et al. 2003. Total mercury, methylmercury and selenium in mercury polluted areas in the province Guizhou, China. Science of the Total Environment 304, 231–56.

IOM (Institute of Medicine), 1981. Costs of Environment-Related Health Effects: A Plan for Continuing Study. National Academy Press. IOM, Washington, USA.

Jacobson, J. L., Muckle, G., Ayotte, P., et al. 2015. Relation of prenatal methylmercury expo-sure form environmental sources to childhood IQ. Environmental Health Perspectives 123, 827–33.

JECFA, 2003. Summary and Conclusions of the Sixty-First Meeting of the Joint FAO/WHO Expert Committee on Food Additives. JECFA, Rome, Italy.

Jeong, K. S., Park, H., Ha, E., et al. 2017. High maternal blood mercury level is associated with low verbal IQ in children. Journal of Korean Medical Science 32, 1097–104.

JFSP, 2011. Joint FAO/WHO Food Standards Programme Codex Committee on Contaminants in Foods, Working Document for Information and Use in Discussions Related to Contaminants and Toxins in the GSCTFF, Fifth Session. JFSP, Hague, Netherlands.

Kelly, J. B.2000. Children's adjustment in conflicted marriage and divorce: A decade review of research. Journal of the American Academy of Child and Adolescent Psychiatry 39, 963–73.

Kritee, K., Barkay, T., Blum, J. D., 2009. Mass dependent stable isotope fractionation of mer-cury during mer mediated microbial degradation of monomethylmercury. Geochimica et Cosmochimica Acta 73, 1285–96.

Kritee, K., Blum, J. D., Johnson, M. W., et al. 2007. Mercury stable isotope fractionation dur-ing reduction of Hg (II) to Hg (0) by mercury resistant microorganisms. Environmental Science & Technology 41, 1889–95.

Kwon, S. Y., Blum, J. D., Carvan, M. J., et al. 2012. Absence of fractionation of mercury isotopes during trophic transfer of methylmercury to freshwater fish in captivity. Environmental Science & Technology 46(14), 7527–34.

Kwon, S. Y., Blum, J. D., Chirby, M. A., et al. 2013. Application of mercury isotopes for trac-ing trophic transfer and internal distribution of mercury in marine fish feeding experi-ments. Environmental Toxicology and Chemistry 23, 2322–30.

Laffont, L., Sonke, J. E., Maurice, L., et al. 2009. Anomalous mercury isotopic compositions of fish and human hair in the Bolivian Amazon. Environmental Science & Technology 43(23), 8985–90.

Laffont, L., Sonke, J. E., Maurice, L., et al. 2011. Hg speciation and stable isotope signa-tures in human hair as a tracer for dietary and occupational exposure to mercury. Environmental Science & Technology 45(23), 9910–6.

Lam, H. S., Kwok, K. M., Chan, P. H. Y., et al. 2013. Long term neurocognitive impact of low dose prenatal methylmercury exposure in Hong Kong. Environment International 54, 59–64.

Landrigan, P. J., Schechter, C. B., Lipton, J. M., et al. 2002. Environmental pollutants and disease in American children: Estimates of morbidity, mortality, and costs for lead poisoning, asthma, cancer, and developmental disabilities. Environmental Health Perspectives 110, 721–28.

Layton, D. W. 1993. Metabolically consistent breathing rates for use in dose assessments. Health Physics 64, 22–36.

Li, M., Schartup, A. T., Valberg, A. P., et al. 2016. Environmental origins of methylmercury accumulated in subarctic estuarine fish indicated by mercury stable isotopes. Environmental Science & Technology 50(21), 11559–68.

Li, M., Sherman, L. S., Blum, J. D., et al. 2014. Assessing sources of human methylmercury exposure using stable mercury isotopes. Environmental Science & Technology 48(15), 8800–6.

Li, P., Du, B., Maurice, L., et al. 2017. Mercury isotope signatures of methylmercury in rice samples from the Wanshan mercury mining area, China: Environmental implications. Environmental Science & Technology 51(21), 12321–8.

Li, P., Feng, X. B., Qiu, G. L. 2010. Methylmercury exposure and health effects from rice and fish consumption: A review. International Journal of Environmental Research and Public Health 7, 2666–91.

Li, P., Feng, X. B., Shang, L. H., et al. 2011. Human co-exposure to mercury vapor and methylmercury in artisanal mercury mining areas, Guizhou, China. Ecotoxicology and Environmental Safety 74, 473–9.

Li, P., Feng, X., Chan, H. M., et al. 2015. Human body burden and dietary methylmercury intake: The relationship in a rice-consuming population. Environmental Science & Technology 49(16), 9682–9.

Li, P., Feng, X., Qiu, G., et al. 2008. Mercury exposure in the population from Wuchuan mercury mining area, Guizhou, China. Science of the Total Environment 395, 72–9.

Li, P., Feng, X., Yuan, X., et al. 2012. Rice consumption contributes to low level methylmercury exposure in southern China. Environment International 49, 18–23.

Li, Y., Zhang, B., Yang, L., et al. 2013. Blood mercury concentration among residents of a historic mercury mine and possible effects on renal function: A cross-sectional study in southwestern China. Environmental Monitoring and Assessment 185, 3049–55.

Liang, L., Bloom, N. S., Horvat, M. 1994. Simultaneous determination of mercury speciation in biological-materials by GC/CVAFS after ethylation and room-temperature precollection. Clinical Chemistry 40, 602–7.

Liang, L., Horvat, M., Cernichiari, E., et al. 1996. Simple solvent extraction technique for elimination of matrix interferences in the determination of methylmercury in environmental and biological samples by ethylation gas chromatography cold vapor atomic fluorescence spectrometry. Talanta 43, 1883–8.

Lindqvist, O., Johansson, K., Aastrup, M., et al. 1991. Mercury in the Swedish environment – recent research on causes, consequences and corrective methods. Water Air and Soil Pollution 55, 1–261.

Lucchini, R. G., Guazzetti, S., Renzetti, S., et al. 2019. Neurocognitive impact of metal exposure and social stressors among schoolchildren in Taranto, Italy. Environmental Health 18, 1–12.

Lucotte, M., Montgomery, S., Begin, M. 1999. Mercury dynamics at the flooded soil-water interface in reservoirs of Northern Quebec: In situ observations. In Mercury in the Biogeochemical Cycle, Natural Environments and Hydroelectric Reservoirs of Northern Quebec. M. Lucotte, R. Schetagne, N. Therien, Eds., Springer, Berlin.

Malm, O., Dorea, J. G., Barbosa, A. C., et al. 2010. Sequential hair mercury in mothers and children from a traditional riverine population of the Rio Tapajos, Amazonia: Seasonal changes. Environmental Research 110, 705–9.

Marinho, J. S., Lima, M. O., Oliveira, E. C., et al. 2014. Mercury speciation in hair of children in three communities of the Amazon, Brazil. Biomed Research International, 945963.

Mason, R. P., Sheu, G. R. 2002. Role of the ocean in the global mercury cycle. Global Biogeochemical Cycle 16, 1–40.

McDowell, M. A., Dillon, C. F., Osterloh, J., et al. 2004. Hair mercury levels in U.S. children and women of childbearing age: Reference range data from NHANES 1999–2000. Environmental Health Perspectives 112, 1165–71.

Mergler, D., Anderson, A. H., Chan, H. M., et al. 2007. Methylmercury exposure and health effects in humans: A worldwide concern. Ambio 36, 3–11.

Muir, T., Zegarac, M. 2001. Societal costs of exposure to toxic substances: Economic and health costs of four case studies that are candidates for environmental causation. Environmental Health Perspectives 109, 885–903.

Murata, K., Dakeishi, M. 2002. Impact of prenatal methylmercury exposure on child neuro-development in the Faroe Islands. Japanese Journal of Hygiene 57, 564–70.

Murata, K., Weihe, P., Araki, S., et al. 1999. Evoked potentials in Faroese children prenatally exposed to methylmercury. Neurotoxicology and Teratology 21, 471–2.

Myers, G. J., Thurston, S. W., Pearson, A. T., et al. 2009. Postnatal exposure to methyl mercury from fish consumption: A review and new data from the Seychelles Child Development Study. Neurotoxicology 30, 338–49.

NHFPC & CFDA, 2017. National Food Safety Standard-Contamination Limit in Food, GB 2762-2017. National Health and Family Planning Commission & China Food and Drug Administration, Beijing.

Niševića, J. R., Prpića, I., Kolić, I., et al. 2019. Combined prenatal exposure to mercury and LCPUFA on newborn's brain measures and neurodevelopment at the age of 18 months. Environmental Research 178, 1–5.

NRC, 2000. Toxicological Effects of Methylmercury. National Academy Press. National Research Council, Washington.

Nuovo, A. G. D., Nuovo, S. D., Buono, S. 2012. Intelligence quotient estimation of mentally retarded people from different psychometric instruments using artificial neural networks. Artificial Intelligence in Medicine 54, 135–45.

Pan, S. X., Lin, L. F., Zeng, F., et al. 2018. Effects of lead, cadmium, arsenic, and mercury co-exposure on children's intelligence quotient in an industrialized area of southern China. Environmental Pollution 235, 47–54.

Perrot, V., Pastukhov, M. V., Epov, V. N., et al. 2012. Higher mass-independent isotope fractionation of methylmercury in the pelagic food web of Lake Baikal (Russia). Environmental Science & Technology 46(11), 5902–11.

Qiu, G., Feng, X., Li, P., et al. 2008. Methylmercury accumulation in rice (Oryza sativa L) grown at abandoned mercury mines in Guizhou, China. Journal of Agricultural and Food Chemistry 56, 2465–8.

Qiu, G. L., Feng, X. B., Wang, S. F., et al. 2006a. Environmental contamination of mercury from Hg-mining areas in Wuchuan, northeastern Guizhou, China. Environmental Pollution 142, 549–58.

Qiu, G. L., Feng, X. B., Wang, S. F., et al. 2005. Mercury and methylmercury in riparian soil, sediments, mine-waste calcines, and moss from abandoned Hg mines in east Guizhou province, southwestern China. Applied Geochemistry 20, 627–38.

Qiu, G. L., Feng, X. B., Wang, S. F., et al. 2006b. Mercury contaminations from historic mining to water, soil and vegetation in Lanmuchang, Guizhou, southwestern China. Science of the Total Environment 368, 56–68.

Qiu, G. L., Feng, X. B., Wang, S. F., et al. 2009. Mercury distribution and speciation in water and fish from abandoned Hg mines in Wanshan, Guizhou province. Science of the Total Environment 407, 5162–68.

Rocha, A. V., Cardoso, B. R., Cominetti, C., et al. 2014. Selenium status and hair mercury levels in riverine children from Rondonia, Amazonia. Nutrition 30, 1318–23.

Rothenberg, S., Yin, R., Hurley, J. P., et al. 2017. Stable mercury isotopes in polished rice (Oryza sativa L.) and hair from rice consumers. Environmental Science & Technology 51(11), 6480–8.

Salkever, D.S., 1995. Updated estimates of earnings benefits from reduced exposure of children to environmental lead. Environmental Research 70, 1–6.

Santos, E. C. O., Camara, V. M., Jesus, I. M., et al. 2002. A contribution to the establishment of reference values for total mercury levels in hair and fish in Amazonia. Environmental Research 90, 6–11.

Schauble, E. A. 2007. Role of nuclear volume in driving equilibrium stable isotope fractionation of mercury, thallium, and other very heavy elements. Geochimica et Cosmochimica Acta 71(9), 2170–89.

Senn, D. B., Chesney, E. J., Blum, J. D., et al. 2010. Stable isotope (N, C, Hg) study of methylmercury sources and trophic transfer in the northern Gulf of Mexico. Environmental Science & Technology 44(5), 1630–7.

Sherman, L. S., Blum, J. D., Basu, N., et al. 2015. Assessment of mercury exposure among small-scale gold miners using mercury stable isotopes. Environmental Research 137, 226–34.

Sherman, L. S., Blum, J. D., Franzblau, A., et al. 2013. New insight into biomarkers of human mercury exposure using naturally occurring mercury stable isotopes. Environmental Science & Technology 47(7), 3403–9.

Smith, C. A., Ackerman, J. T., Yee, J., et al. 2009. Mercury demethylation in waterbird livers: Dose–response thresholds and differences among species. Environmental Toxicology and Chemistry 28, 568–77.

Sonke, J. E., Schäfer, J., Chmeleff, J., et al. 2010. Sedimentary mercury stable isotope records of atmospheric and riverine pollution from two major European heavy metal refineries. Chemical Geology 279(3), 90–100.

Stern, A.H. 2004. A revised probabilistic estimate of the maternal methyl mercury intake dose corresponding to a measured cord blood mercury concentration. Environmental Health Perspectives 113, 155–63.

Stern, A.H. 1997. Estimation of the interindividual variability in the one-compartment pharmacokinetic model for methylmercury: Implications for the derivation of a reference dose. Regulatory Toxicology and Pharmacology 25, 277–88.

Strain, J., Davidson, P., Bonham, M. et al. 2008. Associations of maternal long-chain polyunsaturated fatty acids, methyl mercury, and infant development in the Seychelles Child Development Nutrition Study. Neurotoxicology 29(5), 776–82.

Sun, G., Sommar, J., Feng, X., et al. 2016. Mass-dependent and -independent fractionation of mercury isotope during gas-phase oxidation of elemental mercury vapor by atomic Cl and Br. Environmental Science & Technology 50(17), 9232–41.

Sun, H., Chen, W., Wang, D. Y., et al. 2015. Inverse association between intelligence quotient and urinary retinol binding protein in Chinese school-age children with low blood lead levels: Results from a cross-sectional investigation. Chemosphere 128, 155–60.

Swartout, J., Rice, G. 2000. Uncertainty analysis of the estimated ingestion rates used to derive the methylmercury reference dose. Drug and Chemical Toxicology 23, 293–306.

Taylor, C. M., Kordas, K., Golding, J., et al. 2017. Effects of low-level prenatal lead exposure on child IQ at 4 and 8 years in a UK birth cohort study. Neurotoxicology 62, 162–9.

Tian, W. J., Egeland, G. M., Sobol, I., et al. 2011. Mercury hair concentrations and dietary exposure among Inuit preschool children in Nunavut, Canada. Environment International 37, 42–8.

Trasande, L., Landrigan, P. J., Clyde, S. 2005. Public health and economic consequences of methyl mercury toxicity to the developing brain. Environmental Health Perspectives 113, 590–6.

Tsui, M. T., Blum, J. D., Finlay, J. C., et al. 2014. Variation in terrestrial and aquatic sources of methylmercury in stream predators as revealed by stable mercury isotopes. Environmental Science & Technology 48(17), 10128–35.

Tsui, M. T., Blum, J. D., Kwon, S. Y., et al. 2012. Sources and transfers of methylmercury in adjacent river and forest food webs. Environmental Science & Technology 46(20), 10957–64.

Umbangtalad, S., Parkpian, P., Visvanathan, C., et al. 2007. Assessment of Hg contamination and exposure to miners and schoolchildren at a small-scale gold mining and recovery operation in Thailand. Journal of Environmental Science and Health Part A 42, 2071–9.

US EPA, 1985. Costs and Benefits of Reducing Lead in Gasoline—Final Regulatory Impact Analysis. US EPA, Washington, USA.

US EPA, 2000. Economic Analysis of Toxic Substance Control Act Section 403: Lead-Based Paint Hazard Standards. US EPA, Washington, USA.

US EPA, 1997. Health Effects of Mercury and Mercury Compounds. Mercury Study Report to the Congress, Vol. V. US EPA, Washington, USA.

US EPA, 2002. Mercury in Water by Oxidation, Purge and Trap, and Cold Vapor Atomic Fluorescence Spectrometry (Method 1631, Revision E), EPA-821-R-02-019. US EPA, Washington, USA.

US EPA, 2001. Methylmercury in Water by Distillation, Aqueous Ethylation, Purge and Trap, and CVAFS (Method 1630), EPA-821-R-01-020. US EPA, Washington, USA.

Wang, Y., Chen, A., Dietrich, K. N., et al. 2014. Postnatal exposure to methyl mercury and neuropsychological development in 7-year-old urban inner-city children exposed to lead in the United States. Child Neuropsychology 20, 527–38.

Wang, Y., Goodrich, J. M., Gillespie, B., et al. 2012. An investigation of modifying effects of metallothionein single-nucleotide polymorphisms on the association between mercury exposure and biomarker levels. Environmental Health Perspectives 120, 530–4.

Wechsler, D., Zhang, H. C. 2008. The Wechsler Intelligence Scale for Children–Fourth Edition, Chinese version. King-May Psychological Assessment, Guangdong, China.

Whitaker, S. 2008. WISC-IV and low IQ: Review and comparison with the WAIS-III. Educational Psychology in Practice 24, 129–37.

WHO, 1990. Environmental Health Criteria 101: Methylmercury. World Health Organization, Geneva.

WHO, 1991. Inorganic Mercury Environmental Health Criteria. Vol. 118, World Health Organization, Geneva.

Yaginuma-Sakurai, K., Murata, K., Iwai-Shimada, M., et al. 2012. Hair-to-blood ratio and biological half-life of mercury: Experimental study of methylmercury exposure through fish consumption in humans. Journal of Toxicological Sciences 37, 123–30.

Yiengst, M. J., Shock, N. W. 1962. Blood and plasma volume in adult males. Journal of Applied Physiology 17, 195–8.

Yin, R., Feng, X., Foucher, D., et al. 2010. High precision determination of mercury isotope ratios using online mercury vapor generation system coupled with multicollector inductively coupled plasma-mass spectrometer. Chinese Journal of Analytical Chemistry 38(7), 929–34.

Yin, R., Feng, X., Li, X., et al. 2014. Trends and advances in mercury stable isotopes as a geochemical tracer. Trends in Environmental Analytical Chemistry 2, 1–10.

Yin, R., Feng, X., Meng, B. 2013. Stable mercury isotope variation in rice plants (Oryza sativa L.) from the Wanshan mercury mining district, SW China. Environmental Science & Technology 47(5), 2238–45.

Zhang, G.P., Liu, C.Q., Wu, P., et al. 2004. The geochemical characteristies of mine-waste calcines and runoff from the Wanshan mercury mine, Guizhou, China. Applied Geochemistry 19, 1735–44.

Zhang, H., Feng, X., Larssen, T., et al. 2010d. Fractionation, distribution and transport of mercury in rivers and tributaries around Wanshan Hg mining district, Guizhou Province, Southwestern China: Part 2 - Methylmercury. Applied Geochemistry 25, 642–9.

Zhang, H., Feng, X., Larssen, T., et al. 2010c. Fractionation, distribution and transport of mercury in rivers and tributaries around Wanshan Hg mining district, Guizhou province, southwestern China: Part 1 - Total mercury. Applied Geochemistry 5, 633–41.

Zhang, H., Feng, X. B., Larssen, T., et al. 2010b. Bioaccumulation of methylmercury versus inorganic mercury in rice (Oryza sativa L.) grain. Environmental Science & Technology 44, 4499–504.

Zhang, H., Feng, X. B., Larssen, T., et al. 2010a. In inland China, rice, rather than fish is the major pathway for methylmercury exposure. Environmental Health Perspective 118, 1183–8.

5 Biogeochemical Transformation Process of Mercury in Soils

Bo Meng, Jiang Liu, and Xinbin Feng

5.1 INTRODUCTION

Over the last few decades, mercury (Hg) cycling in rice paddy ecosystems has gained extensive attention (Rothenberg and Feng, 2012; Zhao et al., 2020). In rice paddy soils, inorganic Hg is readily transformed into toxic and bioaccumulative methylmercury (MeHg) and therefore plays an important role in human MeHg exposure. Previous studies have documented that rice (*Oryza sativa* L.) is able to accumulate MeHg from paddy soil (Qiu et al., 2008; Meng et al., 2010; 2011; Liu et al., 2021). Since rice is a staple food for billions of people, MeHg-contaminated rice and the resulting MeHg exposure risks are recognized as a global issue (Cui et al., 2017; Kwon et al., 2018; Liu M. et al., 2019). Therefore, a comprehensive understanding of the biogeochemical cycling of Hg in paddy soils is urgently needed. The transformation of Hg species in rice paddy ecosystems plays a vital role in Hg bioaccumulation and associated human exposure risks. Of particular importance are Hg methylation, demethylation, reduction, and oxidation; most of these processes are predominantly mediated by microorganisms (Bravo and Cosio, 2020). Current studies have mostly focused on methylation and demethylation of Hg, with little attention given to the reduction and oxidation processes. In this chapter, we have summarized the current understanding of Hg methylation, demethylation, reduction, and oxidation processes in rice paddy soils and hope to provide a complete picture of Hg cycling in rice paddy soils.

5.2 BIOGEOCHEMICAL TRANSFORMATION PROCESS OF Hg IN PADDY SOILS

Rice paddy fields are ephemeral wetland systems that undergo wetting and drying rotations (Marschner, 2021). As a result, redox transformation (i.e., reduction and oxidation), methylation, and demethylation of Hg occur in rice paddy soils. Of particular importance is the transformation of Hg species in rice paddy soils, which plays a vital role in Hg bioaccumulation and associated human exposure risks (Zhang et al., 2010; Li et al., 2012; Meng et al., 2014; Liu et al., 2023). In this section, the up-to-date understanding of Hg methylation, demethylation, reduction, and oxidation in paddy soils is introduced.

DOI: 10.1201/9781003404941-5

5.2.1 METHYLATION

Both biotic and abiotic methylation of inorganic Hg have been reported in natural environments, and these processes have been substantially reviewed by Hg-study communities (Ullrich et al., 2001; Beckers and Rinklebe, 2017; Grégoire and Poulain, 2018; Ma et al., 2019; Bravo and Cosio, 2020; Gao et al., 2022; Sonke et al., 2023). Of particular importance is the microbial methylation of inorganic Hg^{II}, which is the main pathway of MeHg production in natural environments (Driscoll et al., 2013). Similar to the situation in rice paddy fields, abiotic methylation, if present at all, is negligible (Liu et al., 2023). Currently, the identified microbial methylators include methanogens, sulfate-reducing bacteria (SRB), and iron-reducing bacteria (IRB) that harbor *hgcAB* genes (Parks et al., 2013; Podar et al., 2015).

It is generally accepted that paddy soil is the unique source for the MeHg that accumulates in rice grains (Strickman and Mitchell, 2017; Liu et al., 2021). Therefore, *in situ* methylation of inorganic Hg^{II} in paddy soils has become an emerging hotspot in recent years. Some relevant reviews can be found in W. Tang et al. (2020), Z. Tang. et al. (2020), and Zhao et al. (2020). Microbial communities involved in Hg methylation in paddy soils have been widely studied, and some novel microorganisms other than SRB and IRB have been identified (Gilmour et al., 2013; Liu et al., 2019; Zhang et al., 2023). In this book, we have a specific chapter describing the microbiological mechanisms in Hg methylation and the identified Hg-methylating microorganisms in paddy soils (Chapter 6).

In addition to the recent emphasis on the genetic basis of Hg methylation, research continues to emerge addressing the fundamental aspects of Hg bioavailability to methylators in paddy soils (Li et al., 2019; Tang W. et al., 2020). In a sulfate-amended paddy soil, the promoted Hg methylation was attributed to the facilitated Hg mobilization from refractory HgS releases. However, changes in the abundances or activities of potential Hg-methylating microorganisms were not significant (Li et al., 2019). This case study further highlighted the role of Hg^{II} bioavailability in methylation. Liu et al. (2022) prepared four geochemically relevant Hg^{II} tracers, including dissolved Hg^{II} ($^{198}Hg(NO_3)_2$), natural organic matter (NOM) bond Hg^{II} (NOM-$^{199}Hg^{II}$), ferrous sulfide adsorbed Hg^{II} ($\equiv$FeS-$^{200}Hg^{II}$), and nanoparticulate mercuric sulfide (nano-^{202}HgS). An anaerobic paddy slurry incubation experiment was conducted by spiking those Hg^{II} tracers to identify the bioavailable Hg^{II} species that can be methylated. They showed that methylation rates using NOM-$^{199}Hg^{II}$ and nano-^{202}HgS as substrates were similar to or greater than rates obtained using the labile $^{198}Hg(NO_3)_2$ substrate (Figure 5.1).

Studies on the bioavailability of nano-HgS can be traced back to Dyrssén and Wedborg (1991), who suggested that the log K value for the formation of $HgOHSH^0(aq)$ (or $HgS^0(aq)$) is -10 according to the solubility of CdS(s) and ZnS(s). Based on this log K of $HgS^0(aq)$, Benoit et al. (1999) suggested that $HgS^0(aq)$ is one of the most bioavailable Hg^{II} species that could be methylated. However, subsequent studies found that the log $K = -10$ of $HgS^0(aq)$ was overestimated due to the presence of nano-HgS (Deonarine and Hsu-Kim et al., 2009; Drott et al., 2013). After the discovery of nano-HgS, Zhang et al. (2012, 2014) reported that nano-HgS is a bioavailable Hg^{II} species that could be methylated either in a pure bacterial culture system or

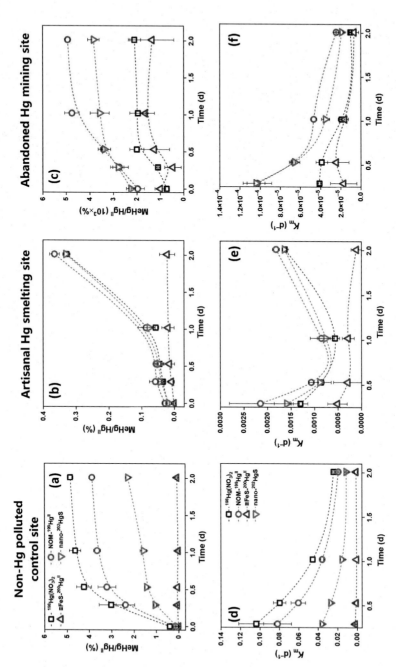

FIGURE 5.1 Methylmercury production (MeHg/Hg^{II}; a, b and c) and methylation rate constant (K_m; d, e, and f) as a function of time for different Hg^{II} tracers in three microcosms. NOM-^{199}Hg^{II} represents natural organic matter-bound Hg^{II}; ≡FeS-^{200}Hg^{II} represents ferrous sulfide-adsorbed Hg^{II}; and nano-^{202}HgS represents nanoparticulate HgS. Error bars indicate the standard deviation (±SD) for replicates ($n = 3$). The non-Hg-polluted control site is at Huaxi, Guiyang, China; the artisanal Hg smelting site and the abandoned Hg mining site are at WSHM, Tongren, China. (Modified from Liu et al., 2022.)

in estuarine sediment microcosms. More recently, Tian et al. (2021) found that the methylation potential of nano-HgS is determined by its crystal structure, and more MeHg production is observed when more of the exposed surface of nano-HgS occurs as the (111) facet. Guo et al. (2023) and Xiang et al. (2023) reported that the methylation of nano-HgS is a passive diffusion-intracellular dissolution-*hgcAB* dependent/ independent methylation process (Figure 5.2). In addition, dissolved organic matter (DOM) could either slow the aggregation of nano-HgS particles in sulfidic environments or promote the dissolution of HgS(s), and both processes could accumulate nano-HgS (Ravichandran et al., 1999; Slowey, 2010; Gerbig et al., 2011; Graham et al., 2012; Pham et al., 2014). With the successful extraction and quantification of nano-HgS in WSHM soils (Manceau et al., 2018; Cai et al., 2022), the role of nano-HgS in net MeHg production in rice paddy soils deserves more work.

Liu et al. (2019) amended $HgCl_2$, α-HgS, β-HgS, nano-HgS, and Hg-DOM complexes in a rice cultivated plot experiment, and bulk MeHg concentrations among treatments were compared. In addition to the methylation of nano-HgS and Hg-DOM, α-HgS and β-HgS dissolution promoted methylation (Figure 5.2). Similar results were also reported by Li et al. (2022), who found that stable HgS(s) could be a source of Hg^{II} in methylation in sulfidic paddy soils. All these findings suggest

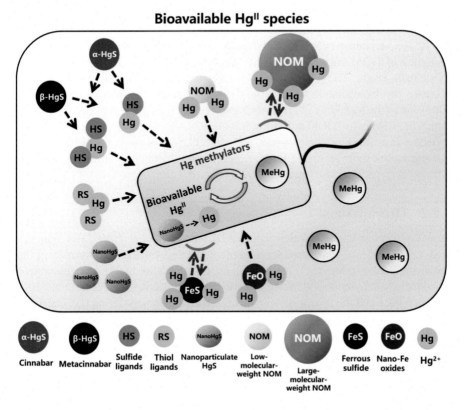

FIGURE 5.2 Current understanding of bioavailable Hg^{II} species that can be methylated in rice paddy soils.

that bioavailable Hg^{II} could also be released from refractory HgS(s) in paddy soils. In particular, β-HgS is the major Hg species in Hg-contaminated paddy soils in the Wanshan Hg mining area (Yin et al., 2016). Previous studies have reported that sulfide and polysulfide (i.e., generated from sulfide and elemental sulfur reactions) promote the dissolution of HgS(s) (Paquette and Helz, 1997; Jay et al., 2000; Liu, 2019). However, the speciation of Hg-polysulfide complexes remains unclear and needs more work.

In a paddy slurry incubation, Liu et al. (2022) found that ≡FeS-^{200}Hg^{II} yielded the lowest methylation rate at all sites, and the formation of FeS is likely a sink for labile ^{198}Hg(NO$_3$)$_2$ in sulfide-rich paddy soils (Figures 5.1 and 5.2). This suggests that the formation of FeS in submerged paddy soils reduced Hg^{II} methylation. This finding is consistent with that of Xiang et al. (2022b), who observed the same results by using an *Escherichia coli* biosensor. Skyllberg et al. (2021) suggested that the presence or absence of FeS determined the transformation processes of Hg (e.g., methylation, demethylation, and reduction) in sediments and in different environments. However, Jonsson et al. (2012) reported comparable bioavailabilities of ≡FeS-Hg(II) and NOM-Hg(II) in estuary sediment, which was likely attributable to the dissolution or desorption of Hg from solids in methylation (Jonsson et al., 2012, 2014). By using a whole-cell biosensor method, Xiang et al. (2022a) found that particulate (Fe$_2$O$_3$ and Fe$_3$O$_4$)-sorbed Hg^{II} was methylated (Figure 5.2), implying divergent bioavailabilities of ≡Feoxides-Hg^{II} and ≡FeS-Hg^{II}.

The bioavailability of DOM bound to Hg^{II} was determined not only by the concentration of DOM but also by the chemical composition of DOM in paddy soils (Abdelhafiz et al., 2023). It is generally accepted that the presence of NOM will decrease the bioavailability of Hg and inhibit MeHg formation (Ravichandran, 2004) due to the formation of large macromolecular Hg-NOM complexes (Hsu-Kim et al., 2013). However, DOM with a lower molecular weight, fewer humic substances, and more autochthonous sources (e.g., low-molecular-weight organic acids, proteins, and sugars) are more favorable for Hg^{II} methylation than highly aromatic or humic substances in paddy soils (Liu et al., 2023) (Figure 5.2).

5.2.2 DEMETHYLATION

Demethylation of MeHg was first reported by Furukawa et al. (1969) and Spangler et al. (1973) and was considered a competitive process with Hg^{II} methylation in the net accumulation of MeHg. Therefore, the net production of MeHg was determined by both Hg^{II} methylation and MeHg demethylation. In paddy fields, Zhao et al. (2016 a, b) first qualified the *in situ* specific methylation and demethylation rate constants (K_m and K_d) in paddy soil profiles during the rice growing season and found that the MeHg levels in rice paddy soil were a function of both methylation and demethylation processes. In addition, studies in the paddy soils of the Wanshan Hg mining area found a lower MeHg but a higher THg concentration at an abandoned Hg mining site than at an artisanal Hg smelting site (Wu et al., 2020; Liu et al., 2022), which is likely due to the differentiation of microbial communities between the two sites. Also, the demethylation rate (%) and K_d of MeHg at the abandoned Hg mining site was higher than that at the artisanal Hg smelting site (Liu et al., 2022).

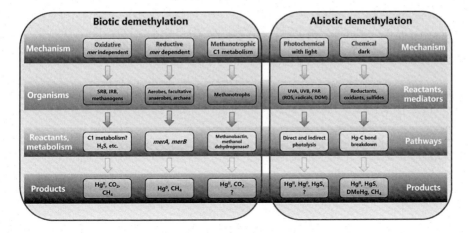

FIGURE 5.3 Potential mechanisms, microorganisms, reactants, and products of both biotic and abiotic pathways of MeHg demethylation in the environment. (Modified from Barkay and Gu, 2022.)

Recently, the demethylation of MeHg was systematically reviewed by Barkay and Gu (2022). Both biotic and abiotic demethylation of MeHg occurs in natural environments. The former includes *mer*-dependent (Hg-resistant) and *mer*-independent processes, and the latter were mainly regulated by photochemical processes with light and some chemical processes in the dark (Figure 5.3). Photochemical process-regulated abiotic demethylation of MeHg is usually found in the overlying water in rice paddy systems but is unlikely to occur in dark paddy soils. Therefore, the photo-degradation of MeHg is of minor importance in paddy fields (solid phase). In an Me^{198}Hg tracer-spiked paddy slurry incubation work, Liu et al. (2023) reported that microbially mediated demethylation of MeHg is predominant in paddy soils. Meanwhile, the low concentration of MeHg was also observed in autoclaved paddy slurries after 2 days, suggesting the existence of abiotic demethylation of MeHg.

Regarding the biotic demethylation of MeHg, Zhou et al. (2020), Liu et al. (2023), and Wu et al. (2023) suggest that *mer*-independent oxidative demethylation (OD) is the dominant demethylation pathway in paddy soils. Oxidative demethylation is a nonspecific co-metabolic process that produces Hg^{II} and CO$_2$ under anoxic conditions (Oremland et al., 1991; Barkay and Gu, 2022). Although it remains challenging to isolate specific microbial strains mediating OD, studies have applied metabolic inhibitors (i.e., molybdate for SRB and BES for methanogens) and previously identified the role of SRB and methanogens in OD (Oremland et al., 1991, 1995; Fuhrmann et al., 2021; Barkay and Gu, 2022). In paddy fields, the role of methanogens in MeHg degradation was highlighted by Wu et al. (2020), who observed the increase in MeHg production and decrease in MeHg demethylation by inhibiting methanogenesis. Hao et al. (2024) further attempted to distinguish the roles of aceticlastic and hydrogenotrophic methanogens in MeHg degradation in paddy soils. However, they found that both methanogen florae facilitated MeHg degradation and potential competition occurred between the two types of methanogens.

Reductive demethylation (RD) was mediated by the Hg resistance system (*mer* operon), with an organo-Hg lyase enzyme (*merB*) (i.e., breaking down the Hg-C bond and generating CH_4) and a Hg reductase (*merA*) (reducing Hg^{II} to Hg^0). RD usually occurs in oxic conditions with high Hg levels (Schaefer et al., 2004). Previous work suggested that OD is the dominant demethylation pathway in paddy soil during anaerobic incubation (Zhou et al., 2020; Liu et al., 2023; Wu et al., 2023). In natural rice paddy fields, RD likely occurs, especially during the drying period (i.e., air-exposed oxic conditions). In a metagenomics study using natural paddy soil samples, Zhang et al. (2023) observed the occurrence of *merB* genes, which indicated *merB*-facilitating aerobic reductive demethylation in paddy soils. In addition to the OD and RD pathways, methanotrophs were found to be involved in MeHg demethylation through cleavage of the Hg-C bond by methanol dehydrogenase (Lu et al., 2017; Barkay and Gu, 2022; Kang-Yun et al., 2022)

Abiotic demethylation of MeHg in rice paddy fields has rarely been studied. However, it is certain that photo-degradation could be the dominant pathway of MeHg demethylation in overlying waters. Direct photolysis was mediated by UV-A and UV-B, whereas indirect photolysis was mediated by free radicals (e.g., ·OH, $^1O_2$, $^3DOM^*$, O_2^-) (Figure 5.3). The role of dark abiotic demethylation cannot be ignored, especially in paddy soil profiles that are out of reach of light. Kronberg et al. (2018) reported that dark abiotic demethylation may be comparable to biotic demethylation in some swamps. As a dark abiotic demethylation pathway, the reaction between MeHg and sulfide generates HgS(s) and dimethylmercury (DMeHg) (Craig and Bartlett, 1978; Kanzler et al., 2018) (Figure 5.4).

In recent years, the production of reactive oxygen species (ROS), such as hydroxyl radicals (·OH), from Fe redox processes in paddy soils has gained much attention (Tong et al., 2016; Dai et al., 2022; Huang et al., 2023), and the produced ROS show significant influences on the oxidation and mobilization of heavy metals (e.g., Cd, As, and organic As) (Dai et al., 2021; Huang et al., 2021a, b). ROS are expected to play an important role in MeHg degradation; however, more studies are needed to verify this hypothesis.

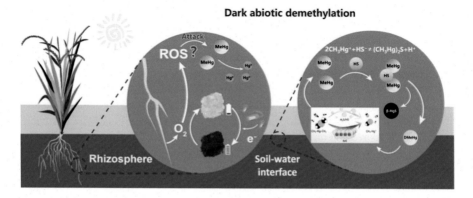

FIGURE 5.4 Illustration of the potential abiotic demethylation of MeHg in paddy soils under dark condition. (Modified according to Dai et al., 2022 and West et al., 2020.)

5.2.3 REDUCTION

Mercury reduction to Hg^0 is responsible for Hg evasion from terrestrial and aquatic ecosystems (Poulain et al., 2007). The oxidation states of Hg include Hg^0, Hg^I, and Hg^{II}. Therefore, the reduction of Hg^{II} should generally be a two-step single-electron transfer process (Gao et al., 2022). However, Hg^I is metastable and is rarely determined in natural environments.

Both biotic and abiotic reductions of Hg have been reported in rice paddy systems (Yin et al., 2013; Qin et al., 2020; Liu et al., 2023). Measurements of soil/water–air Hg^0 fluxes in paddy fields reflect net Hg^0 emissions combined with both biotic and abiotic Hg reductions (Zhu et al., 2011; Fu et al., 2012; Liang et al., 2014). In paddy slurry incubation work (in the dark), the formation of $^{200}Hg^0$ in the headspace of incubation bottles from spiked $^{200}Hg^{II}$ tracers was detected, and microbial-mediated reduction dominated this process (Liu et al., 2023). However, the reduction of $^{200}Hg^{II}$ was 1–2 orders of magnitude lower than the methylation of $^{200}Hg^{II}$, suggesting a predominant role of methylation when compared with the reduction of Hg^{II} in dark paddy soils. It has been assumed that reduction competes with methylation for bioavailable Hg^{II} substrates. However, under incubation conditions, the reduction of Hg^{II} can hardly impact the methylation of Hg^{II} when their fractions of conversion are quantified. Moreover, Hg^0 has been shown to be capable of serving as a substrate for methylation (Colombo et al., 2013; Hu et al., 2013). It is noted that the detected Hg^0 in the incubation of Liu et al. (2023) is the Hg^0 that can be purged out (purgeable Hg^0). Therefore, underestimation of Hg^{II} reduction could occur due to the potential existence of non-purgeable Hg^0 in paddy slurries (e.g., immobilized by solid phases) (Landa, 1978; Wang et al., 2015). However, the influences of Hg^{II} reduction on Hg^{II} methylation could be ignored in dark paddy soils. Over a large scale or long term, Hg^{II} reduction and its subsequent evasion may still contribute to the removal of Hg from rice paddy soils and, therefore, limit the formation of MeHg, especially in uncontaminated paddy soils (i.e., Hg^{II} methylation is constrained by the THg concentration). Therefore, it is critical to tease apart the importance of these two pathways for the proper management of paddy systems (Liu et al., 2023).

Hg^0 can also be generated by MeHg through either reductive demethylation (RD) or oxidative demethylation (OD) followed by reduction. The formation of $^{198}Hg^0$ in the headspace of incubation bottles from spiked $Me^{198}Hg$ tracers was detected, and this Hg^0 formation is a microbially mediated process (Liu et al., 2023). In addition, the volatilization rate constants (K_v) of $Me^{198}Hg$ and $^{200}Hg^{II}$, as well as the formation of $^{198}Hg^0$ and $^{200}Hg^0$, are highly covaried, which implies that the formation of Hg^0 from MeHg tracers was partially the same as Hg^{II} reduction (Liu et al., 2023). However, only a small part of the Hg^{II} degraded from MeHg was further reduced, and the ratio of purgeable $^{198}Hg^0$ to spiked $Me^{198}Hg$ ($^{198}Hg^0/Me^{198}Hg$ %) was 3–4 orders of magnitude lower than the percentage of $Me^{198}Hg$ demethylation (Liu et al., 2023; Wu et al., 2023).

Wu et al. (2023) found the constrained Hg^{II} reduction after inhibiting SRB and methanogens activities using molybdate and BES, respectively. This suggests that Hg^{II} reduction is associated with sulfate reduction and methanogenesis in paddy soils. Following work with anoxygenic phototrophs, Grégoire et al. (2018) discovered that Heliobacteria, a family of spore-forming fermentative photoheterotrophs

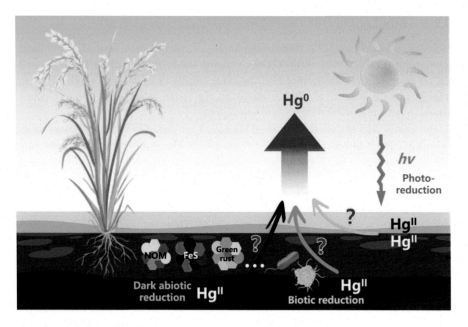

FIGURE 5.5   Illustration of the Hg^{II} reduction pathways and their uncertainties.

typically isolated from rice paddies, were efficient Hg^{II} reducers. No apparent dedi-
cated Hg^{II} reduction machinery, such as *mer*-operon, was observed in the genome of
Heliobacterium modesticaldum Ice1, and Hg^{II} reduction was most likely determined
by reduced redox cofactors and proceeded as a co-metabolic process (Grégoire et al.,
2018; Grégoire and Poulain, 2018).

In addition to the microbially mediated biotic reduction of Hg in paddy fields,
Hg^0 emissions can also result from photo-reduction and abiotic dark reduction. The
photo-reduction of Hg^{II} was traced by the negative mass-independent fractionation
(MIF) of Hg^0 in the ambient air (Yin et al., 2013), and abiotic dark reduction of Hg^{II}
mediated by natural organic matter (NOM) (Gu et al., 2011; Zheng et al., 2012; Jiang
et al., 2015) and some Fe^{II}/Fe^{III}-bearing minerals (e.g., mackinawite, green rust,
magnetite, etc.) (O'Loughlin et al., 2003; Bouffard and Amyot, 2009; Bone et al.,
2014; Schwab et al., 2023) was reported in other environmental settings. However,
the contribution of different Hg^{II} reduction pathways to Hg^0 emissions from paddy
fields remains unknown (Figure 5.5), which largely limits the understanding of Hg
reduction processes in agricultural ecosystems.

5.2.4   OXIDATION

Similar to other transformation processes, the oxidation of Hg could also be regulated
by biotic and abiotic factors. Biotic oxidation of Hg remains one of the most poorly
understood transformations (Grégoire and Poulain, 2018). Colombo et al. (2013)
reported an anaerobic oxidation of Hg^0. The oxidized Hg^{II} was covalently bonded
to cellular thiol functional groups and could be further methylated. Additional
evidence has been documented supporting the presence of the abovementioned

pathway in other obligate and facultative anaerobes (Colombo et al., 2014; Lin et al., 2014; Lu et al., 2016).

In a paddy slurry incubation work, Liu et al. (2023) observed that the spiked Hg^0 tracers were rapidly oxidized to Hg^{II} through abiotic processes. In particular, oxidized Hg^{II} is involved in Hg^{II} methylation (Liu et al., 2023). This suggests that the rapid redox recycling of Hg species contributes to Hg speciation resetting, forming bioavailable Hg^{II} for methylation. In paddy soils, oxidation of Hg^0 could also be regulated by oxidative complexation with thiol functional groups on NOM (Zheng et al., 2012, 2013).

5.2.5 INTEGRATED PROCESSES OF Hg METHYLATION, DEMETHYLATION, REDUCTION, AND OXIDATION

By spiking $^{200}Hg^{II}$, $Me^{198}Hg$, and $^{202}Hg^0$ tracers, Liu et al. (2023) investigated the integrated reactions of methylation, demethylation, reduction, and oxidation simultaneously. In addition to the widely accepted Hg^{II} methylation and MeHg demethylation in paddy soils, direct evidence of Hg^{II} reduction, Hg^0 oxidation/immobilization, Hg^0 methylation, and the formation of Hg^0 from MeHg was provided (Figure 5.6).

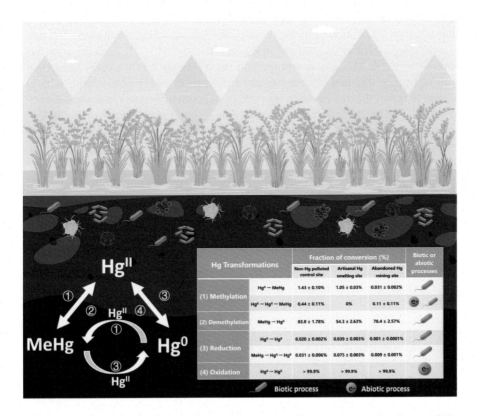

FIGURE 5.6 Schematic diagram illustrating the transformation processes and rates of Hg in paddy soils. The non-Hg-polluted control site is at Huaxi, Guiyang, China; the artisanal Hg smelting site and the abandoned Hg mining site are at WSHM, Tongren, China. (Modified from Liu et al., 2023.)

Moreover, the fraction of conversions for each transformation process of Hg in paddy fields with different total Hg levels was provided (Figure 5.6). Most of the above-mentioned processes are biotically mediated, with the one exception being that Hg^0 oxidation/immobilization is mainly mediated by abiotic processes. Interestingly, the transformation between Hg^0 and MeHg was observed: (1) Hg^0 from the dark reduction of Hg^{II} can be methylated upon reoxidation, and (2) oxidative demethylation of MeHg was coupled with Hg^{II} reduction. These findings highlight that (i) biotically mediated dark reduction of Hg^{II} followed by reoxidation is also a source of Hg^{II} methylation in paddy soils, something that has been largely overlooked previously in redox-fluctuating environments, and (ii) transformation processes for different Hg species (Hg^0, Hg^{II}, and MeHg) in paddy soils are coupled. In addition to Hg^{II} reduction and methylation, as mentioned above, MeHg may also be a source of Hg^0 emission into the atmosphere through oxidative demethylation and then reduction. This highlights the continuous and dynamic nature of Hg transformation in paddy soils (Liu et al., 2023).

5.3   FUTURE RESEARCH NEEDS

The bioavailability of geochemically relevant Hg species remains unclear. For example, nano-Fe oxides sorbed Hg^{II} can be methylated, but FeS sorbed Hg^{II} cannot. In addition, the contribution of MeHg production from nano-HgS is not clear. The role of methanogens and methanotrophs in Hg methylation and MeHg demethylation has been recognized. Mercury transformation processes are likely closely associated with carbon cycling and greenhouse gas emissions in paddy fields. More work is needed to reveal the link between Hg cycling and carbon turnover in changing environments. The production of ROS in paddy soils from redox reactions is a detoxification mechanism by degrading MeHg or a toxification mechanism by mobilizing previously stable Hg, but the mechanism of ROS-mediated abiotic Hg transformation processes in paddy fields remains unknown. It is not clear whether Hg emission from paddy fields is a biotic-dominant or an abiotic-dominant process. The relative contributions of photo-reduction, dark abiotic reduction, and microbially mediated biotic reduction to Hg emissions in paddy fields are unknown. This has limited the estimation of global Hg emissions from agricultural lands.

REFERENCES

Abdelhafiz, M. A., Liu, J., Jiang, T., et al. 2023. DOM influences Hg methylation in paddy soils across a Hg contamination gradient. Environmental Pollution 322, 121237.

Barkay, T., Gu, B. H., 2022. Demethylation - the other side of the mercury methylation coin: A critical review. ACS Environmental Au 2(2), 77–97.

Beckers, F., Rinklebe, J., 2017. Cycling of mercury in the environment: Sources, fate, and human health implications: A review. Critical Reviews in Environmental Science and Technology 47(9), 693–794.

Benoit, J. M., Mason, R. P., Gilmour, C. C., 1999. Estimation of mercury-sulfide speciation in sediment pore waters using octanol-water partitioning and implications for availability to methylating bacteria. Environmental Toxicology and Chemistry 18(10), 2138–2141.

Bone, S. E., Bargar, J. R., Sposito, G., 2014. Mackinawite (FeS) reduces mercury(II) under sulfidic conditions. Environmental Science & Technology 48(18), 10681–10689.

Bouffard, A., Amyot, M., 2009. Importance of elemental mercury in lake sediments. Chemosphere 74(8), 1098–1103.

Bravo, A. G., Cosio, C., 2020. Biotic formation of methylmercury: A bio–physico–chemical conundrum. Limnology and Oceanography 65(5), 1010–1027.

Cai, W. P., Wang, Y. J., Feng, Y., et al. 2022. Extraction and quantification of nanoparticulate mercury in natural soils. Environmental Science & Technology 56(3), 1763–1770.

Colombo, M. J., Ha, J. Y., Reinfelder, J. R., et al. 2013. Anaerobic oxidation of Hg(0) and methylmercury formation by Desulfovibrio desulfuricans ND132. Geochimica et Cosmochimica Acta 112, 166–177.

Colombo, M. J., Ha, J., Reinfelder, J. R., et al. 2014. Oxidation of Hg(0) to Hg(II) by diverse anaerobic bacteria. Chemical Geology 363, 334–340.

Craig, P. J., Bartlett, P. D., 1978. Role of hydrogen-sulfide in environmental transport of mercury. Nature 275 (5681), 635–637.

Cui, W. B., Liu, G. L., Bezerra, M., et al. 2017. Occurrence of methylmercury in rice-based infant cereals and estimation of daily dietary intake of methylmercury for infants. Journal of Agricultural and Food Chemistry 65(44), 9569–9578.

Dai, J., Chen, C. A., Gao, A. X., et al. 2021. Dynamics of dimethylated monothioarsenate (DMMTA) in paddy soils and its accumulation in rice grains. Environmental Science & Technology 55(13), 8665–8674.

Dai, H. Y., Wu, B. B., Chen, B. L., et al. 2022. Diel fluctuation of extracellular reactive oxygen species production in the rhizosphere of rice. Environmental Science & Technology 56(12), 9075–9082.

Deonarine, A., Hsu-Kim, H., 2009. Precipitation of mercuric sulfide nanoparticles in NOM-containing water: Implications for the natural environment. Environmental Science & Technology 43(7), 2368–2373.

Driscoll, C. T., Mason, R. P., Chan, H. M., et al. 2013. Mercury as a global pollutant: Sources, pathways, and effects. Environmental Science & Technology 47(10), 4967–4983.

Drott, A., Bjorn, E., Bouchet, S., et al. 2013. Refining thermodynamic constants for mercury(II)- sulfides in equilibrium with metacinnabar at sub-micromolar aqueous sulfide concentrations. Environmental Science & Technology 47(9), 4179–4203.

Dyrssén, D., Wedborg, M., 1991. The sulphur-mercury(II) system in natural waters. Water, Air, Soil Pollution 56, 507–519.

Fu, X. W., Feng, X. B., Zhang, H., et al. 2012. Mercury emissions from natural surfaces highly impacted by human activities in Guangzhou province, South China. Atmospheric Environment 54, 185–193.

Fuhrmann, B. C., Beutel, M. W., O'Day, P. A., et al. 2021. Effects of mercury, organic carbon, and microbial inhibition on methylmercury cycling at the profundal sediment-water interface of a sulfate-rich hypereutrophic reservoir. Environmental Pollution 268, 115853.

Furukawa, K., Suzuki, T., Tonomura, K., 1969. Decomposition of organic mercurial compounds by mercury-resistant bacteria. Agricultural and Biological Chemistry 33 (1), 128–133.

Gao, Z. Y., Zheng, W., Li, Y. B., et al. 2022. Mercury transformation processes in nature: Critical knowledge gaps and perspectives for moving forward. J. Environment. Science 119, 152–165.

Gerbig, C. A., Kim, C. S., Stegemeier, J. P., et al. 2011. Formation of nanocolloidal metacinnabar in mercury-DOM-sulfide systems. Environmental Science & Technology 45(21), 9180–9187.

Gilmour, C. C., Podar, M., Bullock, A. L., et al. 2013. Mercury methylation by novel microorganisms from new environments. Environmental Science & Technology 47(20), 11810–11820.

Graham, A. M., Aiken, G. R., Gilmour, C. C., 2012. Dissolved organic matter enhances microbial mercury methylation under sulfidic conditions. Environmental Science & Technology 46(5), 2715–2723.

Grégoire, D. S., Lavoie, N. C., Poulain, A. J., 2018. Heliobacteria reveal fermentation as a key pathway for mercury reduction in anoxic environments. Environmental Science & Technology 52(7), 4145–4153.

Grégoire, D. S., Poulain, A. J., 2018. Shining light on recent advances in microbial mercury cycling. Facets 3, 858–879.

Gu, B. H., Bian, Y. R., Miller, C. L., et al. 2011. Mercury reduction and complexation by natural organic matter in anoxic environments. Proceedings of the National Academy of Sciences 108(4), 1479–1483.

Guo, Y. Y., Xiang, Y. P., Liu, G. L., et al. 2023. "Trojan Horse" type internalization increases the bioavailability of mercury sulfide nanoparticles and methylation after intracellular dissolution. ACS Nano 17(3), 1925–1934.

Hao, Z. D., Zhao, L., Liu, J., at al. 2024. Relative importance of aceticlastic methanogens and hydrogenotrophic methanogens on mercury methylation and methylmercury demethylation in paddy soils. Science of the Total Environment 906, 167601.

Hsu-Kim, H., Kucharzyk, K. H., Zhang, T., et al. 2013. Mechanisms regulating mercury bioavailability for methylating microorganisms in the aquatic environment: A critical review. Environmental Science & Technology 47(6), 2441–2456.

Huang, D. Y., Chen, N., Zhu, C. Y., et al. 2023. Dynamic production of hydroxyl radicals during the flooding–drainage process of paddy soil: An in situ column study. Environmental Science & Technology 57, 16340–16347.

Huang, H., Chen, H. P., Kopittke, P. M., et al. 2021a. The voltaic effect as a novel mechanism controlling the remobilization of cadmium in paddy soils during drainage. Environmental Science & Technology 55(3), 1750–1758.

Huang, H., Ji, X. B., Cheng, L. Y., et al. 2021b. Free radicals produced from the oxidation of ferrous sulfides promote the remobilization of cadmium in paddy soils during drainage. Environmental Science & Technology 55(14), 9845–9853.

Hu, H. Y., Lin, H., Zheng, W., et al. 2013. Oxidation and methylation of dissolved elemental mercury by anaerobic bacteria. Nature Geoscience 6(9), 751–754.

Jay, J. A., Morel, F. M. M., Hemond, H. F., 2000. Mercury speciation in the presence of polysulfides. Environmental Science & Technology 34(11), 2196–2200.

Jiang, T., Skyllberg, U., Wei, S. Q., et al. 2015. Modeling of the structure-specific kinetics of abiotic, dark reduction of Hg (II) complexed by O/N and S functional groups in humic acids while accounting for time-dependent structural rearrangement. Geochimica et Cosmochimica Acta 154, 151–167.

Jonsson, S., Skyllberg, U., Nilsson, M. B., et al. 2014. Differentiated availability of geochemical mercury pools controls methylmercury levels in estuarine sediment and biota. Nature Communication 5, 4624.

Jonsson, S., Skyllberg, U., Nilsson, M. B., et al. 2012. Mercury methylation rates for geochemically relevant Hg^{II} species in sediments. Environmental Science & Technology 46(21), 11653–11659.

Kang-Yun, C. S., Liang, X. J., Dershwitz, P., et al. 2022. Evidence for methanobactin "theft" and novel chalkophore production in methanotrophs: Impact on methanotrophic-mediated methylmercury degradation. ISME J 16(1), 211–220.

Kanzler, C. R., Lian, P., Trainer, E. L., et al. 2018. Emerging investigator series: Methylmercury speciation and dimethylmercury production in sulfidic solutions. Environmental Science: Processes & Impacts 20 (4), 584–594.

Kronberg, R. M., Schaefer, J. K., Bjorn, E., et al. 2018. Mechanisms of methylmercury net degradation in alder swamps: The role of methanogens and abiotic processes. Environmental Science & Technology Letter 5 (4), 220–225.

Kwon, S. Y., Selin, N. E., Giang, A., et al. 2018. Present and future mercury concentrations in Chinese rice: Insights from modeling. Global Biogeochemical Cycles 32(3), 437–462.

Landa, E. R., 1978. The retention of metallic mercury vapor by soils. Geochimica et Cosmochimica Acta 42(9), 1407–1411.

Li, H., Li, Y. Y., Tang, W. L., et al. 2022. Bioavailability and methylation of bulk mercury sulfide in paddy soils: New insights into mercury risks in rice paddies. Journal of Hazardous Materials 424, 127394.

Li, P., Feng, X. B., Yuan, X. B., et al. 2012. Rice consumption contributes to low level methylmercury exposure in southern China. Environment International 49, 18–23.

Liang, P., Zhang, C., Yang, Y. K., et al. 2014. A simulation study of mercury release fluxes from soils in wet-dry rotation environment. Journal of Environmental Sciences 26(7), 1445–1452.

Lin, H., Morrell-Falvey, J. L., Rao, B., et al. 2014. Coupled mercury-cell sorption, reduction, and oxidation on methylmercury production by *Geobacter sulfurreducens* PCA. Environmental Science & Technology 48(20), 11969–11976

Liu, J., 2019. Variations of Inorganic Sulfur Species and Their Influence on Mercury Methylation in the Water Level Fluctuation Zone of the Three Gorges Reservoir Area. PhD diss., Southwest University.

Liu, J., Chen, J., Poulain, A. J., et al. 2023. Mercury and sulfur redox cycling affect methylmercury levels in rice paddy soils across a contamination gradient. Environmental Science & Technology 57(21), 8149–8160.

Liu, J., Lu, B. Q., Poulain, A. J., et al. 2022. The underappreciated role of natural organic matter bond Hg(II) and nanoparticulate HgS as substrates for methylation in paddy soils across a Hg concentration gradient. Environmental Pollution 292, 118321.

Liu, J., Meng, B., Poulain, A. J., et al. 2021. Stable isotope tracers identify sources and transformations of mercury in rice (Oryza sativa L.) growing in a mercury mining area. Fundamental Research 1, 259–268.

Liu, J. L., Wang, J. X., Ning, Y. Q., et al. 2019. Methylmercury production in a paddy soil and its uptake by rice plants as affected by different geochemical mercury pools. Environment International. 129, 461–469.

Liu, Y. R., Yang, Z. M., Zhou, X. Q., et al. 2019. Overlooked role of putative non-Hg methylators in predicting methylmercury production in paddy soils. Environmental Science & Technology 53(21), 12330–12338.

Liu, M. D., Zhang, Q. R., Cheng, M. H., et al. 2019. Rice life cycle-based global mercury biotransport and human methylmercury exposure. Nature Communication 10, 5164.

Li, Y. Y., Zhao, J. T, Zhong, H., et al. 2019. Understanding enhanced microbial MeHg production in mining-contaminated paddy soils under sulfate amendment: Changes in Hg mobility or microbial methylators? Environmental Science & Technology 53(4), 1844–1852.

Lu, X., Gu, W. Y., Zhao, L. D., et al. 2017. Methylmercury uptake and degradation by methanotrophs. Science Advance 3(5), e1700041.

Lu, X., Liu, Y. R., Johs, A., et al. 2016. Anaerobic mercury methylation and demethylation by *Geobacter bemidjiensis* Bem. Environmental Science & Technology 50(8), 4366–4373.

Ma, M., Du, H. X., Wang, D. Y., 2019. Mercury methylation by anaerobic microorganisms: A review. Critical Reviews in Environmental Science & Technology 49(20), 1893–1936.

Manceau, A., Wang, J. X., Rovezzi, M., et al. 2018. Biogenesis of mercury-sulfur nanoparticles in plant leaves from atmospheric gaseous mercury. Environmental Science & Technology 52(7), 3935–3948.

Marschner, P., 2021. Processes in submerged soils - linking redox potential, soil organic matter turnover and plants to nutrient cycling. Plant Soil 464(1–2), 1–12.

Meng, B., Feng, X. B., Qiu, G. L., et al. 2010. Distribution patterns of inorganic mercury and methylmercury in tissues of rice (Oryza sativa L.) plants and possible bioaccumulation pathways. Journal of Agricultural and Food Chemistry 58(8), 4951–4958.

Meng, B., Feng, X. B., Qiu, G. L., et al. 2014. Localization and speciation of mercury in brown rice with implications for pan-Asian public health. Environmental Science & Technology 48(14), 7974–7981.

Meng, B., Feng, X. B., Qiu, G. L., et al. 2011. The process of methylmercury accumulation in rice (Oryza sativa L.). Environmental Science & Technology 45(7), 2711–2717.

O'Loughlin, E. J., Kelly, S. D., Kemner, K. M., et al. 2003. Reduction of Ag^I, Au^{III}, Cu^{II}, and Hg^{II} by Fe^{II}/Fe^{III} hydroxysulfate green rust. Chemosphere 53(5), 437–446.

Oremland, R. S., Culbertson, C. W., Winfrey, M. R., 1991. Methylmercury decomposition in sediments and bacterial cultures? Involvement of methanogens and sulfate reducers in oxidative demethylation. Applied and Environmental Microbiology 57(1), 130–137.

Oremland, R. S., Miller, L. G., Dowdle, P., et al. 1995. Methylmercury oxidative-degradation potentials in contaminated and pristine sediments of the Carson River, Nevada. Applied and Environmental Microbiology 61(7), 2745–2753.

Paquette, K. E., Helz, G. R., 1997. Inorganic speciation of mercury in sulfidic waters: The importance of zero-valent sulfur. Environmental Science & Technology 31(7), 2148–2153.

Parks, J. M., Johs, A., Podar, M., et al. 2013. The genetic basis for bacterial mercury methylation. Science 339(6125), 1332–1335.

Pham, A. L., Morris, A., Zhang, T., et al. 2014. Precipitation of nanoscale mercuric sulfides in the presence of natural organic matter: Structural properties, aggregation, and biotransformation. Geochimica et Cosmochimica Acta 133, 204–215.

Podar, M., Gilmour, C. C., Brandt, C. C., et al. 2015. Global prevalence and distribution of genes and microorganisms involved in mercury methylation. Science Advance 1(9), e1500675.

Poulain, A. J., Ní Chadhain, S. M., Ariya, P. A., et al. 2007. Potential for mercury reduction by microbes in the high Arctic. Applied and Environmental Microbiology 73(7), 2230–2238.

Qin, C. Y., Du, B. Y., Yin, R. S., et al. 2020. Isotopic fractionation and source appointment of methylmercury and inorganic mercury in a paddy ecosystem. Environmental Science & Technology 54(22), 14334–14342.

Qiu, G. L., Feng, X. B., Li, P., et al. 2008. Methylmercury accumulation in rice (Oryza sativa L.) grown at abandoned mercury mines in Guizhou, China. Journal of Agricultural and Food Chemistry 56(7), 2465–2468.

Ravichandran, M., 2004. Interactions between mercury and dissolved organic matter - A review. Chemosphere 55(3), 319–331.

Ravichandran, M., Aiken, G. R., Ryan, J. N., et al. 1999. Inhibition of precipitation and aggregation of metacinnabar (mercuric sulfide) by dissolved organic matter isolated from the Florida Everglades. Environmental Science & Technology 33(9), 1418–1423.

Rothenberg, S. E., Feng, X., 2012. Mercury cycling in a flooded rice paddy. Journal of Geophysical Research: Biogeosciences 117, 1–16.

Schaefer, J. K., Yagi, J., Reinfelder, J. R., et al. 2004. Role of the bacterial organomercury lyase (merB) in controlling methylmercury accumulation in mercury-contaminated natural waters. Environmental Science & Technology 38(16), 4304–4311.

Schwab, L., Gallati, N., Reiter, S. M., et al. 2023. Mercury isotope fractionation during dark abiotic reduction of Hg(II) by dissolved, surface-bound, and structural Fe(II). Environmental Science & Technology 57(40), 15243–15254.

Skyllberg, U., Persson, A., Tjerngren, I., et al. 2021. Chemical speciation of mercury, sulfur and iron in a dystrophic boreal lake sediment, as controlled by the formation of mackinawite and framboidal pyrite. Geochimica et Cosmochimica Acta 294, 106–125.

Slowey, A. J., 2010. Rate of formation and dissolution of mercury sulfide nanoparticles: The dual role of natural organic matter. Geochimica et Cosmochimica Acta 74, 4693–4708.

Sonke, J. E., Angot, H., Zhang, Y. X., et al. 2023. Global change effects on biogeochemical mercury cycling. Ambio 52, 853–876.

Spangler, W. J., Spigarelli, J. L., Rose, J. M., et al. 1973. Methylmercury - bacterial degradation in lake sediments. Science 180 (4082), 192–193.

Strickman, R. J., Mitchell, C. P. J., 2017. Accumulation and translocation of methylmercury and inorganic mercury in Oryza sativa: An enriched isotope tracer study. Science of the Total Environment 574, 1415–1423.

Tang, Z. Y., Fan, F. L., Deng, S. P., et al. 2020. Mercury in rice paddy fields and how does some agricultural activities affect the translocation and transformation of mercury - A critical review. Ecotoxicology and Environmental Safety 202, 110950.

Tang, W. L., Liu, Y. R., Guan, W. Y., et al. 2020. Understanding mercury methylation in the changing environment: Recent advances in assessing microbial methylators and mercury bioavailability. Science of the Total Environment 714, 136827.

Tian, L., Guan, W. Y., Ji, Y. Y., et al. 2021. Microbial methylation potential of mercury sulfide particles dictated by surface structure. Nature Geoscience 14(6), 409–416.

Tong, M., Yuan, S. H., Ma, S. C., et al. 2016. Production of abundant hydroxyl radicals from oxygenation of subsurface sediments. Environmental Science & Technology 50(1), 214–221.

Ullrich, S. M., Tanton, T. W., Abdrashitova, S. A., 2001. Mercury in the aquatic environment: A review of factors affecting methylation. Crit. Rev. Environmental Science & Technology 31(3), 241–293.

Wang, Y. M., Li, Y. B, Liu, G. L., et al. 2015. Elemental mercury in natural waters: Occurrence and determination of particulate Hg(0). Environmental Science & Technology 49(16), 9742–9749.

West, J., Graham, A. M., Liem-Nguyen, V., et al. 2020. Dimethylmercury degradation by dissolved sulfide and mackinawite. Environmental Science & Technology 54(21), 13731–13738.

Wu, Q. Q., Hu, H. Y., Meng, B., et al. 2020. Methanogenesis is an important process in controlling MeHg concentration in rice paddy soils affected by mining activities. Environmental Science & Technology 54(21), 13517–13526.

Wu, Q. Q., Wang, B. L., Hu, H. Y., et al. 2023. Sulfate-reduction and methanogenesis are coupled to Hg (II) and MeHg reduction in rice paddies. Journal of Hazardous Materials. 460, 132486.

Xiang, Y. P., Guo, Y. Y., Liu, G. L., et al. 2023. Direct uptake and intracellular dissolution of HgS nanoparticles: Evidence from a bacterial biosensor approach. Environmental Science & Technology 57(40), 14994–15003.

Xiang, Y. P., Guo, Y. Y., Liu, G. L., et al. 2022a. Particle-bound Hg(II) is available for microbial uptake as revealed by a whole-cell biosensor. Environmental Science & Technology 56(10), 6754–6764.

Xiang, Y. P., Zhu, A. L., Guo, Y. Y., et al. 2022b. Decreased bioavailability of both inorganic mercury and methylmercury in anaerobic sediments by sorption on iron sulfide nanoparticles. Journal of Hazardous Materials 424, 127399.

Yin, R. S, Feng, X. B, Meng, B., 2013. Stable mercury isotope variation in rice plants (Oryza sativa L.) from the Wanshan mercury mining district, SW China. Environmental Science & Technology 47(5), 2238–2245.

Yin, R. S., Gu, C. H., Feng, X. B., et al. 2016. Distribution and geochemical speciation of soil mercury in Wanshan Hg mine: Effects of cultivation. Geoderma. 272, 32–38.

Zhang, R., Aris-brosou, S., Storck, V., et al.2023. Mining-impacted rice paddies select for Archaeal methylators and reveal a putative (Archaeal) regulator of mercury methylation. ISME Communication 3(1), 74.

Zhang, H., Feng, X. B., Larssen, T., et al. 2010. In inland China, rice, rather than fish, is the major pathway for methylmercury exposure. Environmental Health Perspectives 118(9), 1183–1188.

Zhang, T., Kim, B., Levard, C., et al. 2012. Methylation of mercury by bacteria exposed to dissolved, nanoparticulate, and microparticulate mercuric sulfides. Environmental Science & Technology 46(13), 6950–6958.

Zhang, T., Kucharzyk, K. H., Kim, B., et al. 2014. Net methylation of mercury in estuarine sediment microcosms amended with dissolved, nanoparticulate, and microparticulate mercuric sulfides. Environmental Science & Technology 48(16), 9133–9141.

Zhao, L., Anderson, C. W. N., Qiu, G. L., et al. 2016a. Mercury methylation in paddy soil: Source and distribution of mercury species at a Hg mining area, Guizhou Province, China. Biogeosciences 13(8), 2429–2440.

Zhao, L., Meng, B., Feng, X. B., 2020. Mercury methylation in rice paddy and accumulation in rice plant: A review. Ecotoxicology and Environmental Safety 195, 110462.

Zhao, L., Qiu, G. L., Anderson, C. W. N., et al. 2016b. Mercury methylation in rice paddies and its possible controlling factors in the Hg mining area, Guizhou province, Southwest China. Environment. Pollution. 215, 1–9.

Zheng, W., Liang, L. Y., Gu, B. H., 2012. Mercury reduction and oxidation by reduced natural organic matter in anoxic environments. Environmental Science & Technology 46(1), 292–299.

Zheng, W., Lin, H., Mann, B. F., et al. 2013. Oxidation of dissolved elemental mercury by thiol compounds under anoxic conditions. Environmental Science & Technology 47(22), 12827–12834.

Zhou, X. Q., Hao, Y. Y., Gu, B. H., et al. 2020. Microbial communities associated with methylmercury degradation in paddy soils. Environmental Science & Technology 54(13), 7952–7960.

Zhu, J. S., Wang, D. Y., Liu, X., Zhang, Y. T., 2011. Mercury fluxes from air/surface interfaces in paddy field and dry land. Applied Geochemistry 26(2), 249–255.

6 Microbial Communities Responsible for Hg Transformations in Soils

Haiyan Hu, Baolin Wang, Qingqing Wu, Xile Liu, and Xinbin Feng

6.1 INTRODUCTION

Mercury (Hg) is a global toxic element, and its toxicity level highly depends on its chemical form. The most common chemical forms of Hg in nature are elemental Hg [Hg(0)], inorganic Hg [Hg(II)], and methylated Hg (CH_3Hg^+, MeHg), with MeHg being the most concerning one due to its high neurotoxicity and bioaccumulation in the food chain. Hg enters into environments mainly in its inorganic forms, i.e., Hg(II) or Hg(0), with the former able to be methylated to the neurotoxic form, MeHg, by certain strains of anaerobic microorganisms. The net MeHg formation in the environment depends on two opposite processes: Hg(II) methylation and MeHg demethylation. Hg(II) methylation is mainly a microbial process mediated by some anaerobic microorganisms, while MeHg demethylation occurs through biotic or abiotic processes. Microorganisms take part in all Hg transformation reactions; especially Hg methylation is demonstrated to be primarily a microbial process, and thus microorganisms play a key role in Hg biogeochemical cycling, modulating Hg toxicity (Figure 6.1).

Fish consumption has long been considered the main route of MeHg exposure (Clarkson 1997). More recently though, rice consumption has been recognized as an important MeHg exposure route in many parts of the world where rice is the staple food (Feng et al., 2008; Qiu et al., 2008; Zhang et al. 2010a). Intensive studies on MeHg formation in soils/sediments and its accumulation by rice were conducted in the past decades, and they revealed that the source of MeHg in rice is mostly rice paddies, recognized as a "hotspot" for Hg methylation (Zhang et al., 2010b; Meng et al., 2011). Hg(II) methylation is a complex process that is largely controlled by the uptake of Hg(II) and the activity of Hg methylators, which were demonstrated to be some species from sulfate-reducers, iron-reducers, methanogens, etc. (Liu et al., 2018; Vishnivetskaya et al., 2018; Zhou et al., 2020). Microbial MeHg demethylation occurs through a reductive (RD) or oxidative (OD) pathway, which is distinguished by the end-products of demethylation, with the former ending with CH_4 and Hg(0) and the latter ending with CO_2 and Hg(II). The choice between RD and OD is controlled by Hg concentration and redox factors in rice paddies.

Both Hg(II) reduction to Hg(0) and Hg(0) oxidation to Hg(II) control the availability of Hg(II) for methylation; thus the two processes have a significant impact on MeHg formation (Barkay and Wagner-Dobler, 2005). Microbial Hg(II) reduction

DOI: 10.1201/9781003404941-6

105

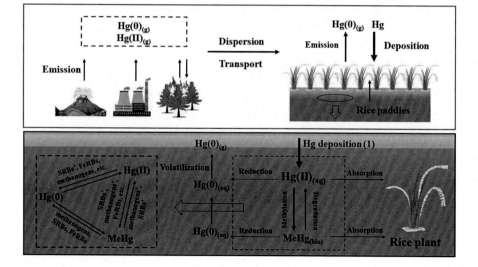

FIGURE 6.1 Biogeochemical cycling of Hg in rice paddy soils. The arrows depict transformation reactions and transport pathways, with microbial guilds involved in the reactions dipicted on the arrows. The asterisk (*) indicates the main microbial guild for each pathway, with one asterisk for SRBs and one asterisk for methanogens. (Modified from Wu et al., 2023.)

is mediated by Hg-resistant bacteria through the mercuric reductase of MerA from *mer*-operon or by some Hg-sensitive bacteria through the cell surface functional group (Hu et al., 2013a). Although Hg(0) oxidation has long been recognized to occur in aerobic conditions, Hg(0) oxidation in anaerobic environments has been poorly studied.

6.2 MICROBIAL Hg METHYLATION

6.2.1 Hg Speciation and Bioavailability for Methylation

Microbial Hg methylation is likely to occur in the intracellular cells of methylators (Gilmour et al., 2011; Schaefer et al., 2011; An et al., 2019). Thus, the transport of inorganic Hg substrate from the extracellular cellular surroundings to the inner side of methylator cells is a critical step for Hg methylation. In most of the environmental settings (sediments, wetlands, rice paddy soils, etc.), there are various Hg compounds (e.g., Hg complexes with chloride, inorganic sulfide, dissolved organic matter, minerals, or particles) to which the methylators are exposed. These Hg compounds have different fractionation sizes and mobilities, resulting in a difference in availability for Hg methylators. Mercury in soil is operationally classified into dissolved, colloidal, and particulate fractions according to its ability to pass through filters with different pore sizes.

However, with the size-based method it is difficult to determine Hg species and their bioavailability, because there is no natural cut-off to distinguish between dissolved Hg and particulate Hg, as dissolved Hg can absorb to filters. More recently, diffusive gradient thin film (DGT) passive sampling devices have been deployed to estimate the "chemically labile" Hg concentration, since presumably only aqueous dissolved Hg complexes can diffuse through the membrane/gel layer and accumulate on the resin of the DGT through the chelation of functional groups (e.g., thiolate ligands) (Diviš et al., 2009; Fernandez-Gomez et al., 2011).

Both laboratory experiments and field studies have shown that the neutrally charged complexes $Hg(SH)_2$, low-molecular-weight Hg-thiols, and HgS nanoparticles (HgS_{NP}, which was previously suggested as $HgS_{(aq)}$) are important Hg species available for methylation and could be significant to MeHg production in the environment (Benoit et al., 1999, 2001; Drott et al., 2007; Zhang et al., 2012; Graham et al., 2013; Mazrui et al., 2016; Zhou et al., 2017).

6.2.2 PATHWAYS AND MECHANISMS OF Hg UPTAKE BY MICROORGANISM

The uptake of Hg by methylators may occur through the pathways as follows: active transport, passive transport, a Mer-based transport system, or facilitated diffusion based on a transmembrane protein channel (Hsu-Kim et al., 2013; An et al., 2019; Regnell and Watras, 2019). To better understand the process of Hg methylation, it is necessary to elucidate how these methylators acquire Hg, as it is the first and a limiting step of Hg methylation (Benoit et al., 2003; Schaefer et al., 2011; Graham et al., 2012).

Passive transport means that Hg (inorganic Hg for methylation) diffuses passively across the cellular envelope, which involves the movement of solutes down a concentration gradient without any energy requirements. Both laboratory experiments and field studies showed that the neutrally charged complexes $Hg(SH)_2^0$ (aq) and HgS^0(aq) entered into cells primarily via the passive diffusion pathway (Benoit et al., 1999, 2001; Drott et al., 2007). HgS nanoparticles (HgS_{NP}) and low-molecular-weight Hg-thiols, which are suggested to be important Hg species for methylation, are likely acquired by microbial cells through passive diffusion and could be significant to MeHg production in the environment (Zhang et al., 2012; Graham et al., 2013; Mazrui et al., 2016; Zhou et al., 2017). Notably, the passive transport of Hg is still controversial, with some studies pointing out that passive diffusion is unlikely to occur (Eckley and Hintelmann, 2006; Acha et al., 2011), since it is difficult to distinguish between Hg adsorption to cells and transmembrane uptake.

Active transport of Hg into cells involves Hg passing through cell membrane against a concentration gradient, which requires energy (ATP) consumption and the specific membrane transporters/proteins. The well-known example for active Hg transport is Mer-based transport of divalent inorganic Hg(II) by those with the *mer*-resistance system, whose structure and regulation are described below. However, most Hg methylators, including all the obligatory anaerobic bacteria, don't have *mer* operon, as can be inferred from the lack of a *mer* sequence in their genomes. Most of the identified Hg methylators are Gram negative bacteria (Ranchou-Peyruse et al., 2009; Gilmour et al., 2011). Obviously, in addition to the Mer-based transporters, alternative Hg transport pathways would exist, and that would be different between Gram negative and positive microorganisms since the latter lack an outer membrane lipid bilayer and possess a thicker peptidoglycan layer outside the cytoplasmic membrane.

Furthermore, a number of studies showed that essential metal transporters would be involved in Hg uptake (Schaefer et al., 2011; An et al., 2019). It was demonstrated that metal binding sites are not strictly specific (e.g., they are not specific enough to exclude unwanted metal ions), and thus Hg could be acquired by microbial cells via the essential metal transport channel (Ma et al., 2009; Szczuka et al., 2015). This hypothesis was supported by the studies showing that the presence of Zn(II) and Cd(II) reduced Hg uptake and/or methylation by the model Hg methylators (*Geobacter sulfurreducens* PCA and *Desulfovibrio desulfuricans* ND132) (Hintelmann et al., 2000; Schaefer et al., 2014) and Hg uptake by non-Hg methylators (*Shewanella oneidensis* MR-1 and *E. coli mer*-lux bioreporter equipped with a *merR* gene but lacking *mer* transporter genes) (Szczuka et al., 2015).

6.2.3 Hg Methylation Genes

Tremendous efforts have been made by researchers worldwide to reveal the molecular mechanism of Hg methylation, ever since the severe Hg poisoning event in Minamata, Japan, in 1956. This notorious Hg event was caused by the poisoning MeHg produced from inorganic Hg released from nearby industrial activities. It is generally believed that Hg methylation was associated with the reductive acetyl–coenzyme A (CoA) (Choi et al., 1994). However, there is no firm evidence showing the connection between the acetyl-CoA pathway and Hg methylation ability, limiting understanding of the methylation at a molecular level and hence the ability to track MeHg formation.

Hg methylation is mediated by some anaerobic microorganisms, typically sulfate-reducing bacteria (Compeau and Bartha, 1985; Gilmour et al., 1992), iron-reducing bacteria (Fleming et al., 2006), and methanogens (Hamelin et al., 2011; Yu et al., 2012). Most recently, using competitive genomics and structural biology tools, scientists from the Oak Ridge National Laboratory identified two genes, *hgcA* and *hgcB*, that are responsible for Hg methylation. The gene *hgcA* encodes a putative corrinoid protein (HgcA), which mediates the Hg methylation reaction by transferring methyl (CH_3^+) to inorganic Hg, while *hgcB* encodes a 2[4Fe-4S] ferredoxin (HgcB), which acts as the electron donor required for corrinoid cofactor reduction (Parks et al., 2013) (Figure 6.2).

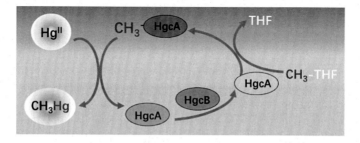

FIGURE 6.2 A mechanistic model for the roles of HgcA (putative corrinoid protein) and HgcB (a 2[4Fe-4S]). The methylated MerA protein transfers a methyl group to Hg(II). HgcB protein is required for HgcA turnover. Different shades of gray for the HgcA protein indicate different redox states of the corrinoid HgcA enzyme. THF = tetrahydrofolate. (Illustrated on the basis of Parks et al., 2013, and Poulain and Barkay, 2013.)

Based on these findings, Poulain and Barkay (2013) proposed a mechanistic model for the transfer of a methyl group from the methylated HgcA protein to inorganic Hg(II) and HgcA turnover by an HgcB protein, and they hypothesized that the C terminus of HgcA may be membrane-embedded, possibly coupling methylation to the transport of Hg(II) and/or methylmercury across the cell wall (Figure 6.2).

6.2.4 MICROBIAL COMMUNITY RESPONSIBLE FOR Hg METHYLATION

Early in 1969, Hg methylation was found to be driven by microbes (Jensen and Jernelöv, 1969). This was speculated based on the fact that inorganic Hg was converted to MeHg in the sediment and this methylation process was greatly inhibited in the sterilized sediment. Thereafter, Hg methylation was demonstrated to be mediated by pure cultures of bacteria and fungi (Landner, 1971; Yamada and Tonomura, 1972; Vonk and Sijpesteijn, 1973). Compeau and Bartha (1985) reported that Hg methylation in salt marsh sediments was greatly inhibited (95%) by molybdate (20 mmol · L^{-1}), an inhibitor of SRB, while it was greatly increased by sodium 2-bromoethylsulfonate (30 mmol·L^{-1}), a specific inhibitor of methanogens (Compeau and Bartha, 1985).Thereafter, by using the molybdate inhibition method, SRBs were demonstrated to be the main Hg methylators in marine, estuarine, and freshwater sediments (Gilmour et al., 1992; Choi et al., 1994; Pak and Bartha, 1998a; King et al., 2000). Therefore, sulfate-reducing bacteria are considered the main methylation bacteria in anaerobic sediments. However, further studies showed that not all SRBs can methylate Hg, and Hg methylation ability is poorly related to the taxonomic status of microorganisms. Hg methylation SRB strains are randomly distributed in the phylogenetic tree (Devereux et al., 1996).

In iron-rich and sulfate-limited environments, iron-reducing bacteria (FeRBs), rather than SRBs, were found to be the main Hg methylators. Fleming et al. (2006) found that the addition of molybdate completely inhibited the activity of SRB, while slightly inhibiting Hg methylation in sediment. Later on, an FeRB strain, *Geobacter* sp. strain CLFeRB, isolated from sediment was found to methylate Hg in pure culture, and its Hg methylation ability was greater than that of most SRB strains, indicating that Hg methylation was dominated by FeRBs rather than SRBs.

Since the discovery of Hg methylation genes *hgcAB*, more and more microorganisms have been found to have the ability to convert inorganic Hg(II) into MeHg and these microorganisms are phylogenetically and environmentally diverse. There are at least 140 predicted methylators based on multiple BLASTP searches for homologs of HgcA and HgcB, and Hg methylation might occur in some unexpected niches, such as animal gut and extremes of pH and salinity (Gilmour et al., 2013). Besides SRBs and FeRBs, methanogens and syntrophic, acetogenic, and fermentative Firmicutes were also demonstrated to have the ability to methylate Hg by measuring MeHg production in their pure cultures. With the discovery of Hg methylation genes and the development of sequencing technology, *hgcAB* is not only used as an effective means to discover new Hg-methylation microorganisms, but also used as an important basis for identification of Hg-methylation microorganisms in the environment.

Paddy fields are a notable "hotspot" for Hg methylation. MeHg in rice paddies can be accumulated by rice grains, causing a great risk to the health of rice consumers (Feng et al., 2008; Zhang et al., 2010a). Consumption of Hg-contaminated rice is the main pathway of human exposure to MeHg in Hg-contaminated areas in China, such as Hg mining regions (Qiu et al., 2006; Li et al., 2011; Meng et al., 2014) and places near coal-fired power plants, energy-saving-lamp factories, urban industrial parks, and e-waste recycling areas (Horvat et al., 2003; Fu et al., 2008; Cheng et al., 2013; Liang et al., 2015). The elevated MeHg concentration was also observed in rice grown in mercury-contaminated soils worldwide (Zarcinas et al., 2004; Krisnayanti et al., 2012; Sarkar et al., 2012; Liu et al., 2019).

Since the discovery of MeHg accumulation in rice grain, great efforts have been made to explore the methylation process and the underlying mechanism of Hg methylation in rice paddies. By using the combination of third-generation PacBio long-read sequencing, Illumina short-read metagenomic sequencing, and quantitative PCR analyses, Liu et al. (2018) revealed that Hg-methylating communities in Hg-polluted paddy soils from the southwestern part of China were dominated by iron-reducing bacteria (i.e., *Geobacter*) and methanogens (Figure 6.3). Studies have shown that

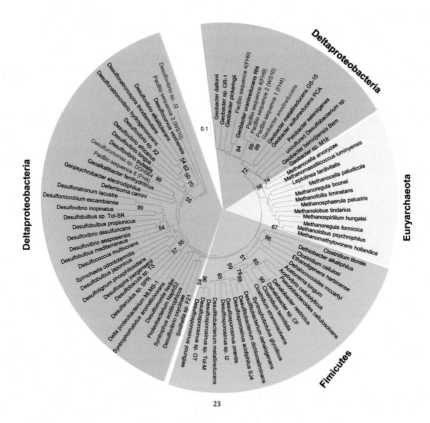

FIGURE 6.3 Maximum likelihood trees of hgcA sequences. The translated representative PacBio sequences are indicated in blue and red type. The phlya (classes) of Deltaproteobacteria, Euryarchaeota, and Firmicutes are marked in purple, yellow, and green, respectively. Bootstrap support values of >50 are shown, with consensus based on 100 replicates. (Reprinted with permission from Liu et al., 2018.)

Proteobacteria, *Actinobacteria*, *Chloroflexi*, *Acidobacteria*, *Euryarchaeota*, and *Crenarchaeota* were dominant in rice paddies at Hg mining areas in Guizhou province and the microbial communities at high THg and high MeHg appear to be adapted by species that are Hg-resistant (Vishnivetskaya et al., 2018). To investigate the contribution of different microbial groups to MeHg production and degradation in rice paddies across an Hg contamination gradient, Wu et al. (2020) combined the specific microbial inhibitors and stable isotope tracers in incubation experiments, and they revealed that methanogens had an important role in controlling MeHg concentration in Hg-contaminated areas due to their ability of demethylation of MeHg (Figure 6.4). This case study also showed that the main Hg methylators may vary with Hg contamination levels, with SRBs being the dominant methylators at the control site while complex microbial guilds were involved in mining areas. Besides the indispensable role of methylators in

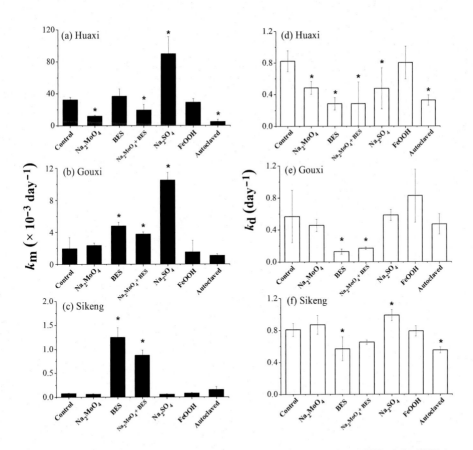

FIGURE 6.4 Potential methylation/demethylation rate constants (k m ± STD, k d ± STD) in rice paddies under different treatments with inhibitors/stimulants. Huaxi (a and d, the control site); Gouxi (b and e, the artisanal Hg mining site); Sikeng (c and f, the abandoned Hg mining site). An asterisk denotes significant difference from control treatment, $p < 0.05$. (Reprinted with permission from Wu et al., 2020.)

the formation of MeHg, putative non-Hg methylators were suggested to also be important for MeHg formation in boreal peatlands (Wang et al., 2021) and rice paddy soils (Liu et al., 2019).

6.3   MICROBIAL MeHg DEMETHYLATION

6.3.1   REDUCTIVE DEMETHYLATION (RD)

Reductive demethylation largely refers to the reaction mediated by Hg-resistant microorganisms, which carry a *mer* system to break the carbon-mercury (C-Hg) bond by the organomercury lyase (MerB) to produce CH_4 and Hg(II). The produced Hg(II) is then reduced to Hg(0) by the mercuric reductase (MerA). Thus, *mer*-mediated (MerB and MerA) reductive demethylation converts MeHg to CH_4 and Hg(0) (Barkay and Wagner-Dobler, 2005; Barkay and Gu, 2022). This *mer* operon-dependent demethylation has been found both in the laboratory and in natural environments such as lake sediments, phytoplankton biofilms, and fish (Tonomura et al., 1968; Furukawa et al., 1969; Spangler et al., 1973a, b).

The *mer* system is broadly distributed among aerobic prokaryotes, resulting in their resistance to organic and inorganic Hg by degrading the neurotoxic organic Hg (typically MeHg) to Hg(II) followed by reduction to Hg(0). Besides MerA and MerB, the *mer* system consists of a variety of other components playing an important function in Hg transportation and regulation, among which MerT is a membrane-bound protein for uptake of Hg(II) and MerR is both a repressor and an activator for functional genes (Barkay et al., 2003). Those *mer* genes are co-located in the *mer* operon, and their arrangements can be quite diverse in various microorganisms. Furthermore, *merA* and *merB* are not always co-occurring in Hg-resistant bacteria (in other words, the *merA*-carrying bacteria do not necessarily carry the *merB* gene; thus these bacteria have resistance only to inorganic Hg but not to organic Hg. The bacteria that carry both *merA* and *merB* genes (resistance to organic Hg and inorganic Hg) are so called broad-spectrum Hg resistant, while those only have the *merA* gene (only resistance to inorganic Hg) are defined having narrow-spectrum resistance. Notably, recent studies showed that horizontal gene transfer is commonly observed for the Hg resistance genes *merA* and *merB*, causing it to be difficult to distinguish the phylogeny of Hg-resistant bacteria.

It has been demonstrated that the *mer* is an inducible operon, with the *mer* expressions only at certain Hg concentrations, which were largely influenced by the redox condition and microbial strains (Schaefer et al., 2002). The Hg(II) and/or MeHg compounds bind to the Hg(II)-responsive regulatory protein, MerR, inducing the transcription of a polycistronic message which encodes MerA and MerB (Brown et al., 2003). It is suggested that the rate of reductive demethylation is likely dependent on the Hg concentration, since the induction of *mer* expression is proportional to the amount of Hg, i.e., the higher the Hg level, the higher the level of *mer* expression (Ralston and O'Halloran, 1990; Rasmussen et al., 1997).

Recently, a researcher group from Yunnan University isolated an endophytic bacterium (*Pseudomonas* sp. AN-B15) from rice, which could efficiently volatilize (reduce highly toxic Hg^{2+} to low-toxic and volatile Hg^0) and inactivate Hg (form stable HgS).

At the same time, the strain also has a growth-promoting effect on rice. Further studies have found that the molecular mechanism of Hg reduction by the endophytic bacterium is mainly regulated by the *merA* operon, coupled with amino acid, lipid, and carbohydrate metabolism to produce reducing power (NADPH).

6.3.2 OXIDATIVE DEMETHYLATION (OD)

The discovery of MeHg oxidative demethylation was thanks to the usage of ^{14}C-MeHg in measuring demethylation potentials. This method found that there were both CH_4 and CO_2 in the gaseous C products pool (Korthals and Winfrey, 1987). Besides *mer*-dependent reductive demethylation by Hg-resistant bacteria producing CH_4, there exist other pathways of MeHg demethylation producing CO_2 (Winfrey and Rudd, 1990). Very shortly after this discovery, Oremland et al. (1991), to distinguish the process from reductive demethylation (RD), coined the term "oxidative demethylation (OD)" to describe the formation of CO_2 during demethylation. Thereafter, Pak and Bartha (1998b) applied C isotope $^{14}CH_3HgI$, as a spike, to investigate the demethylation process and found that the gaseous C product was $^{14}CH_4$ rather than $^{14}CO_2$. The distinction between OD and RD is based on the oxidation state of Hg rather than the state of C, since the oxidation state of C is the same in both RD and OD. In RD the product of Hg is Hg(0), while in OD it is Hg(II), resulting in the potential re-methylation-demethylation cycle (Schaefer et al., 2004).

Compared to *mer*-mediated RD in high Hg level and oxic environments, fewer studies have been made on OD in low Hg level and anoxic environments; thus little is known about the mechanism of OD and the microbes involved. SRB and methanogens are confirmed to be involved in MeHg demethylation, both in pure cultures and in freshwater sediments (Pak and Bartha, 1998a). Similarly, Bridou et al. (2011) tested more than a dozen SRB strains for demethylation and found that all of them were able to degrade MeHg to Hg(II), suggesting that SRB strains contributed to MeHg degradation under anoxic conditions, with the process consistent with the OD pathway. Further studies conducted by Oremland et al. (1991) showed that the addition of C1 compounds such as methanol, methylamine, and methylsulfide significantly inhibited demethylation, suggesting that OD is probably related to the one-carbon (C1) metabolism of SRB and methanogens. Wu et al. (2023) determined that OD is absolutely dominant in MeHg demethylation in both highly contaminated and less Hg contaminated paddy soils, with methanogens and SRBs being involved in OD (Figure 6.5).

As described above, Hg transformations in the rice paddy ecosystem greatly control the net MeHg formation and consequently the Hg accumulation in rice seed. Thus, most recent studies have focused on Hg methylation in paddy soils, the accumulation pathway of Hg, the distribution of Hg and MeHg in plants, etc., while many fewer studies have beeen made, and consequently less knowledge obtained, about Hg speciation transformations inside the rice plant. Until recently, MeHg was demonstrated to be demethylated inside the rice plant by using both the synchrotron radiation and the isotope tracing techniques (Xu et al., 2016; Liu et al., 2021a). It was also found that plant leaf may oxidize elemental Hg and thus immobilize Hg in the leaf (Du and Fang, 1983; Patra and Sharma, 2000; Meng et al., 2012; Liu et al., 2021b).

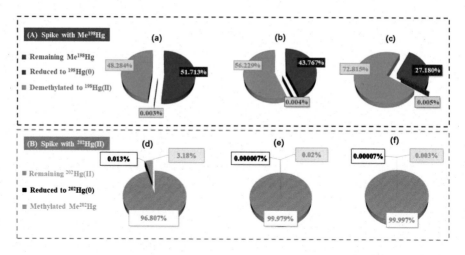

FIGURE 6.5 The fate of the isotopic tracers of Me[198]Hg (A: a, b, c) and [202]Hg(II) (B: d, e, f) amended in a gradient of Hg-contaminated rice paddy soils after spiking in the microcosm incubations for 24 h. (a and d) Huaxi, the control site; (b and e) Gouxi, the artisanal Hg mining site; (c and f) Sikeng, the abandoned Hg mining site. (Reprinted with permission from Wu et al., 2023.)

These studies suggested that Hg speciation transformations occur in plant tissues. However, researchers are still unclear about the pathways (chemically or biologically) of these conversions and the underlying mechanisms. Various studies have shown that the endophytic communities of rice are rich and diverse, with the abundant species including *Proteobacteria, Firmicutesa, Actinobacteria,* etc. (Hu, 2010; Sha, 2018; Khaskheli et al., 2020), and the communities and their relative abundance are varied in Hg contamination (Pietro-Souza et al., 2017; Durand et al., 2018; Ustiatik et al., 2021). However, whether these endophytic microorganisms involve Hg transformations and the underlaying pathways need further study.

6.4 MICROBIAL Hg REDUCTION

6.4.1 Hg(II) Reduction by Hg-resistant Bacteria

Ionic mercury [Hg(II)] and elemental mercury [Hg(0)] are the two main formations of Hg that enter the environment from power generation and other industrial processes. Hg(II) is the most active species of Hg, which undergoes methylation, reduction, sorption, and complexation reactions in natural environments. As mentioned above, Hg(II) can be methylated in anoxic environments by certain microorganisms, resulting in the formation of the most toxic species, MeHg, which is a public health concern because of its accumulation and biomagnification. Meanwhile, Hg(II) also readily undergoes reduction through both biotic and abiotic processes to Hg(0), which volatilizes and thus can potentially be removed as a substrate for microbial methylation (O'Loughlin et al., 2003; Warner et al., 2003; Poulain et al., 2004; Wiatrowski et al., 2006; Gu et al., 2011). Studies have shown that abiotic Hg(II) reduction can be mediated by the low concentrations of naturally dissolved organic matter (DOM) (Gu et al., 2011; Zheng et al., 2012) and minerals containing Fe(II), such as green rust and magnetite (O'Loughlin et al., 2003).

The most well-known microbial Hg reduction is conferred by the Hg resistance (*mer*) operon, a genetic system encoding mercuric reductase (MerA) that catalyzes Hg(II) reduction to Hg(0), and several other function proteins, such as periplasmic Hg binding protein (MerP), the inner (cytosolic) membrane protein (MerT), and the metal-responsive regulatory protein MerR, as illustrated in Figure 6.6.

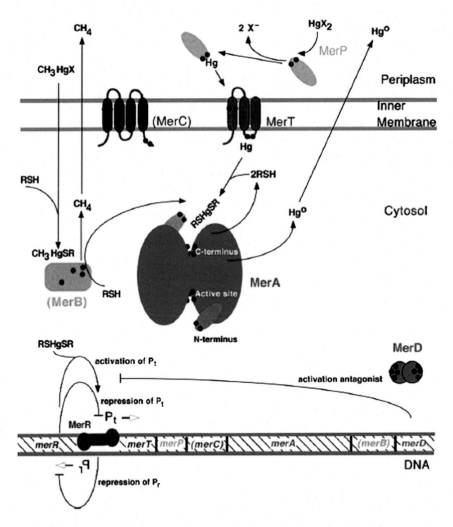

FIGURE 6.6 Model of a typical Gram-negative Hg resistance (*mer*) operon. The symbol ● indicates a cysteine residue. X refers to a generic solvent nucleophile. RSH is the low-molecular-mass, cytosolic thiol redox buffer such as glutathione. Parentheses around gene or protein designations indicate proteins/genes that do not occur in all examples of the operon. (Reprinted with permission from Barkay, 2003.)

The *mer* operon is a tightly regulated genetic system consisting of genes encoding proteins for Hg transport, transformations, and regulation (Barkay et al., 2003; Barkay and Wagner-Dobler, 2005). These functional components are tightly regulated. Comprehensive reviews of the *mer* system, its regulation, and its utility in environmental management and in monitoring of Hg contamination were already published (Barkay et al., 2003; Brown et al., 2003; Barkay and Wagner-Dobler, 2005). MerA, the heart agent of Hg(II) reduction, is located in the cytoplasm, and it is a cytosolic flavin disulfide oxidoreductase (homodimer 120kDa) which uses NAD(P)H as a source of electrons (Furukawa and Tonomura, 1972; Summers and Sugarman, 1974). It has been shown that there are four core C-terminal cysteines in this catalytic enzyme, which was predicted to be involved in the Hg(II) binding pathway and the formation of the actual reducible Hg(II) complex (Miller et al., 1989; Moore et al., 1992).

To date, hundreds of Hg-resistant bacterial strains and *mer* operons have been reported, which were mostly defined in "crown" species of heterotrophic aerobic bacteria, organisms belonging to recently evolved lineages, the Proteobacteria, and the high and low G + C Gram-positive bacteria (Barkay and Wagner-Dobler, 2005). Studies have shown that Hg stress would increase the relative abundance of Hg-resistant bacteria (Rasmussen et al., 2000; Schaefer et al., 2002). However, few studies on Hg-resistant bacteria in rice paddy soils have been conducted. More studies are needed to expand the organisms representing the known prokaryotic diversity and to identify the Hg-resistant ones in the rice paddy system.

6.4.2 Hg(II) Reduction by Hg-sensitive Bacteria

Besides the *mer*-mediated Hg(II) reduction conducted by Hg-resistant bacteria, a number of dissimilatory metal-reducing bacteria, such as *Geobacter metallireducens* GS-15, *Geobacter sulfurreducens* PCA, and *Shewanellaoneidensis* MR-1, are also reported to be able to reduce Hg(II) (Lovley et al., 1993; Wiatrowski et al., 2006), and the mechanism is distinct from *mer* operon-induced Hg reduction. The Hg resistance level of these dissimilatory metal-reducing bacteria is much lower than those of *mer*-carrying bacteria; thus we called them Hg-sensitive bacteria. Unlike *mer*-dependent Hg(II) reduction, which is only induced at the μM Hg level and is not very effective under anoxic conditions (Schaefer et al., 2002), the Hg-sensitive strains are capable of reducing Hg(II) to Hg(0) at much lower Hg concentration (Takeuchi et al., 1999). Meanwhile Hg(II) could also be sorbed by microbial cells through the surface functional groups such as carboxyls, hydroxyls, and amines (Das et al., 2007; Mishra et al., 2011). In order to reveal the interplay between Hg(II) reduction and surface complexation by dissimilatory metal-reducing bacteria, Hu et al. (2013a) used a typical Hg-sensitive strain, *G. sulfurreducens* PCA, which is an important group of microorganisms known to methylate Hg(II) (Kerin et al., 2006; Schaefer and Morel, 2009), to determine the Hg(II) reduction

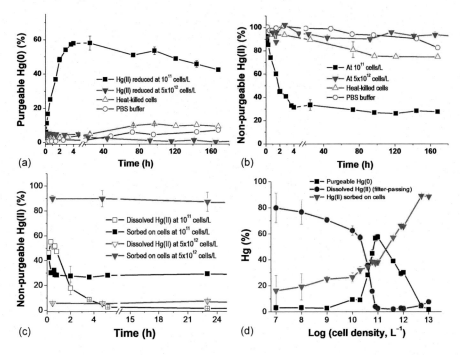

FIGURE 6.7 The kinetics of Hg(II) reduction and surface complexation by the cell of *G. sulfurreducens* in phosphate buffer saline (PBS). (a) Hg(II) reduction, expressed as purgeable gaseous Hg(0) (%), by washed cells (at 10^{11} and 5×10^{12} cells/L). The initial Hg(II): 50 nM. (b) Hg(II) remaining in the cell suspension (unfiltered) after purging. (c) Analysis of dissolved Hg(II) in solution (after purging) and sorbed Hg(II) on cells by filtering through a 0.2-μm syringe filter. (d) Hg(II) reduction and sorption onto *G. sulfurreducens* cells at varying cell concentrations (10^8 –10^{13} L^{-1}). Error bars represent one standard deviation. (Reprinted with permission from Hu et al., 2013a.)

and complexation by this microorganism. The main findings of this case study are presented in Figures 6.7 and 6.8: (1) the two competing processes of Hg(II) reduction and surface complexation, which occur simultaneously, with the latter happening much faster than the former, are related to different cell surface functional groups; (2) Hg(II) reduction extent and rates depend on the growth stage of cells, cell density, and the presence of various organic compounds; (3) Hg(II) reduction requires direct contact with *G. sulfurreducens* cells, possibly through c-cytochromes on cell surfaces, and the reduction occurs faster than complexation. Based on these findings, Hu et al. (2013a) proposed a schematic diagram showing the competition between Hg(II) reduction and surface complexation by the strain of *G. sulfurreducens* PCA, and one of the most important findings is that once Hg(II) is bound on the strong binding functional group, it will be hardly reduced (Figure 6.8).

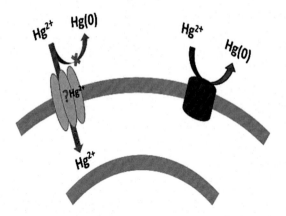

FIGURE 6.8 A schematic diagram of Hg(II) reduction and surface complexation by the strain of *G. sulfurreducens* PCA. (Reprinted with permission from Hu et al., 2013a.)

6.5 MICROBIAL Hg OXIDATION

The oxidation of Hg occurs in the atmosphere (Lindberg et al., 2002), natural waters (Siciliano et al., 2002), and soils (Thöming et al., 2000), converting the vaporable Hg(0) to the active Hg(II). Hg(0) oxidation, rather than volatilization, was suggested to be the sink for Hg(0) in nature; thus it may be critical to MeHg production in natural environments by increasing the substrate of Hg methylation, Hg(II) (Amyot et al., 1997; Lalonde et al., 2001). A number of aerobic microbes, including *E. coli*, *Bacillus*, and *Streptomyces*, were demonstrated to be able to oxide Hg(0) to Hg(II), and bacterial hydroperoxidases KatG and, to a lesser extent, KatE and other bacterial Hg oxidases are likely involved in this process (Smith et al., 1998). For a very long time, microbial Hg(0) oxidation was recognized to be mediated by aerobic microorganisms. However, recently, Hu et al. (2013b) identified a previously unrecognized reaction pathway of Hg(0) oxidation in anoxic environments by some anaerobic microorganisms, such as *Desulfovibriode sulfuricans* ND132 and *Desulfovibrio alaskensis* G20 (Figure 6.9). This case study also revealed that *D. desulfuricans* ND132, a model strain for Hg methylation, is capable of utilizing Hg(0) as a sole source for methylation, while *D.alaskensis* G20 cannot produce MeHg from Hg(0) although it can oxidize Hg(0) to Hg(II).The typical iron reducer of Hg methylator, *G. sulfurreducens* PCA, can neither oxidize nor methylate Hg(0), suggesting that cellular oxidation of Hg(0) is essential for methylation (Hu et al., 2013b). Thus, the ability of bacteria to oxidize Hg(0) with subsequent methylation differs greatly among different bacterial strains, probably due to species-specific biochemical mechanisms and cell surface characteristics. In a broader context, the findings of microbial oxidation and methylation of Hg(0) have important implications for Hg geochemical cycling and net methyl-Hg production leading to its bioaccumulation in aquatic food chains.

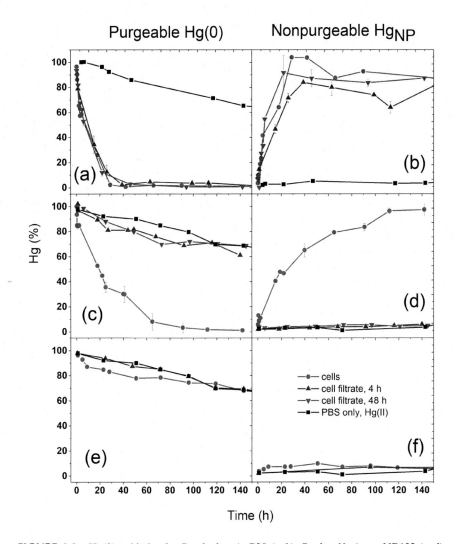

FIGURE 6.9 Hg(0) oxidation by *D. alaskensis* G20 (a, b), *D. desulfuricans* ND132 (c, d), and *G. sulfurreducens* PCA (e, f), which was expressed by the changes in purgeable Hg(0) and nonpurgeable HgNP with time. The initial concentration of dissolved elemental Hg(0) was ~25 nM. "Cell filtrates" were obtained by pre-incubating washed cells in the phosphate buffer for either 4 h or 48 h and then filtering through a 0.2-μm syringe filter to remove cells. (Reprinted with permission from Hu et al., 2013b.)

REFERENCES

Acha, D., Hintelmann, H., Yee, J., 2011. Importance of sulfate reducing bacteria in mercury methylation and demethylation in periphyton from Bolivian Amazon region. Chemosphere 82(6), 911–916.

Amyot, M., Gill, G. A., Morel, F. M. M., 1997. Production and loss of dissolved gaseous mercury in coastal seawater. Environmental Science & Technology 31(12), 3606–3611.

An, J., Zhang, L. J., Lu, X., et al., 2019. Mercury uptake by *Desulfovibrio desulfuricans* ND132: Passive or active? Environmental Science & Technology 53(11), 6264–6272.

Barkay, T., Gu, B. H., 2022. Demethylation—the other side of the mercury methylation coin: A critical review. ACS Environmental Au, 2, 77–97.

Barkay, T., Miller, S. M., Summers, A. O., 2003. Bacterial mercury resistance from atoms to ecosystems. FEMS Microbiology Reviews 27(2–3), 355–384.

Barkay, T., Wagner-Dobler, I., 2005. Microbial transformations of mercury: Potentials, challenges, and achievements in controlling mercury toxicity in the environment. Advances in Applied Microbiology 57, 1–52.

Benoit J.M., Gilmour C.C., Heyes A., et al., 2003. Geochemical and Biological Controls over Methylmercury Production and Degradation in Aquatic Ecosystems. American Chemical Society.

Benoit, J. M., Gilmour, C. C., Mason, R. P., 2001. The influence of sulfide on solid phase mercury bioavailability for methylation by pure cultures of *Desulfobulbus propionicus* (1pr3). Environmental Science & Technology 35(1), 127–132.

Benoit, J. M., Mason, R. P., Gilmour, C. C., 1999. Estimation of mercury-sulfide speciation in sediment pore waters using octanol-water partitioning and implications for availability to methylating bacteria. Environmental Toxicology and Chemistry 18(10), 2138–2141.

Bridou, R., Monperrus, M., Gonzalez, P.R., et al., 2011. Simultaneous determination of mercury methylation and demethylation capacities of various sulfate-reducing bacteria using species-specific isotopic tracers. Environmental Toxicology and Chemistry 30(2), 337–344.

Brown, N. L, Stoyanov, J. V, Kidd, S. P, et al., 2003. The MerR family of transcriptional regulators. FEMS Microbiology Reviews 27(2–3), 145–63.

Cheng, J.P., Zhao, W. C., Wang, Q., et al., 2013. Accumulation of mercury, selenium and PCBs in domestic duck brain, liver and egg from a contaminated area with an investigation of their redox responses. Environmental Toxicology and Pharmacology 35(3), 388–394.

Choi, S. C., Chase, T., Bartha, R., 1994. Metabolic pathways leading to mercury methylation in *Desulfovibrio desulfuricans* LS. Applied and Environmental Microbiology 60(11), 4072–4077.

Clarkson, T. W., 1997. The toxicology of mercury. Critical Reviews in Clinical Laboratory Sciences 34(4), 369–403.

Compeau, G. C., Bartha, R., 1985. Sulfate-reducing bacteria – Principal methylators of mercury in anoxic estuarine sediment. Applied and Environmental Microbiology 50(2), 498–502.

Das, S. K., Das, A. R., Guha, A. K., 2007. A study on the adsorption mechanism of mercury on *Aspergillus versicolor* biomass. Environmental Science & Technology 41(24), 8281–8287.

Devereux, R., Winfrey, M.R., Winfrey, J., et al., 1996. Depth profile of sulfate-reducing bacterial ribosomal RNA and mercury methylation in an estuarine sediment. FEMS Microbiology Ecology 20(1), 23–31.

Diviš, P., Szkandera, R., Brulík, L., et al., 2009. Application of new resin gels for measuring mercury by diffusive gradients in a thin-films technique. Analytical Sciences 25(4), 575–578.

Drott, A, Lambertsson, L, Bjorn, E, et al., 2007. Importance of dissolved neutral mercury sulfides for methyl mercury production in contaminated sediments. Environmental Science & Technology 41(7), 2270–2276.

Du, S. H., Fang, S. C., 1983. Catalase activity of C-3 and C-4 species and its relationship to mercury-vapor uptake. Environmental and Experimental Botany 23(4), 347–353.

Durand, A., Maillard, F., Alvarez-Lopez, V., et al., 2018. Bacterial diversity associated with poplar trees grown on a Hg-contaminated site: Community characterization and isolation of Hg-resistant plant growth-promoting bacteria. Science of the Total Environment 622, 1165–1177.

Eckley, C. S., Hintelmann, H., 2006. Determination of mercury methylation potentials in the water column of lakes across Canada. Science of the Total Environment 368(1), 111–125.

Feng, X. B., Li, P., Qiu, G. L., et al., 2008. Human exposure to methylmercury through rice intake in mercury mining areas, Guizhou province, China. Environmental Science & Technology 42(1), 326–332.

Fernandez-Gomez, C., Dimock, B., Hintelmann, H., et al., 2011. Development of the DGT technique for Hg measurement in water: Comparison of three different types of samplers in laboratory assays. Chemosphere 85(9), 1452–1457.

Fleming, E. J., Mack, E. E., Green, P. G., et al., 2006. Mercury methylation from unexpected sources: Molybdate-inhibited freshwater sediments and an iron-reducing bacterium. Applied and Environmental Microbiology 72(1), 457–464.

Furukawa, K., Suzuki, T., Tonomura, K., 1969. Decomposition of organic mercurial compounds by mercury-resistant bacteria. Agricultural and Biological Chemistry 33(1), 128–130.

Furukawa, K. Tonomura, K., 1972. Induction of metallic mercury-releasing enzyme in mercury-resistant pseudomonas. Agricultural and Biological Chemistry 36(13), 2441–2448.

Fu, J. J., Zhou, Q.F., Liu, J.M., et al., 2008. High levels of heavy metals in rice (*Oryza sativa* L.) from a typical e-waste recycling area in southeast China and its potential risk to human health. Chemosphere 71(7), 1269–1275.

Gilmour, C. C., Elias, D. A., Kucken, A. M., et al., 2011. Sulfate-reducing bacterium *Desulfovibrio desulfuricans* ND132 as a model for understanding bacterial mercury methylation. Applied and Environmental Microbiology 77(12), 3938–3951.

Gilmour, C. C., Henry, E. A., Mitchell, R., 1992. Sulfate stimulation of mercury methylation in fresh-water sediments. Environmental Science & Technology 26(11), 2281–2287.

Gilmour, C. C., Podar, M., Bullock, A. L., et al., 2013. Mercury methylation by novel microorganisms from new environments. Environmental Science & Technology 47(20), 11810–11820.

Graham, A. M., Aiken, G. R., Gilmour, C. C., 2012. Dissolved organic matter enhances microbial mercury methylation under sulfidic conditions. Environmental Science & Technology 46(5), 2715–2723.

Graham, A. M., Aiken, G. R., Gilmour, C. C., 2013. Effect of dissolved organic matter source and character on microbial Hg methylation in Hg-S-DOM solutions. Environmental Science & Technology 47(11), 5746–5754.

Gu, B. H., Bian, Y. R., Miller, C. L., et al., 2011. Mercury reduction and complexation by natural organic matter in anoxic environments. The Proceedings of the National Academy of Sciences, USA 108(4), 1479–1483.

Hamelin, S., Amyot, M., Barkay, T., 2011. Methanogens: Principal methylators of mercury in lake periphyton. Environmental Science & Technology 45(18), 7693–7700.

Hintelmann, H., Keppel-Jones, K., Evans, R. D., 2000. Constants of mercury methylation and demethylation rates in sediments and comparison of tracer and ambient mercury availability. Environmental Toxicology and Chemistry 19(9), 2204–2211.

Horvat, M., Nolde, N., Fajon, V., et al., 2003. Total mercury, methylmercury and selenium in mercury polluted areas in the province Guizhou, China. Science of the Total Environment 304(1), 231–256.

Hsu-Kim, H., Kucharzyk, K. H., Zhang, T., et al., 2013. Mechanisms regulating mercury bioavailability for methylating microorganisms in the aquatic environment: A critical review. Environmental Science & Technology 47(6), 2441–2456.

Hu, G. P. 2010. Study on the Community Diversity of the Endophytic and Rhizosphere Microorganism of Rice (*Oryza sativa L.*). PhD diss., Fujian Agriculture and Forestry University.

Hu, H. Y., Lin, H., Zheng, W., et al., 2013a. Mercury reduction and cell-surface adsorption by *Geobacter sulfurreducens* PCA. Environmental Science & Technology 47(19), 10922–10930.

Hu, H. Y., Lin, H., Zheng, W., et al., 2013b. Oxidation and methylation of dissolved elemental mercury by anaerobic bacteria. Nature Geoscience 6(9), 751–754.

Jensen, S., Jernelöv, A., 1969. Biological methylation of mercury in aquatic organisms. Nature 223, 753–754.

Kerin, E. J., Gilmour, C. C., Roden, E., et al., 2006. Mercury methylation by dissimilatory iron-reducing bacteria. Applied and Environmental Microbiology 72(12), 7919–7921.

Khaskheli M. A., Wu L., Chen G., et al., 2020. Isolation and characterization of root-associated bacterial endophytes and their biocontrol potential against major fungal phytopathogens of rice (*Oryza sativa* L.). Pathogens 9(3), 1–28.

King, J. K., Kostka, J. E., Frischer, M. E., et al., 2000. Sulfate-reducing bacteria methylate mercury at variable rates in pure culture and in marine sediments. Applied and Environmental Microbiology 66(6), 2430–2437.

Korthals E. T., Winfrey M. R., 1987. Seasonal and spatial variations in mercury methylation and demethylation in an oligotrophic lake. Applied and Environmental Microbiology 53(10), 2397–2404.

Krisnayanti, B. D., Anderson, C. W., Utomo, W. H., et al., 2012. Assessment of environmental mercury discharge at a four-year-old artisanal gold mining area on Lombok Island, Indonesia. Journal of Environmental Monitoring 14(10), 2598–2607.

Lalonde, J. D., Amyot, M., Kraepiel, A. M. L., et al., 2001. Photooxidation of Hg(0) in artificial and natural waters. Environmental Science & Technology 35(7), 1367–1372.

Landner, L., 1971. Biochemical model for the biological methylation of mercury suggested from methylation studies in vivo with *Neuospora crassa*. Nature 230, 452–454.

Liang, P., Feng, X. B., Zhang, C., et al., 2015. Human exposure to mercury in a compact fluorescent lamp manufacturing area: By food (rice and fish) consumption and occupational exposure. Environmental Pollution 198, 126–132.

Li, P., Feng, X. B., Shang, L. H., et al., 2011. Human co-exposure to mercury vapor and methylmercury in artisanal mercury mining areas, Guizhou, China. Ecotoxicology and Environmental Safety 74(3), 473–479.

Lindberg, S. E., Brooks, S., Lin, C. J., et al., 2002. Dynamic oxidation of gaseous mercury in the Arctic troposphere at polar sunrise. Environmental Science & Technology 36(6), 1245–1256.

Liu, Y. R., Johs, A., Bi, L, et al., 2018. Unraveling microbial communities associated with methylmercury production in paddy soils. Environmental Science & Technology 52(22), 13110–13118.

Liu, J., Meng, B., Poulain, A.J., et al., 2021a. Stable isotope tracers identify sources and transformations of mercury in rice (*Oryza sativa* L.) growing in a mercury mining area. Fundamental Research 1(3), 259–268.

Liu, Y. W, Tao, H., Wang, Y., et al., 2021b. Gaseous elemental mercury Hg(0) oxidation in poplar leaves through a two-step single-electron transfer process. Environmental Science & Technology Letters 8(12), 1098–1103.

Liu, Y. R., Yang, Z. M., Zhou, X. Q., et al., 2019. Overlooked role of putative non-Hg methylators in predicting methylmercury production in paddy soils. Environmental Science & Technology 53(21), 12330–12338.

Lovley, D. R., Giovannoni, S. J., White, D. C., et al., 1993. *Geobacter metallireducens* gen. nov. sp. nov., a microorganism capable of coupling the complete oxidation of organic-compounds to the reduction of iron and other metals. Archives of Microbiology 159(4), 336–344.

Ma, Z, Jacobsen, F. E., Giedroc, D. P., 2009. Coordination chemistry of bacterial metal transport and sensing. Chemical Reviews 109(10), 4644–4681.

Marvin-DiPasquale, Mark C., Oremland, R. S., 1998. Bacterial methylmercury degradation in Florida Everglades peat sediment. Environmental Science & Technology 32(17), 2556–2563.

Mazrui, N. M., Jonsson, S., Thota, S., et al., 2016. Enhanced availability of mercury bound to dissolved organic matter for methylation in marine sediments. Geochimica et Cosmochimica Acta, 194, 153–162.

Meng, B., Feng, X. B., Qiu, G. L., et al., 2011. The process of methylmercury accumulation in rice (*Oryza sativa* L.). Environmental Science & Technology 45(7), 2711–2717.

Meng, B., Feng, X. B., Qiu, G. L., et al., 2012. Inorganic mercury accumulation in rice (*Oryza sativa* L.). Environmental Toxicology and Chemistry 31(9), 2093–2098.

Meng, B., Feng, X. B., Qiu, G. L., et al., 2014. Localization and speciation of mercury in brown rice with implications for pan-Asian public health. Environmental Science & Technology 48(14), 7974–7981.

Miller, S. M., Moore, M. J., Massey, V., et al., 1989. Evidence for the participation of Cys558 and Cys559 at the active-site of mercuric reductase. Biochemistry 28(3), 1194–1205.

Mishra, B., O'Loughlin, E. J., Boyanov, M. I., et al., 2011. Binding of HgII to high-affinity sites on bacteria inhibits reduction to Hg0 by mixed FeII/III phases. Environmental Science & Technology 45(22), 9597–9603.

Moore, M. J., Miller, S. M., Walsh, C. T., 1992. C-terminal cysteines of Tn501 mercuric ion reductase. Biochemistry 31(6), 1677–1685.

O'Loughlin, E. J., Kelly, S. D., Kemner, K. M., et al., 2003. Reduction of Ag(I), Au(III), Cu(II), and Hg(II) by Fe(II)/Fe(III) hydroxysulfate green rust. Chemosphere 53(5), 437–446.

Oremland, R. S., Culbertson, C. W., Winfrey, M. R., 1991. Methylmercury decomposition in sediments and bacterial cultures: Involvement of methanogens and sulfate reducers in oxidative demethylation. Applied and Environmental Microbiology 57(1), 130–137.

Pak, K., Bartha, R., 1998b. Products of mercury demethylation by sulfidogens and methanogens. Bulletin of Environmental Contamination and Toxicology 61(5), 690–694.

Pak, K. R., Bartha, R., 1998a. Mercury methylation and demethylation in anoxic lake sediments and by strictly anaerobic bacteria. Applied and Environmental Microbiology 64(3), 1013–1017.

Parks, J. M., Johs, A., Podar, M, et al., 2013. The genetic basis for bacterial mercury methylation. Science 339(6125), 1332–1335.

Patra, M., Sharma, A., 2000. Mercury toxicity in plants. Botanical Review 66(3), 379–422.

Pietro-Souza, W., Mello, I. S., Vendruscullo, S. J., et al., 2017. Endophytic fungal communities of *Polygonum acuminatum* and *Aeschynomene fluminensis* are influenced by soil mercury contamination. Plos One 12(7), 1–24.

Poulain, A. J., Amyot, M., Findlay, D., et al., 2004. Biological and photochemical production of dissolved gaseous mercury in a boreal lake. Limnol. Oceanography 49(6), 2265–2275.

Poulain, A. J. and Barkay T., 2013.Cracking the Mercury Methylation Code. Science, 339(6125), 1280–1281.

Qiu, G. L., Feng, X. B, Li, P., et al., 2008. Methylmercury accumulation in rice (*Oryza sativa L*) grown at abandoned mercury mines in Guizhou, China. Journal of Agricultural and Food Chemistry 56(7), 2465–2468.

Qiu, G. L., Feng, X. B., Wang, S. F., et al., 2006. Environmental contamination of mercury from Hg-mining areas in Wuchuan, northeastern Guizhou, China. Environmental Pollution 142(3), 549–558.

Ralston, D. M., O'Halloran, T. V., 1990. Ultrasensitivity and heavy-metal selectivity of the allosterically modulated MerR transcription complex. Proceedings of the National Academy of Sciences of the United States of America 87(10), 3846–3850.

Ranchou-Peyruse, M., Monperrus, M., Bridou, R., et al., 2009. Overview of mercury methylation capacities among anaerobic bacteria including representatives of the sulphate-reducers: Implications for environmental studies. Geomicrobiology Journal 26(1), 1–8.

Rasmussen, L. D., Serrensen, S. J., Turner, R. R., et al., 2000. Application of a mer-lux biosensor for estimating bioavailable mercury in soil. Soil Biology and Biochemistry 32, 639–646.

Rasmussen, L. D., Turner, R. R., Barkay, T., 1997. Cell-density-dependent sensitivity of a mer-lux bioassay. Applied and Environmental Microbiology 63(8), 3291–3293.

Regnell, O., Watras, C. J., 2019. Microbial mercury methylation in aquatic environments: A critical review of published field and laboratory studies. Environmental Science & Technology 53(1), 4–19.

Sarkar, A., Aronson, K. J., Patil, S., et al., 2012. Emerging health risks associated with modern agriculture practices: A comprehensive study in India. Environmental Research 115, 37–50.

Schaefer, J. K., Letowski, J., Barkay, T., 2002. Mer-mediated resistance and volatilization of Hg(II) under anaerobic conditions. Geomicrobiology Journal 19(1), 87–102.

Schaefer, J. K., Morel, F. M. M., 2009. High methylation rates of mercury bound to cysteine by *Geobacter sulfurreducens*. Nature Geoscience 2(2), 123–126.

Schaefer, J. K., Rocks, S. S., Zheng, W., et al., 2011. Active transport, substrate specificity, and methylation of Hg(II) in anaerobic bacteria. Proceedings of the National Academy of Sciences of the United States of America 108(21), 8714–8719.

Schaefer, J. K., Szczuka, A., Morel, F. M. M., 2014. Effect of divalent metals on Hg(II) uptake and methylation by bacteria. Environmental Science & Technology 48(5), 3007–3013.

Schaefer, J. K., Yagi, J., Reinfelder, J. R., et al., 2004. Role of the bacterial organomercury lyase (MerB) in controlling methylmercury accumulation in mercury-contaminated natural waters. Environmental Science & Technology 38(16), 4304–4311.

Sha, Y. X., 2018. Diversity of bacterial endophytic community in different rice tissues. Acta Microbiologica Sinica 58(9), 2216–2228.

Siciliano, S. D., O'Driscoll, N. J., Lean, D. R. S., 2002. Microbial reduction and oxidation of mercury in freshwater lakes. Environmental Science & Technology 36(14), 3064–3068.

Smith, T., Pitts, K., McGarvey, J. A., et al., 1998. Bacterial oxidation of mercury metal vapor, Hg(0). Applied and Environmental Microbiology 64(4), 1328–1332.

Spangler, W. J., Spigarelli, J. L., Rose, J. M., et al., 1973a. Degradation of methylmercury by bacteria isolated from environmental samples. Applied Microbiology 25(4), 488–493.

Spangler, W. J., Spigarelli, J. L., Rose, J. M., et al., 1973b. Methylmercury-bacterial degradation in lake sediments. Science 180(4082), 192–193.

Summers, A. O., Sugarman, L. I., 1974. Cell-free mercury (II)-reducing activity in a plasmid-bearing strain of Escherichia-coli. Journal of Bacteriology 119(1), 242–249.

Szczuka, A., Morel, F. M. M., Schaefer, J. K., 2015. Effect of thiols, zinc, and redox conditions on Hg uptake in *Shewanella oneidensis*. Environmental Science & Technology 49(12), 7432–7438.

Takeuchi, F., Iwahori, K., Kamimura, K., et al., 1999. Isolation and some properties of *Thioibacillus ferrooxidans* strains with differing levels of mercury resistance from natural environments. Journal of Bioscience and Bioengineering 88, 387–392.

Thöming, J., Kliem, B. K., Ottosen, L. M., 2000. Electrochemically enhanced oxidation reactions in sandy soil polluted with mercury. Science of the Total Environment 261(1–3), 137–147.

Tonomura, K., Nakagami, T., Futai, F., et al., 1968. Studies on action of mercury-resistant microorganisms on mercurials. 1. Isolation of mercury-resistant bacterium and binding of mercurials to cells. Journal of Fermentation Technology 46(6), 506–512.

Ustiatik, R., Nuraini, Y. L, Suharjono, S., et al., 2021. Mercury resistance and plant growth promoting traits of endophytic bacteria isolated from mercury-contaminated soil. Bioremediation Journal 26(3), 208–227.

Vishnivetskaya, T. A., Hu, H. Y., Van Nostrand, J. D., et al., 2018. Microbial community structure with trends in methylation gene diversity and abundance in mercury-contaminated rice paddy soils in Guizhou, China. Environmental Science-Processes & Impacts 20(4), 673–685.

Vonk, J. W., Sijpesteijn, A. K., 1973. Studies on the methylation of mercuric chloride by pure cultures of bacteria and fungi. Antonie van Leeuwenhoek 39, 505–513.

Wang, B. L., Zhong, S. Q., Bishop, K., et al., 2021. Biogeochemical influences on net methylmercury formation proxies along a peatland chronosequence. Geochimica et Cosmochimica Acta 308, 188–203.

Warner, K. A., Roden, E. E., Bonzongo, J. C., 2003. Microbial mercury transformation in anoxic freshwater sediments under iron-reducing and other electron-accepting conditions. Environmental Science & Technology 37(10), 2159–2165.

Wiatrowski, H. A., Ward, P. M., Barkay, T., 2006. Novel reduction of mercury(II) by mercury-sensitive dissimilatory metal reducing bacteria. Environmental Science & Technology 40(21), 6690–6696.

Winfrey, M. R., Rudd, J. W. M., 1990. Environmental factors affecting the formation of methylmercury in low pH lakes. Environmental Toxicology and Chemistry 9(7), 853–869.

Wu Q. Q., Wang B. L., Hu H. H. et al. 2023. Sulfate-reduction and methanogenesis are coupled to Hg(II) and MeHg reduction in rice paddies. Journal of hazardous materials. 460, 132486.

Wu, Q. Q., Hu, H. Y., Meng, B., et al., 2020. Methanogenesis is an important process in controlling MeHg concentration in rice paddy soils affected by mining activities. Environmental Science & Technology 54(21), 13517–13526.

Xu, X. H., Zhao, J. T., Li, Y. Y., et al., 2016. Demethylation of methylmercury in growing rice plants: An evidence of self-detoxification. Environmental Pollution 210, 113–120.

Yamada, M., Tonomura, K., 1972. Microbial methylation of mercury in hydrogen sulfide-evolving environments. Journal of Fermentation Technology 50(12), 901–909.

Yu, R. Q., Flanders, J. R., Mack, E. E., et al., 2012. Contribution of coexisting sulfate and iron reducing bacteria to methylmercury production in freshwater river sediments. Environmental Science & Technology 46(5), 2684–2691.

Zarcinas, B. A., Ishak, C. F., McLaughlin, M. J., et.al. 2004. Heavy metals in soils and crops in Southeast Asia. 1. Peninsular Malaysia. Environmental Geochemistry and Health 26(4), 343–357.

Zhang, H., Feng, X. B., Larssen, T., et al., 2010a. In inland China, rice, rather than fish, is the major pathway for methylmercury exposure. Environmental Health Perspectives 118(9), 1183–1188.

Zhang, H., Feng, X. B., Larssen, T., et al., 2010b. Bioaccumulation of methylmercury versus inorganic mercury in rice (*Oryza sativa L.*) grain. Environmental Science & Technology 44(12), 4499–4504.

Zhang, T., Kim, B., Leyard, C., et al., 2012. Methylation of mercury by bacteria exposed to dissolved, nanoparticulate, and microparticulate mercuric sulfides. Environmental Science & Technology 46(13), 6950–6958.

Zheng, W., Liang, L.Y., Gu, B.H., 2012. Mercury reduction and oxidation by reduced natural organic matter in anoxic environments. Environmental Science & Technology 46(1), 292–299.

Zhou, J., Smith, M. D., Cooper, S. J., et al., 2017. Modeling of the passive permeation of mercury and methylmercury complexes through a bacterial cytoplasmic membrane. Environmental Science & Technology 51(18), 10595–10604.

Zhou, X. Q, Hao, Y. Y., Gu, B. H., et al., 2020. Microbial communities associated with methylmercury degradation in paddy soils. Environmental Science & Technology 54(13), 7952–7960.

7 Redox Transformation of Mercury in Soils

Jianxu Wang, Jörg Rinklebe, and Xinbin Feng

7.1 INTRODUCTION

Mercury (Hg) is a redox-sensitive toxic element; thus, changing the redox potential (E_h) can significantly impact Hg mobilization and methylation in soils and sediments. Redox potential, known as oxidation/reduction potential (ORP), is the tendency of oxidized agents (electron acceptors) to accept electrons from reduced agents (electron donors). E_h represents the free energy available for reduction or the equivalent electromotive force of the reactions, explained as the intensity of reduction (Zhang and Furman, 2021). Reduction reactions dominate under low E_h conditions, whereas oxidation reactions prevail under high E_h conditions (Zhang and Furman, 2021). Flooding of soils and sediments causes depletion of oxygen and then ignites a sequence of redox reactions. Zhang and Furman (2021) reviewed soil redox dynamics under dynamic hydrologic regimes and presented a diagram to show a sequence of common redox pairs and their conceptual zonation of the subsurface (Figure 7.1). The common reduction and oxidation reactions in soil systems are shown in Table 7.1, and their common combinations are presented in Table 7.2.

Variations in soil E_h are related to flooding conditions and input of organic materials (Tano et al., 2020). The flooding of paddy fields leads to the decreasing of E_h as a result of exhausting the oxygen in soils. A change in flooding conditions can

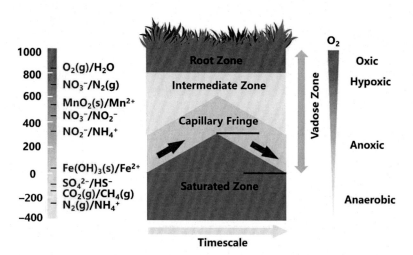

FIGURE 7.1 Diagram of redox ladder and the conceptual zonation of the subsurface (pH 7, 25°C). (From Zhang and Furman, 2021 with modification.)

DOI: 10.1201/9781003404941-7

TABLE 7.1

Common Reduction and Oxidation Reactions in Soil Systems at pH 7 for 25°C

Reduction		Oxidation	
Reactions	E_h^0 **(V)**	**Reactions**	E_h^0 **(V)**
O			
$O_2(g) + 4H_2^+ + 4e = 2H_2O$	0.811		
C		C	
$CH_2O + 2H^+ + 2e^- = CH_3OH$	−0.178	$CH_2O + H_2O = CO_2(g) + 4H^+ + 4e^-$	−0.484
$CO_2(g) + 8H^+ + 8e^- = CH_4(g) + 2H_2O$	−0.244		
N		N	
$2NO_3^- + 12H^+ + 10e^- = N_2(g) + 6H_2O$	0.746	$NH_4^+ + 3H_2O = NO_3^- + 10H^+ + 8e^-$	0.363
$NO_3^- + 10H^+ + 8e^- = NH_4^+ + 3H_2O$	0.363		
Fe		Fe	
$FeOOH(s) + 3H^+ + e = 2H_20 + Fe^{2+}$	−0.236	$FeCO_3(s) + 2H_2O = FeOOH(s) +$ $HCO_3^-(10^{-3}) + 2H^+ + e$	0.047
Mn		Mn	
$MnO_2(s) + 4H^+ + 2e^- = Mn^{2+} + 2H_2O$	0.519	$MnCO_3(s) + 2H_2O = MnO_2(s) +$ $HCO_3^-(10^{-3}) + 3H^+ + 2e^-$	0.525
S		S	
$SO_4^{2-} + 9H^+ + 8e = HS + 4H_2O$	−0.221	$HS^- + 4H_2O = SO_4^{2-} + 9H^+ + 8e^-$	−0.221

Source: Modified from Zhang and Furman (2021).

TABLE 7.2

Common Redox Processes in Soil Systems Based on Table 7.1

Reactions	Reduction	Oxidation
Aerobic respiration	$O_2(g) + 4H_2^+ + 4e^- = 2H_2O$	$CH_2O + H_2O = CO_2(g) + 4H^+ + 4e^-$
Fermentation	$CH_2O + 2H^+ + 2e^- = CH_3OH$	$CH_2O + H_2O = CO_2(g) + 4H^+ + 4e^-$
Methane fermentation	$CO_2(g) + 8H^+ + 8e^- = CH_4(g) + 2H_2O$	$CH_2O + H_2O = CO_2(g) + 4H^+ + 4e^-$
Nitrification	$O_2(g) + 4H_2^+ + 4e^- = 2H_2O$	$NH_4^+ + 3H_2O = NO_3^- + 10H^+ + 8e^-$
Denitrification	$2NO_3^- + 12H^+ + 10e^- = N_2(g) + 6H_2O$	$CH_2O + H_2O = CO_2(g) + 4H^+ + 4e^-$
Nitrate reduction	$NO_3^- + 10H^+ + 8e^- = NH_4^+ + 3H_2O$	$CH_2O + H_2O = CO_2(g) + 4H^+ + 4e^-$
Ferrous oxidation	$O_2(g) + 4H_2^+ + 4e^- = 2H_2O$	$FeCO_3(s) + 2H_2O = FeOOH(s) +$ $HCO_3^-(10^{-3}) + 2H^+ + e^-$
Production of soluble Fe(II)	$FeOOH(s) + 3H^+ + e^- = 2H_20 + Fe^{2+}$	$CH_2O + H_2O = CO_2(g) + 4H^+ + 4e^-$
Mn(II)oxidation	$O_2(g) + 4H_2^+ + 4e^- = 2H_2O$	$MnCO_3(s) + 2H_2O = MnO_2(s) +$ $HCO_3^-(10^{-3}) + 3H^+ + 2e^-$
Production of soluble Mn(II)	$MnO_2(s) + 4H^+ + 2e^- = Mn^{2+} + 2H_2O$	$CH_2O + H_2O = CO_2(g) + 4H^+ + 4e^-$
Sulfide oxidation	$O_2(g) + 4H_2^+ + 4e^- = 2H_2O$	$HS^- + 4H_2O = SO_4^{2-} + 9H^+ + 8e^-$
Sulfate reduction	$SO_4^{2-} + 9H^+ + 8e^- = HS^- + 4H_2O$	$CH_2O + H_2O = CO_2(g) + 4H^+ + 4e^-$

Modified from Zhang and Furman (2021).

lead to variation in E_h. For example, Peng et al. (2012) reported that the E_h value of a flooded paddy soil was between 0 and 225 mV, but when the soil became aerobic the E_h value increased to 408–575 mV. The recorded redox potential of paddy field soils in previous studies is shown in Table 7.3. The lowest and highest E_h a soil can reach are –319 mV and 679 mV, respectively (Pan et al., 2016; Yu et al., 2001). The E_h of a soil can be further decreased by amendment with organic materials such as straw, as these materials can serve as a carbon source to enhance microbial activities, thereby promoting reduction-oxidation reactions. An et al. (2022) reported that the soil E_h value of a paddy field decreased from –78–142 mV to –106–87 mV after straw amendment.

In addition to flooding conditions and input of organic materials, biogeochemical factors of soil, including organic carbon, Fe/Mn oxides, sulfate, etc., are closely associated with soil redox potential. Organic carbon serves as both an electron donator and an electron acceptor in soils, and its composition affects functions. The decomposition of organic carbon produces dissolved organic carbon (DOC), which is available for microorganisms (Husson, 2013). Iron (Fe) is the most studied element in soils and sediments, as it is extremely sensitive to E_h. When O_2 was exhausted,

TABLE 7.3
Redox Potential of Paddy Soil

Location	Soil Type	E_h (mV)	References
China	Paddy soil	–239 to 294	Yu et al., 2001
United States	Paddy soil	–316 to 390	Yu et al., 2001
Nanjing, China	Paddy soil	–152 to 118	An et al., 2022
Guizhou, China	Paddy soil	–26 to 198	Wang et al., 2014
Guangdong, China	Paddy soil	–6 to 220	Peng et al., 2012
Hubei, China	Paddy soil	–48 to 198	Xu et al., 2013
Sichuan, China	Paddy soil	–125 to 325	Wang et al., 2014
Tsukuba, Japan	Paddy soil	–222 to 233	Lu et al., 2012
Jiangxi, China	Paddy soil	–201 to 389	Schmidt et al., 2011
Zhejiang, China	Paddy soil	–288 to 679	Pan et al., 2016
Jiangsu, China	Paddy soil	–173 to 514	Sha et al., 2020
Zhejiang, China	Paddy soil	–159 to 147	Ge et al., 2021
Kerala, India	Paddy soil	–80 to 190	Krishnani et al., 2011
Bagerhat, Bangladesh	Paddy soil	–39 to 139	Azam et al., 2023
Hokuriku, Japan	Paddy soil	–120 to 588	Honma et al., 2012
China	Paddy soil	–273 to 315	Du et al., 2019
Jiangsu, China	Paddy soil	–170 to 143	Liu et al., 2021
Jiangsu, China	Paddy soil	–134 to 183	Peng et al., 2011
Hunan, China	Paddy soil	–137 to 228	Yin et al., 2015
Zhejiang, China	Paddy soil	–376 to 216	Yang et al., 2022
Central Japan	Paddy soil	–227 to 89	Honma et al., 2016
Zhejiang, China	Paddy soil	–95 to 143	Yuan et al., 2017

reductive dissolution of Fe oxides (ferrihydrite) became prevalent. In the dissolution of Fe oxides, Fe^{3+} serves as a terminal electron acceptor, receiving electrons from microorganisms through metabolic oxidation of organic matter (Mansfeldt et al., 2012 Zhang et al., 2021). The reductive dissolution of Fe oxides produces Fe^{2+}, which is oxidized to Fe^{3+} to form Fe oxides when soil becomes aerated. In addition to Fe, manganese (Mn) is also highly sensitive to E_h and serves as an electron acceptor. The reductive dissolution of Mn oxides produces Mn^{2+}, which is oxidized to Mn^{4+} to form Mn oxides when soil becomes aerated (Reddy and Delaune, 2008). In soils, a certain amount of Hg is bound to Fe/Mn oxides and organic matter. For example, Wang et al. (2011) used a sequential extraction procedure to study the Hg fraction in Hg-polluted soil collected from Wanshan Hg mining region in China, and results showed that the concentrations of Fe/Mn oxide bound Hg and organic matter bound Hg were 4.61 and 54.8 mg/kg, respectively. Therefore, the changing of redox potential to an anaerobic condition could lead to the dissolution of Fe/Mn oxides and consequently lead to mobilization of the Hg associated with Fe/Mn oxides.

7.2 THE TRANSFORMATION OF Hg IN SOIL AS A FUNCTION OF REDOX POTENTIAL

Understanding redox dynamics is particularly important for revealing biogeochemical reactions, which is important for predicting the fate of Hg in soils and sediments. A precise control of redox potential (E_h) is a prerequisite to study the impact of E_h on Hg transformation in soils. Fortunately, Yu and Rinklebe (2011) developed an automated biogeochemical microcosm system, which enables precise control and pre-setting of redox changes through an automatic-valve regulation system along with high temporal resolution monitoring of E_h, pH, and temperature, which can be exploited to simulate changing environmental conditions. Figure 7.2 shows a schematic of an automated redox potential–pH controller with temperature control and gas analysis system. Thanks to this automated biogeochemical microcosm system, scientists were able to investigate the geochemical behavior of heavy metals at a pre-defined E_h window, exploring the effect of E_h on transformation of heavy metals in a polluted soil. Figure 7.3 shows a temporal course of pH-E_h of a soil slurry, generated by the automated biogeochemical microcosm system developed by Yu and Rinklebe (2011). As shown in Figure 7.3, at each E_h window, a soil sample was maintained for 48 h, by which time E_h-induced biogeochemical reactions would reach equilibrium. The recorded E_h in Chinese soil ranged from −333 mV to +306 mV, covering the E_h range of global wetlands and paddy fields. The pH of soil was lower at low E_h and higher at high E_h. This phenomenon might be attributed to the acidification of soil by CO_2 and organic acids originating from microbial activities and decomposing of organic matter. It should be noted that Wang et al. (2021) spiked a certain amount of powdered wheat straw and glucose into the soil to eliminate any carbon-limitation effect. The input of carbon sources will lead to production of CO_2 and organic acids.

By using the above biogeochemical microcosm system, Wang et al. (2021) studied the effect of stepwise increases of E_h on Hg mobilization and methylation in Hg-polluted paddy soil collected from China. The authors found a clear E_h-dependent behavior of Hg in the soil. The dissolved Hg concentration was higher at lower E_h

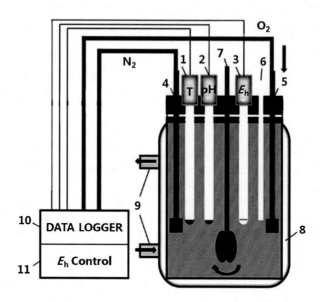

FIGURE 7.2 A schematic of a microcosm. The MC components (bottom) include (1) thermometer; (2) pH electrode; (3) redox potential (E_h) electrode;(4) dispersion tube for N_2; (5) dispersion tube for O_2; (6) sampling tube; (7) overhead stirrer; (8) double-hull incubation vessel; (9) temperature control by a thermostat and water circulation; (10) data logger for E_h, pH, and temperature; (11) automatic redox regulation by N_2 and O_2 valves. (Reprinted with permission from Yu and Rinklebe, 2011.)

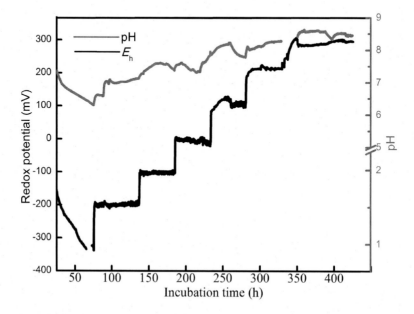

FIGURE 7.3 Temporal course of pH-E_h of the soil slurry measured every 10 min under predefined E_h conditions. (Reprinted with permission from Wang et al., 2022.)

windows and lower at higher E_h windows. Later, Xing et al. (2022) also observed a similar redox behavior of Hg in Hg-polluted soil collected from the Wanshan Hg mining region in China. Also, Beckers et al. (2019) studied the mobilization of Hg in Hg-polluted floodplain soil collected from Germany, and they found that the concentration of dissolved Hg in soil solution was 28–29 µg/L at an E_h of –110 to –92 mV, and it decreased to less than 10 µg/L at an E_h of higher than +250 mV. It seemed that, regardless of soil type, Hg presented a similar E_h-dependent behavior. These results point to the fact that high E_h favors the immobilization of Hg in soils, while low E_h enhances the mobilization of Hg. Colloidal Hg is a fraction of Hg that is bound to small soil particles (<8µm), and it has limited mobility compared to dissolved Hg. The E_h behavior of colloidal Hg was studied by Wang et al. (2021). The colloidal Hg showed the opposite distribution pattern from dissolved Hg. At an E_h range of –300–100 mV, the concentrations of colloidal Hg were rather low, whereas The concentration of colloidal Hg was higher at E_h of 0 to 300 mV than that at E_h range of –300 to –100 mV. In previous studies, the variation of MeHg in soil during E_h changes was investigated (Wang et al., 2021; Xing et al., 2022). The dissolved MeHg showed a similar distribution pattern to that of dissolved total Hg in soils as a function of E_h. The higher concentration of MeHg was observed at low E_h windows, and the lower concentration of MeHg presented at higher E_h windows. The distribution pattern of colloidal MeHg as a function of E_h was different from that of dissolved MeHg. The higher concentration of colloidal MeHg presented at an E_h of 0 mV, and the lower concentration of MeHg presented at both high and low E_h conditions (Figure 7.4).

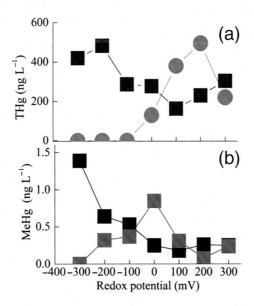

FIGURE 7.4 Concentration of total Hg (THg) (a) and MeHg (b) in the dissolved and colloidal phase in the soil of each E_h condition. The circle and square in (a) indicate dissolved THg and colloidal THg, respectively." In (b), "red" is changed to "gray." "The black square and gray square (b) indicate dissolved MeHg and colloidal MeHg, respectively. (Modified from Wang et al., 2022.)

7.3 MECHANISM OF Hg (IM)MOBILIZATION IN SOIL UNDER DIFFERENT E_h CONDITIONS

The geochemical behavior of Hg under different E_h conditions can be attributed to the following aspects. Firstly, the pH of soil was acidic (pH was around 6.0) under low E_h conditions. This acidic environment could lead to the mobilization of Hg because the dissolution of carbonate and Fe/Mn/Al(oxyhydr)oxide could release the associated Hg and consequently enhance mobilization of Hg. Wang et al. (2021) used a mixture of acids (pH = 4.2) to extract Hg from soil to investigate the extent of Hg mobilization by acidification. Results showed that potentially mobile Hg, quantified through extraction with dilute acid (pH = 4.2), was 50 ng/L in the bulk soil, and this sets a maximum limit for Hg mobilization that can be attributed to acidification. The dissolved total Hg (THg) concentration (483 ng/L) at an E_h of −200 mV was over 8 times higher than the Hg mobilized from the bulk soil via the simple dilute acid (pH = 4.2) extraction procedure. This result indicated that, in addition to acidification, Hg mobilization under low E_h conditions could be driven by further biogeochemical processes. Secondly, the redox chemistry of Fe/Mn/Al(oxyhydr) oxide controlled Hg mobilization in soils. The concentration of dissolved Fe in the soil solution was determined to reveal the extent of dissolution of Fe(oxyhydr)oxides. Prior studies had found that the concentration of dissolved Fe in soils was higher at lower E_h windows than at higher E_h windows, indicating a noticeable mobilization of Fe(oxyhydr)oxides (Wang et al., 2021; Xing et al., 2022). These results demonstrated that reductive dissolution of Fe/Mn/Al(oxyhydr)oxide could have contributed to Hg mobilization. The concentration of dissolved Fe was decreased at high E_h windows. This is because high E_h favors the precipitation of dissolved Fe to poorly crystallized Fe(oxyhydr)oxides, which can absorb Hg to remove it from the soil solution. Also, the poorly crystallized Fe(oxyhydr)oxides are a component of colloid, which can absorb Hg. Therefore, there was a significant linear correlation between dissolved Fe and dissolved Hg in soil (Figure 7.5). It appeared that the precipitation of dissolved Fe could have contributed to Hg immobilization. Wang et al. (2021) observed a significant linear correlation between dissolved Fe and dissolved Hg in soil. The above results provide solid evidence that the redox chemistry of Fe(oxyhydr)oxides

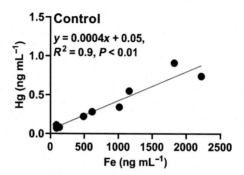

FIGURE 7.5 The correlation between dissolved Fe and dissolved Hg in soil solution. (Reprinted with permission from Xing et al., 2022.)

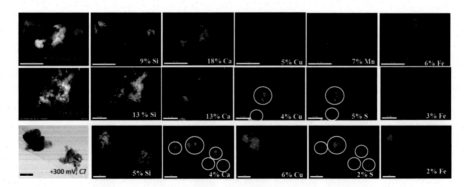

FIGURE 7.6 Elemental scanning electron microscope (ESEM) images of the colloidal particles (–300, 0, and +300 mV) and ESEM-energy dispersive spectroscopy (EDS) digital images of silicon (Si), calcium (Ca), copper (Cu), manganese (Mn), aluminum (Al), iron (Fe), and sulfur (S) in the particles. The white circles indicate a similar distribution pattern of Cu and S at an E_h of 0 mV and of Ca and S at an E_h of +300 mV. (Reprinted with permission from Wang et al., 2022.)

determined Hg mobilization in soils. Thirdly, DOC affected Hg mobilization in soil. There was a significant correlation between DOC and dissolved total Hg in soil solution, which indicates that DOC enhanced Hg mobilization by acting as a carrier (Wang et al., 2021). Fourthly, colloidal particles played a critical role in affecting Hg mobility in soils. The presence of colloidal particles depends on redox potential. Wang et al. (2021) separated colloidal particles from soil solution by ultracentrifugation, and they found that the amount of colloidal particles under aerobic conditions was higher than under anaerobic conditions. Colloidal particles consisted of $CaSO_4$, amorphous Fe(oxyhydr)oxides, Cu_xS, and salts (e.g., KCl) (Figure 7.6). Those colloidal particles were able to absorb Hg from solution to immobilize Hg. Therefore, as shown in Figure 7.4, colloidal Hg displayed the opposite behavior from dissolved Hg. Fifthly, sulfate played an important role in immobilization of Hg, as microbial-mediated sulfate reduction could produce sulfide, which can bind with Hg to form HgS complexes. Generally, reaction of sulfate reduction to sulfide was significant under anaerobic conditions. However, in the study of Wang et al. (2021), sulfate concentration was higher under anaerobic conditions than under aerobic conditions, and they attributed this phenomenon to the following two reasons. On the one hand, preferential or concurrent reduction of NO_3^- and Fe(hydr)oxides preserves sulfate, since these compounds are more thermodynamically favorable for reduction than sulfate. Secondly, the newly formed Fe(hydr)oxides could adsorb sulfate, as proposed by Sparks (2003), who reported that sulfate could be absorbed by Fe(hydr)oxides via the formation of surface outer- and inner-sphere complexes.

7.4 MECHANISM OF Hg (DE)METHYLATION IN SOIL UNDER DIFFERENT E_h CONDITIONS

MeHg is transformed from inorganic Hg by Hg-methylation microorganisms. As shown in Figure 7.4, MeHg shows an E_h-dependent behavior, with the high concentration of MeHg presenting at low E_h windows. The high concentration of dissolved

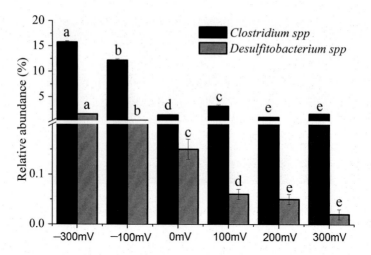

FIGURE 7.7   Relative abundance of *Clostridium spp.* (summarization of relative abundance of *Clostridium_sensu_stricto_1* and *Clostridium_sensu_stricto_12*) and *Desulfitobacterium spp.* in the soil as a function of redox potential. (Reprinted with permission from Wang et al., 2022.)

total Hg at low E_h conditions would be favorable for the formation of MeHg (Figure 7.4). In addition to Hg availability, microorganisms play a critical role in MeHg formation. Wang et al. (2021) studied microbial communities in soil under different redox conditions. Particularly, they focused on *Desulfitobacterium spp.* and *Clostridium spp.*, which were considered as Hg methylators and Hg demethylators, respectively. Many bacteria in *Desulfitobacterium spp.* (e.g., *Desulfitobacteriummetallireducens*, *Desulfitobacteriumdehalogenans*) had been identified as Hg methylators, and two in *Clostridium spp.* were considered as Hg demethylators (*Clostridium_sensu_stricto_1* and *Clostridium_sensu_stricto_12*). The relative abundance of *Clostridium spp.* and *Desulfitobacterium spp.* significantly decreased as a function of E_h rising (Figure 7.7). The high concentration of MeHg at low E_h windows could be partially attributed to the high relative abundance of Hg-methylation microorganisms (*Desulfitobacterium spp.*). However, it should be noted that the relative abundance of Hg-demethylation microorganisms was also high at low E_h windows. This phenomenon was attributed to the greater MeHg production rate than demethylation rate at low E_h windows. With E_h rising, Hg methylation became rather weak, and the MeHg demethylation rate thus exceeded its production rate.

7.5   IMPACT OF AMENDMENT OF BIOCHAR ON REDOX BEHAVIOR OF Hg IN SOILS

Biochar has been proposed as an environmentally friendly amendment for remediation of Hg-polluted sediments and soils. As shown in the previous section, the redox potential is variable in soils and sediments due to the changing of water level. This variation in redox potential could have a certain impact on the performance of amendments in Hg remediation. Xing et al. (2022) used a biogeochemical

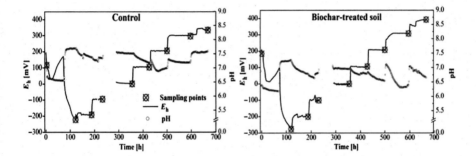

FIGURE 7.8 pH-E_h plots for both non-biochar treated soil (left) and biochar-treated soil (right). (Reprinted with permission from Xing et al., 2022.)

microcosm system to study the impact of rice hull biochar amendment on Hg mobilization and methylation under changing redox conditions. Plots of pH-E_h for both non-biochar treated soil and biochar-treated soil are shown in Figure 7.8. As shown in Figure 7.8, the E_h of biochar-treated soil was 109 mV larger than that of non-biochar treated soil, showing that biochar widened the E_h range of soil. It is interpreted that biochar could enhance redox reactions through the following two mechanisms. On the one hand, biochar could donate electrons via phenolic groups and accept electrons via quinones/polycondensed aromatic structures. On the other hand, biochar could induce inter-species electron transfer via conduction-based mechanisms.

The average pH of biochar-treated soil was 0.63 unit lower than that of non-biochar treated soil, showing that biochar treatment resulted in the acidification of soil. This result was inconsistent with previous finding that biochar could lead to alkalization of soil and was interpreted as resulting from decomposition of small organic molecules of biochar mediated by microorganism-produced organic acids and CO_2, which caused acidification of the soil. The clear impact of biochar on E_h and pH affected the mobilization and methylation of Hg in the soil. The concentration of dissolved total Hg in the biochar-treated soil solution was 29–268% higher than that in the non-biochar treated soil, and the extent of increase was greater under low E_h conditions (Figure 7.9).

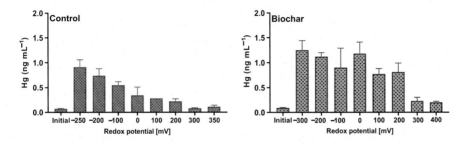

FIGURE 7.9 The concentrations of dissolved total Hg in soil suspensions under different redox conditions. (Modified from Xing et al., 2022.)

To explain the enhanced Hg mobilization by biochar under dynamic E_h conditions, Xing et al. (2022) studied the impact of biochar amendment on various biogeochemical factors in soils.

1. *Fe/Mn redox chemistry*: Biochar-treated soil had higher dissolved Fe and Mn concentrations than the non-treated control, demonstrating that biochar amendment enhanced reductive dissolution of Fe/Mn oxides. This is expected, as E_h was lower in the biochar treatment than in the non-biochar treatment.
2. *Dissolved organic carbon (DOC)*: The average concentration of DOC was increased by 56% in the biochar-treated soil compared to the non-treated control. It is interpreted that the elevated DOC concentration in biochar-treated soil was caused by biochar-promoted formation of DOC from native soil organic matter (Jiang et al., 2018) and/or microbial-mediated decomposition of small organic molecules that were bound at the surface of the biochar (Yuan et al., 2017). Very interestingly, Xing et al. (2022) found a significant linear correlation between dissolved Hg and DOC in non-biochar treated soil, but no such correlation was observed in biochar-treated soil. Their results showed that DOC played an important role in the mobilization of Hg in non-biochar treated soil, whereas in biochar-treated soil the composition of DOC was diverse due to biochar amendment and DOC was variable in binding to Hg. It has been reported that the effect of DOC on Hg mobilization was largely affected by its composition. For example, Jiang et al. (2018) reported an opposite effect of allochthonous and autochthonous DOC on Hg availability in three Chinese lakes, since allochthonous DOC inhibited Hg availability for Hg-methylation microorganisms while autochthonous DOC stimulated MeHg formation by enhancing the activity of microbial communities.
3. *Sulfate*: The average concentration of sulfate in biochar-treated soil was lower than that in non-treated soil. Sulfate reduction to sulfide under anaerobic conditions could cause a decreasing of sulfate concentration in soil. Therefore, the promotion of microbial-mediated sulfate reduction to sulfide by biochar was believed to be the main process for decreasing the sulfate concentration. The sulfide could be eliminated by binding to Hg^{2+}, Fe^{2+}, Cu^{2+}, etc., to form Hg sulfide, FeS, and Cu_xS complexes.

As displayed above, many biogeochemical factors were related to Hg mobilization. Xing et al. (2022) performed multivariate regression analyses for dissolved total Hg concentration with biogeochemical factors under different redox conditions. Results indicated that Hg mobilization was mainly related to Fe/Mn redox chemistry. It appears that the integrated effects of multiple biogeochemical factors on Hg mobilization were complicated.

The effect of biochar on Hg methylation was studied by Xing et al. (2022). Unlike in previous field study (Xing et al., 2020), the addition of biochar increased MeHg concentration in soil under dynamic redox conditions using the biogeochemical microcosm system. The biogeochemical process controlling the formation of MeHg in the biochar-treated soil was different from that in the non-biochar treated soil. In the non-biochar treated soil, MeHg formation was more related to the availability of Hg, as indicated by a strong linear correlation between dissolved total Hg and MeHg concentration in soil, whereas in the biochar-treated soil, MeHg formation was mediated by both dissolved Hg and DOC, as indicated by a linear correlation between Ln(MeHg) and Ln(THg/DOC) (Xing et al., 2022). Therefore, in non-biochar treated soil, the increasing of Hg availability by biochar could enhance the formation of MeHg. However, in biochar-treated soil, the increasing of DOC was unfavorable for MeHg formation, which was likely because the biochar-induced DOC molecules were too large to be methylated by microorganisms (Benoit et al., 2001; Liu et al., 2019). Further, Xing et al. (2022) analyzed organic matter composition in soils and found that a certain group of organic matter in soil, such as lipids, alkanes/alkenes, fatty acids, alkyl esters, sterols, alkyl-aromatics, and suberin, might have affected MeHg by stimulating Hg-methylating bacterial populations through providing carbon food sources.

Overall, there is a certain effect on Hg mobilization and MeHg formation by rice hull biochar in paddy soils under dynamic E_h conditions; one should fully assess this risk before amendment of rice hull biochar into soil with a dynamic potential redox environment.

7.6 IMPACT OF AMENDMENT OF SUGAR BEET FACTORY LIME ON REDOX BEHAVIOR OF Hg IN SOILS

Sugar beet factory lime (SBFL) is a low-cost sorbent for potentially toxic elements, and it has great potential in remediation of Hg-polluted soils. Beckers et al. (2019) studied the impact of SBFL amendment on Hg mobilization, methylation, and demethylation in Hg-polluted soil under dynamic conditions. There was no clear trend of variation of E_h in SBFL-treated soil compared to the non-treated control. The effect of SBFL amendment on Hg mobilization at different E_h windows was clear. Generally, the concentration of dissolved Hg in SBFL-treated soil was lower than that of the control throughout the experiment, particularly under low E_h conditions (Beckers et al., 2019). For example, the concentration of dissolved Hg in SBFL-treated soil was lower than 10 ng/mL at low E_h windows, while in non-SBFL-treated soil it was higher than 10 ng/mL (Beckers et al., 2019). It appears that the SBFL noticeably reduced Hg mobility in soil under changing redox conditions. The immobilization of Hg by SBFL was attributed to the adsorption and precipitation of Hg by $CaCO_3$ and SiO_2 in the SBFL. The effect of SBFL amendment on MeHg and EtHg formation depended on the redox potential. Generally, the concentration of MeHg was lower at low redox windows in SBFL-treated soil than in the non-treated control. Nevertheless, it was higher at high redox windows in SBFL-treated soil than in the non-treated control. It appears that the effect of SBFL on MeHg and EtHg formation was complicated under changing redox conditions. Also, Beckers et al. (2019) studied biogeochemical factors affecting Hg mobilization, methylation, and ethylation. They reported a significant linear correlation between dissolved total Hg and DOC in the non-treated control, but no such correlation was observed in the SBFL-treated soil. They also studied the role of Fe/Mn redox chemistry, Cl^-, sulfate, and phosphate, but no clear relations were observed between Hg and these factors.

7.7 SUMMARY

Mercury shows a redox-dependent behavior through mobilization under anaerobic conditions and immobilization under aerobic conditions. Redox-sensitive biogeochemical factors and processes in soils, including microorganisms, Fe/Mn redox chemistry, dissolved organic carbon (DOC), sulfate, pH, etc., have a significant impact on the mobilization and methylation of Hg. Soils differ in their properties and have thus a different extent of effect on the Hg behavior under dynamic redox conditions. The performance of amendments (e.g., biochar, sugar beet factory lime) on the immobilization of Hg in soil was variable under changing redox conditions. It is recommended to further assess the impact of various amendments on Hg mobilization and methylation in soil before their application to soils and sediments under changing redox conditions. Within this context, field trials are essential.

REFERENCES

An, Y. H., Jiao, X. Y., Gu, Z., et al. 2022. Effects of straw return and aeration on oxygen status and redox environment in flooded soil. Soil and Water Research 17, 29–35.

Azam, M. S., Shafiquzzaman, M., & Haider, H. 2023. Arsenic release dynamics of paddy field soil during groundwater irrigation and natural flooding. Journal of Environmental Management 343, 118204.

Beckers, F., Awad, Y. M., Beiyuan, J. Z., et al. 2019. Impact of biochar on mobilization, methylation, and ethylation of mercury under dynamic redox conditions in a contaminated floodplain soil. Environment International 127, 276–290.

Beckers, F., Mothes, S., Abrigata, J., et al. 2019. Mobilization of mercury species under dynamic laboratory redox conditions in a contaminated floodplain soil as affected by biochar and sugar beet factory lime. Science of the Total Environment 672, 604–617.

Benoit, J. M., Mason, R. P., Gilmour, C. C., et al. 2001. Constants for mercury binding by dissolved organic matter isolates from the Florida Everglades. Geochimica et Cosmochimica Acta 65, 4445–4451.

Du, S. Y., Wang, X. X., Zhang, T. L., et al. 2019. Kinetic characteristics and predictive models of methylmercury production in paddy soils. Environmental Pollution 253, 424–428.

Ge, Y., Ma, J. C., Zou, P., et al. 2021. Improving water management to reduce Cd accumulation in rice in lightly Cd-polluted paddy soils. Journal of Irrigation and Drainage 40, 79–86.

Honma, T., Kaneko, A., Ohba, H., et al. 2012. Effect of application of molasses to paddy soil on the concentration of cadmium and arsenic in rice grain. Soil Science and Plant Nutrition 58, 255–260.

Honma, T., Ohba, H., Kaneko-Kadokura, A., et al. 2016. Optimal soil E_h, pH, and water management for simultaneously minimizing arsenic and cadmium concentrations in rice grains. Environmental Science & Technology 50, 4178–4185.

Husson, O. 2013. Redox potential (E_h) and pH as drivers of soil/plant/microorganism systems: A transdisciplinary overview pointing to integrative opportunities for agronomy. Plant and Soil 362, 389–417.

Jiang, T., Bravo, A. G., Skyllberg, U., et al. 2018. Influence of dissolved organic matter (DOM) characteristics on dissolved mercury (Hg) species composition in sediment porewater of lakes from southwest China. Water Research 146, 146–158.

Krishnani, K. K., Gupta, B. P., Muralidhar, M., et al. 2011. Soil and water characteristics of traditional paddy and shrimp fields of Kerala. Indian Journal of Fisheries 58, 71–77.

Liu, P., Ptacek, C. J., and Blowes, D. W. 2019. Mercury complexation with dissolved organic matter released from thirty-six types of biochar. Bulletin of Environmental Contamination and Toxicology 103, 175–180.

Liu, S. C., Wang, D. X., Zhu, C. Y., et al. 2021. Effect of straw return on hydroxyl radical formation in paddy soil. Bulletin of Environmental Contamination and Toxicology 106, 211–217.

Lu, W. W., Riya, S., Zhou, S., et al. 2012. In situ dissimilatory nitrate reduction to ammonium in a paddy soil fertilized with liquid cattle waste. Pedosphere 22, 314–321.

Mansfeldt, T., Schuth, S., Hausler, W., et al. 2012. Iron oxide mineralogy and stable iron isotope composition in a gleysol with petrogleyic properties. Journal of Soils and Sediments 12, 97–114.

Pan, Y. Y., Koopmans, G. F., Bonten, L. T. C., et al. 2016. Temporal variability in trace metal solubility in a paddy soil not reflected in uptake by rice (*Oryza sativa* L.). Environmental Geochemistry and Health 38, 1355–1372.

Peng, S. Z., Hou, H. J., Xu, J. Z., et al. 2011. Nitrous oxide emissions from paddy fields under different water managements in southeast China. Paddy and Water Environment 9, 403–411.

Peng, X. Y., Liu, F. J., Wang, W. X., et al. 2012. Reducing total mercury and methylmercury accumulation in rice grains through water management and deliberate selection of rice cultivars. Environmental Pollution 162, 202–208.

Reddy, K. R., & Delaune, R. D., 2008. Iron and manganese. Biogeochemistry of Wetlands: Science and Applications. 405–445. CRC Press/Taylor & Francis.

Schmidt, H., Eickhorst, T., and Tippkotter, R. 2011. Monitoring of root growth and redox conditions in paddy soil rhizotrons by redox electrodes and image analysis. Plant and Soil 341, 221–232.

Sha, Z. M., Chen, Z., Feng, Y. F., et al. 2020. Minerals loaded with oxygen nanobubbles mitigate arsenic translocation from paddy soils to rice. Journal of Hazardous Materials 398, 122818.

Sparks, DL. 2003. Environmental Soil Chemistry. Elsevier.

Tano, B. F., Brou, C. Y., Dossou-Yovo, E. R., et al. 2020. Spatial and temporal variability of soil redox potential, pH and electrical conductivity across a toposequence in the Savanna of West Africa. Agronomy-Basel 10.

Wang, H. N., Wang, X. C., Tao, S. S., et al. 2014. Effect of straw returning on soil reducing substance and rice grain yield in gleyed paddy field. Agricultural Research in the Arid Areas 32, 179–183.

Wang, J. X., Feng, X. B., Anderson, C. W. N., et al. 2011. Ammonium thiosulphate enhanced phytoextraction from mercury contaminated soil – Results from a greenhouse study. Journal of Hazardous Materials 186, 119–127.

Wang, J. X., Shaheen, S. M., Jing, M., et al. 2021. Mobilization, methylation, and demethylation of mercury in a paddy soil under systematic redox changes. Environmental Science & Technology 55, 10133–10141.

Xing, Y., Wang, J. X., Kinder, C. E. S., et al. 2022. Rice hull biochar enhances the mobilization and methylation of mercury in a soil under changing redox conditions: Implication for Hg risks management in paddy fields. Environment International 168, 107484.

Xing, Y., Wang, J. X., Shaheen, S. M., et al. 2020. Mitigation of mercury accumulation in rice using rice hull-derived biochar as soil amendment: A field investigation. Journal of Hazardous Materials 388, 121747.

Xu, X. Y., Zhang, Z. Y., Wang, J., et al. 2013. Effect of ridging and fertilization on soil redox in cold waterlogged paddy fields. Chinese Journal of Eco-Agriculture 21, 666–673.

Yang, X., Hinzmann, M., Pan, H., et al. 2022. Pig carcass-derived biochar caused contradictory effects on arsenic mobilization in a contaminated paddy soil under fluctuating controlled redox conditions. Journal of Hazardous Materials 421, 126647.

Yin, L. C., Zhang, L., Yi, Y. N., et al. 2015. Effects of long-term groundwater management and straw application on aggregation of paddy soils in subtropical China. Pedosphere 25, 386–391.

Yu, K. W., and Rinklebe, J. 2011. Advancement in soil microcosm apparatus for biogeochemical research. Ecological Engineering 37, 2071–2075.

Yu, K. W., Wang, Z. P., Vermoesen, A., et al. 2001. Nitrous oxide and methane emissions from different soil suspensions: Effect of soil redox status. Biology and Fertility of Soils 34, 25–30.

Yuan, J., Meng, J., Liang, X., et al. 2017. Organic molecules from biochar leacheates have a positive effect on rice seedling cold tolerance. Frontiers in Plant Science 8, 1624.

Zhang, Z., & Furman, A. 2021. Soil redox dynamics under dynamic hydrologic regimes – A review. Science of the Total Environment 763, 143026.

8 Studying the Availability of Mercury Using the DGT Technique

Jinling Liu, Zhe Liu, and Shaochen Yang

8.1 OVERVIEW OF STUDIES ON THE BIOAVAILABILITY OF Hg

Mercury (Hg) is one of the most toxic heavy metals and poses significant risks to human health and the environment. Due to its unique properties, Hg can exist in different forms such as elemental mercury (Hg^0), methylmercury (MeHg), and inorganic mercury (Hg^{2+}). Concentration of total mercury (THg) can show the extent of Hg pollution in the environment (O'Connor et al., 2019); however, it cannot indicate the mobility and toxicity of Hg and thus provides a poor assessment of the bioaccumulation risk of Hg (Natasha et al., 2020). Therefore, measuring the bioavailable fraction of Hg is crucial for assessing its potential impact on ecosystems.

Bioavailability was first proposed in the 1960s, when it was defined as the available extent of pollutants during biotransfers and bioreactions in liquid phase; it was subsequently extended to solid phases such as soils and sediments (Ruby et al., 1993). The bioavailability of Hg refers to the fraction of Hg that is highly mobile and labile for organisms in the environment. The concentration of bioavailable Hg can better indicate the potential risks of Hg in soil, sediment, and water columns (Natasha et al., 2020).

A number of ex-situ methods were used to study the bioavailability of Hg in the environment, including direct instrument analysis (DIA), plant bioaccumulation elevation (PBE), and the sequential extraction method (SEC) (Table 8.1). DIA uses X-ray diffraction (XRD), secondary ion mass spectrometry (SIMS), infrared spectroscopy (IR), and inductively coupled plasma mass spectrometry (ICP-MS) integrated with liquid chromatography (LC) or ion chromatography (IC) to measure Hg species in samples. The DIA method can yield accurate results for Hg species; however, the instruments are expensive for Hg bioavailability investigation (Borowska and Jankowski, 2020; Hong et al., 2002). PBE is applied to assess the Hg bioavailability in soils by comparing Hg concentration in plants with Hg concentrations in soils (Morosini et al., 2021). This method is discouraged due to the long time frame required for plants to grow and the fact that bioavailable Hg fractions are not analyzed (Xiang et al., 2021). SEC methods for Hg mainly include the Kingston sequential extraction, Bloom sequential extraction, and Boszke sequential extraction methods (Bloom et al., 2003; Boszke et al., 2008; Han et al., 2003). The Kingston sequential extraction method operationally divides Hg into three fractions: mobile Hg, semi-mobile Hg, and non-mobile Hg fractions. Mobile Hg is defined as the bioavailable pool of Hg (Han et al., 2003). Bloom sequential extraction operationally

DOI: 10.1201/9781003404941-8

TABLE 8.1

The Methodologies Employed for Assessing the Bioavailability of Mercury in Environmental Studies

Method	Mechanism	Application	Environmental Media	Ex Situ/ In Situ
Direct instrument analysis	Detecting the forms and contents of Hg through the spectrum produced by particles in various instruments	XRD, SIMS, IR, IC-ICP-MS, LC-ICP-MS, etc.	Soil, sediment, and water	Ex situ
Plant bioaccumulation elevation	Assessing the Hg bioavailability by comparing the Hg concentration absorbed by plants with the THg contents in the ambient environment	Soybean cultivation, Pteris vittata cultivation, etc.	Soil	Ex situ
Sequential chemical extraction	Separating Hg with different chemical reagents or reagent combinations according to the differences in bioavailability between different forms of Hg	One-step extraction, Kingston sequential extraction, Bloom sequential extraction, Boszke sequential extraction, etc.	Soil and sediment	Ex situ
In situ passive sampling	Measuring labile Hg according to the concentration differences between sampler and environmental medium	Peepers, diffusive equilibration in thin films, diffusive gradient in thin films, etc.	Soil, sediment, and water	In situ

divides Hg into five fractions: water-soluble Hg, stomach-acid-soluble Hg, organic chelated Hg, elemental Hg, and sulfide Hg. Among these fractions, water-soluble and stomach-acid-soluble forms are considered bioavailable (Bloom et al., 2003). Boszke sequential extraction categorizes Hg into organic Hg, water-soluble Hg, acid-soluble Hg, humus-bound Hg, and sulfide-bound Hg. Among these fractions, organic Hg, water-soluble Hg, and acid-soluble Hg are defined as bioavailable forms (Boszke et al., 2008). SEC methods offer easy-to-use procedures for assessing Hg bioavailability. However, the ex-situ methods mentioned above lack reliability due to their potential impact on the ambient environment of the samples.

In situ passive sampling techniques have been applied to determine the bioavailability of Hg in environmental samples in the past few decades (Davison and Zhang, 1994; Hesslein, 1976). This method can collect pollutants with minimal disturbances to their ambient environment and is recommended for studying pollutant bioavailability in the environment (Wang et al., 2022). The peepers method works based on the equilibration of pollutants with the ambient environment by a dialysis membrane and can be utilized for studying Hg bioavailability (Hesslein, 1976). However, due to its complex operational procedures and extended experimental period, the accuracy of the peepers method is limited (Liu et al., 2011). The diffusive equilibration in thin films (DET) method was developed by relying on Fick's law of diffusion (Davison et al., 1991). The DET method involves placing a thin film or membrane between two compartments containing different concentrations of the target analyte. The analyte then diffuses through the membrane until it reaches equilibrium, allowing for accurate measurement of its concentration. DET has been employed to assess the bioavailability of various elements such as iron (Fe), manganese (Mn), and cobalt (Co) (Davison et al., 1991). However, hydrogels used in DET are incapable of eliminating interference from the non-targeted elements, thereby limiting its use in assessing Hg bioavailability (Gao, 2020). Furthermore, the diffusive gradient in thin films (DGT) technique is a sister technique of the DET method. The technique works by using a resin gel that selectively binds with target elements and allows them to diffuse through a thin film into an adjacent receiving phase where they can be quantified. The advantages of DGT over DET lie in its ability to establish a consistent gradient concentration during sampling and selectivity toward elements that can penetrate the diffusion layer (Davison and Zhang, 1994). Additionally, DGT demonstrates remarkable efficiency in revealing the resupply capacity of labile metal pools within soil (Liu et al., 2011; 2012; Wang et al., 2022; Wei et al., 2018).

Here, we conducted a literature search on DGT and mercury bioavailability using the database of Web of Science, resulting in a collection of relevant papers. Figure 8.1 illustrates the number of publications prior to 2022, revealing a limited number of

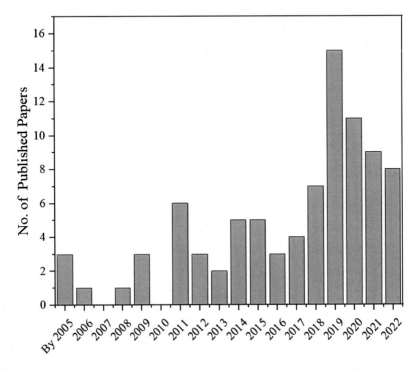

FIGURE 8.1 Number of papers published each year that are related to DGT Hg bioavailability, as of December 2022.

studies on DGT and Hg by 2005 but an increasing trend after 2018. The subsequent sections present the fundamental principles of DGT and its application for investigating Hg bioavailability.

8.2 THE PRINCIPLE OF DGT

8.2.1 DGT CONCENTRATION CALCULATION

When the DGT device is placed at the test site for a period of time, a linear concentration gradient is established between the test solution and the binding layer (Davison and Zhang, 1994), which can be described by Fick's law of diffusion (Eq. 8.1). Thus, the flux of elements passing through the diffusion layer and reaching the binding layer (represented as F, mol·cm^{-2}·s^{-1}) can be presented as in Eq. 8.2.

$$F = M/(A \cdot t) \tag{8.1}$$

$$F = D \cdot (dC/dx) \tag{8.2}$$

where M represents the mass of the measured substance (mol), obtained by eluting from the binding layer; A is the area of the exposure window (cm^2); t is the deployment time (s); D is the diffusion coefficient of the measured substance in the diffusive layer (cm^2·s^{-1}); and dC/dx is the concentration gradient (mol·cm^{-4}).

If the diffusion coefficient of the substance to be measured in the environmental medium is equivalent to that in the diffusion layer, Eq. 8.2 can be reformulated as Eq. 8.3.

$$F = D(C - C')/(\Delta g + \delta) \tag{8.3}$$

where C represents the concentration of the measured substance in the environmental medium (mol·cm^{-3}); C' is the concentration of the measured substance between the binding layer and the diffusion boundary layer (DBL) (mol·cm^{-3}); Δg refers to the thickness of both the diffusive membrane and the filter membrane (cm); and δ stands for the thickness of the DBL (cm). If equilibrium is immediately reached by the measured substance and if saturation does not occur in the binding layer, then C' within the DBL can be considered as 0. Additionally, the thickness of the DBL (δ) can be ignored compared to the thickness of the diffusive layer (Δg). Therefore, Eq. 8.3 can be reformulated as Eq. 8.4, as shown below:

$$F = D \cdot C/\Delta g \tag{8.4}$$

The concentration of the measured substance can be calculated using Eq. 8.1, Eq. 8.4, and Eq. 8.5:

$$C = M \cdot \Delta g/(D \cdot A \cdot t) \tag{8.5}$$

8.2.2 DGT DEVICE STRUCTURE

There are four structural types for DGT devices: piston-type DGT, flat-type DGT, dual-mode DGT, and liquid-binding-phase DGT (Figure 8.2).

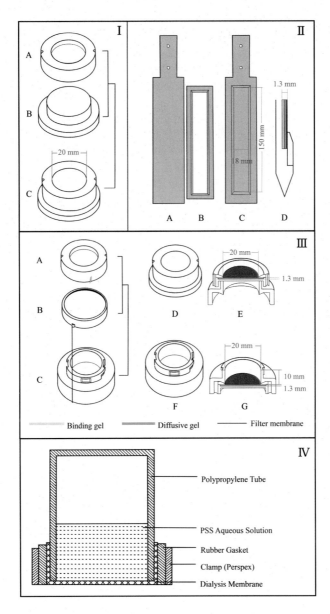

FIGURE 8.2 Four structural types for DGT device, including (I) Piston-type DGT (A, B and C are the cap, base and their assembled form, respectively), (II) Flat-type DGT (A, B, and C are the Cap, Base and their assembled form, respectively; D is membrane which consists of a filter membrane, A diffusive gel and A Binding gel), (III) Dual-mode DGT (A and B are the "O-shape" ring and recessed Base of the DGT core, respectively; C is the hollow base (open cavity) for accommodation of the DGT core; D and F are the two different assembled forms of the DGT core and the open cavity for measurements in solution/water and soil, respectively; E and G are the cutaway views of D and F, respectively), and (IV) Liquid-binding-phase DGT (volume of PSS solution = 2.0 mL, volume of polypropylene tube = 10 mL, area of interface = 1.54 cm^2; the membrane is replaced by placing the device membrane facing up and leaving for 60 min to allow the PSS liquid to flow to the bottom of the tube).

The piston-type DGT consists of a plastic shell and membranes (Figure 8.2I), including a filter membrane, a diffusive gel, and a binding gel (Davison and Zhang, 1994). The filter membrane is utilized for particle filtration; the diffusive gel facilitates the diffusion of the target element into the DGT device, while the binding gel absorbs the target element. A 20-mm-diameter window is situated on the plastic shell through which the target chemical substances diffuse into the diffusion layer (Luo et al., 2011). This type of DGT is commonly used in water columns and soil solutions.

Similar to the piston-type DGT, the flat-type DGT also features a plastic casing and three layers of membranes (a filter membrane, a diffusive gel, and a binding gel) (Figure 8.2II). As shown in Figure 8.2II-C, the device features a rectangular groove in its center. The dimensions of the groove area are about 150 mm × 18 mm. Within this groove, three layers of film are arranged (Figure 8.2II-D), allowing for convenient testing of samples using the plastic cover. The flat-type DGT is suitable for analyzing environmental media with significant spatial heterogeneity, such as sediment and wetland soil. It enables the acquisition of vertical or two-dimensional profile information regarding target elements (Gao, 2020; Liu et al., 2011).

The dual-mode DGT is a modification of the piston-type DGT conducted by Ding et al. (2016). The dual-mode DGT holder can be configured as a piston-type (press-type holder) (part IIID of Figure 8.2) or as a hollow cylinder (open cavity) with dimensions of 10 mm depth and 20 mm diameter (Figure 8.2 III-F). In the latter configuration, soil paste is placed in contact with the exposed surface of the DGT unit at the bottom of the open cavity. The open cavity-type holder was observed to have satisfactory consistency with the existing press-type holder in measuring P, As, Cd, and Pb concentrations in soils. This holder configuration reduced measurement variability by 42% due to eliminating errors from manual pressing of soil paste in the piston-type DGT (Ding et al., 2016).

The liquid-binding-phase DGT is designed to utilize a solution binding phase that is based on the metal binding properties of the poly(4-styrenesulfonate) (PSS) (Li et al., 2003). The device is constructed by securely attaching a 5.0-cm-diameter dialysis membrane onto a polypropylene tube that features an opening with a diameter of 1.4 cm and contains 2.0 mL of 0.020 M PSS solution (Figure 8.2IV). The DGT device of this type is deployed with the membrane facing downward in order to ensure an optimal interface between the PSS solution and the dialysis membrane. The liquid-binding-phase DGT facilitates contact between the polymer solution and the diffusion layer, enabling analysis of the element concentration without elution steps and reducing sampling workload. However, it is limited in aquatic environments.

8.2.3 DIFFUSION AND BINDING LAYERS IN THE DGT FOR MERCURY DETECTION

The selection of diffusion layer and binding layer in the DGT unit can have a significant impact on the absorption efficiency for Hg. The diffusion layer is typically composed of either polyacrylamide (PAAm) or agarose (AG) (Table 8.2). Gao et al. (2014) investigated the absorption efficiency of MeHg by both PAAm and AG, and they observed a significantly lower absorption efficiency of MeHg by PAAm-DGT than by AG-DGT due to the formation of complexes between PAAm and MeHg in the diffusion layer. However, PAAm-DGT is capable of detecting labile Hg in water bodies enriched with organic matter (Fernandez-Gomez et al., 2014). Therefore,

TABLE 8.2

Overview of the Diffusive and Binding Layers Typically Present in DGT Units for Mercury

Binding Layer	Diffusive Layer	Hg Species	Environment	Reference
Chelex-100	PAAm	DTHg	water, soil, sediment	Garmo et al., 2003
	AG	DTHg	river water, sediment	Divis et al., 2005
SH-Thiol	AG	DTHg	river water	Divis et al., 2005
		Hg^{2+}, CH_3Hg^+	soil	Cattani et al., 2008
		Hg^{2+}, CH_3Hg^+	water, soil	Cattani et al., 2009
		THg, DTHg	water	Turull et al., 2018
		THg, organism Hg	sediment	Marziali and Valsecchi, 2021
3MFS	PAAm	CH_3Hg^+	water	Clarisse and Hintelmann, 2006
		Hg^{2+}, CH_3Hg^+	water	Clarisse et al., 2008
		CH_3Hg^+	water	Clarisse et al., 2012
		CH_3Hg^+	soil	Liu et al., 2011, 2012
		CH_3Hg^+	water	Fernandez-Gomez et al., 2015
		THg, DTHg	sediment	Wang et al., 2016
		Hg^{2+}	water	Diez and Giaggio, 2018
		Hg^{2+}, CH_3Hg^+	soil	Turull et al., 2019
	AG	Hg^{2+}, CH_3Hg^+	water	Hong et al., 2011
		Hg^{2+}, CH_3Hg^+	sediment	Amirbahman et al., 2013
		CH_3Hg^+	water	Gao et al., 2014
		THg, CH_3Hg^+	water, sediment	Hong et al., 2014
		Hg^{2+}, HgS(nanoparticles)	water	Pham et al., 2015
		Hg^{2+}, CH_3Hg^+	sediment	Noh et al., 2016
		THg, Hg^{2+}, CH_3Hg^+	soil	Nguyen et al., 2019
		THg, DTHg	water	Xu et al., 2019
		THg, DTHg	water	Noh et al., 2020
		Hg^{2+}, CH_3Hg^+	water	Bretier et al., 2020
		THg, DTHg	soil	Nguyen et al., 2021
	PAAm, AG	Hg^{2+}	water	Fernandez-Gomez et al., 2011
		CH_3Hg^+	water	Fernandez-Gomez et al., 2014

(Continued)

TABLE 8.2 *(Continued)*

Overview of the Diffusive and Binding Layers Typically Present in DGT Units for Mercury

Binding Layer	Diffusive Layer	Hg Species	Environment	Reference
Duolite GT73	AG	DTHg	water	Divis et al., 2009
		Hg^{2+}, CH_3Hg^+, $C_2H_5Hg^+$, $C_6H_5Hg^+$	water	Pelcova et al., 2014
		Hg^{2+}, CH_3Hg^+, $C_2H_5Hg^+$, $C_6H_5Hg^+$	water	Pelcova et al., 2015
		DTHg	water, sediment	Divis et al., 2016
		Hg^{2+}	water	Pelcova et al., 2018
		Hg^{2+}, CH_3Hg^+	soil	Ridoskova et al., 2019
Ambersep GT74	AG	Hg^{2+}, CH_3Hg^+, $C_2H_5Hg^+$, $C_6H_5Hg^+$	water	Pelcova et al., 2014, 2015
		THg, Hg^{2+}	water	Pelcova et al., 2017
		Hg^{2+}, CH_3Hg^+	soil	Pelcova et al., 2019
		Hg^{2+}, CH_3Hg^+	soil	Ridoskova et al., 2019
		THg, Hg^{2+}, CH_3Hg^+, $C_2H_5Hg^+$, $C_6H_5Hg^+$	soil	Pelcova et al., 2020
		THg, Hg^{2+}, CH_3Hg^+	soil	Pelcova et al., 2021
		THg, Hg^{2+}, CH_3Hg^+	water	Pelcova et al., 2022

when using DGT technology to study the bioavailability of Hg, AG is chosen as the diffusion phase in most experiments (Divis et al., 2009; Nguyen et al., 2019; Pelcova et al., 2014, 2015, 2019, 2020, 2021, 2022; Ridoskova et al., 2019; Xu et al., 2019).

The binding layers of DGT for Hg exhibit a wide diversity (Table 8.2). Initially, a cationic chelation resin layer known as Chelex-100 was employed for Hg, but its efficiency was low (Docekalova and Divis, 2005). Subsequently, Spheron-Thiol (SH-Thiol), 3-mercaptopropyl functionalized silica resin gel (3MFS), Duolite GT73, Ambersep GT74, and thiol-modified carbon nanoparticle (SH-CNP) were employed as binding layers for Hg due to their exceptional efficiency in capturing Hg (Cattani et al., 2009; Divis et al., 2016; Liu et al., 2011, 2012; Marziali and Valsecchi, 2021; Pelcova et al., 2018, 2022; Turull et al., 2018). Currently, the most commonly used binding layers for Hg are SH-Thiol, 3MFS, Duolite GT73, and Ambersep GT74, due to their low cost and high efficiency in absorbing Hg from the environment.

8.3 APPLICATION OF THE DGT TECHNIQUE TO STUDY Hg BIOAVAILABILITY IN THE ENVIRONMENT

The application of DGT has been widely employed in the investigation of heavy metal bioavailability in soils, sediments, and aquatic environments. Given its high toxicity, mercury (Hg) has garnered significant attention, prompting numerous global researchers to explore the utilization of DGT for assessing bioavailable Hg (Liu, 2011; Liu et al., 2012; Nguyen et al., 2019; Wang et al., 2022).

8.3.1 USING DGT TO STUDY MERCURY BIOAVAILABILITY IN WATER

Hg, a hazardous heavy metal with the potential to cause severe health issues in both humans and wildlife, presents challenges for comprehending its bioavailability and impact on aquatic ecosystems due to its typically low concentration in natural water bodies (Liu et al., 2011). However, DGT technology has great potential for studying Hg bioavailability in natural water by concentrating it from water bodies (Clarisse and Hintelmann, 2006). Some studies have documented the use of DGT technology for assessing Hg accumulation in aquatic animals. For example, Clarisse et al. (2012) investigated the bioavailability of MeHg to the Baltic clam (*Macoma balthica*) using DGT, and they discovered a significant positive correlation ($r = 0.94$) between MeHg flux measured by DGT and MeHg content in clams, suggesting that DGT can serve as an indicator of the MeHg accumulation process in clams. Similarly, Pelcova et al. (2017) examined the bioavailability of Hg to carp (*Cyprinus carpio*) using DGT, and they observed a significant positive correlation between Hg flux determined by DGT and Hg concentration in various tissues of carp including gills, skin, scales, and eyes ($0.73 < r < 0.95$). Subsequently, Pelcova et al. (2018) conducted a study on the determination of Hg bioavailability using DGT in the presence of chloride ions and humic acid (HA). The investigation revealed that both chloride ions and HA exerted an influence on Hg concentrations in various tissues of carp (*Cyprinus carpio* L.), including skin, gills, and scales. Specifically, it was observed that the presence of chloride ions enhanced Hg accumulation in fish tissues while HA mitigated it. These findings imply that environmental factors play a crucial role in determining the bioavailability and toxicity of heavy metals such as Hg to aquatic animals. Furthermore, DGT has been employed to assess the bioavailability of Hg in water to aquatic plants. Pelcova et al. (2022) investigated Hg bioavailability to submerged aquatic plants (*Ceratophyllumdemersum*, *Myriophyllum spicatum*, *Elodea canadensis*) and one floating plant (*Eichhornia crassipes*). They observed a robust positive correlation ($r > 0.66$) between Hg content in the roots and leaves of aquatic plants and Hg flux measured by DGT. These findings suggest that DGT holds promise for predicting Hg bioavailability in aquatic ecosystems, thereby contributing significantly to our understanding of pollutant accumulation within food webs and its impact on ecosystem health. Further investigations are warranted to explore potential influences of other environmental variables on Hg uptake by fish and other aquatic organisms.

8.3.2 USING DGT TO STUDY Hg BIOAVAILABILITY IN SEDIMENT

Sediment is an important sink of pollutants in aquatic environments, and the exchange of pollutants at the sediment-water interface significantly influences their diffusion into water bodies. Therefore, assessing the bioavailability of Hg in sediment is imperative for accurately estimating the environmental risk posed by Hg in aquatic ecosystems (Gu et al., 2022).

Amirbahman et al. (2013) employed the DGT technique to investigate the mobility of MeHg and inorganic Hg (IHg) in sediment collected from the Penobscot River estuary in Winterport, Maine. Their findings revealed that MeHg bound to sediment is more easily released than IHg bound to sediment. Additionally, they employed DGT to study Hg bioavailability to three species, namely the estuarine amphipod (*Leptocheirusplumulosus*), the estuarine polychaete (*Nereis virens*), and the marine clam (*Macoma nasuta*), in sediments. The authors observed that the MeHg/THg ratio in *Nereis virens* and *Macoma nasuta* exhibited similarities with their corresponding ratios for the DGTs, which were significantly higher than those found in pore water and sediment. These results suggested that measuring MeHg content in sediment and pore water may not be a reliable predictor of MeHg bioaccumulation levels, thus highlighting the effectiveness of DGT as a valuable biomonitometric tool for assessing MeHg bioavailability (Amirbahman et al., 2013). Similarly, Marziali and Valsecchi (2021) employed the DGT technique to investigate the bioavailability of Hg in sediment to dipteran species (*Chironomus riparius*). The results revealed a strong correlation between Hg contents in dipterans and the Hg flux measured by DGT ($0.74 < r < 0.99$). Therefore, DGT can be utilized to study the uptake of Hg by benthic organisms residing in sediments. Gu et al. (2022) assessed the bioavailability of IHg and MeHg in Daya Bay sediments using the DGT technique. This study provided an initial evaluation of the comprehensive toxicity posed by mixtures of different Hg forms on the aquatic organisms within sediment. The authors proposed that the combined probability of ecological risk posed by IHg and MeHg in sediments to aquatic biota be deemed acceptable (Gu et al., 2022). This study represents a pioneering effort in integrating DGT-measured Hg concentrations with environmental ecological models to evaluate the potential risk of sediment-derived Hg to aquatic organisms. We recommend further emphasis on the future application of DGT for investigating the ecological risk of Hg.

Moreover, DGTs have been employed to elucidate the mechanisms underlying Hg methylation processes in sedimentary ecosystems. Neal-Walthall et al. (2022) utilized a combination of DGT and stable isotope labeling techniques to investigate the mechanisms of Hg methylation in aquatic ecosystems. The study revealed a positive correlation between the concentration of MeHg in sediments and the flux of IHg measured by DGT, suggesting that IHg obtained through DGT provides a reliable indicator of sedimentary methylation. However, this investigation overlooked potential variations in both abundance and activity of microbial methylators across different seasons within wetlands. Additionally, it is crucial to consider MeHg degradation processes (Neal-Walthall et al., 2022). Therefore, caution should be exercised when employing DGT for studying Hg methylation processes, while taking into account the aforementioned factors.

8.3.3 Using DGT to Study Hg Bioavailability in Soil

Since the discovery by Leeuwen et al. (2005) that the diffusion in DGT closely resembles that of plants in soil, DGT, as compared to other techniques such as the permeation liquid membrane or Donnan membrane technique, has gained widespread usage for predicting heavy metal levels in soils. For example, Ma et al. (2020) reported that the DGT method exhibited a good correlation with grain Cd concentrations ($r = 0.51$). Subsequently, the authors demonstrated that DGT is a more suitable approach for evaluating Cd bioavailability to barley than chemical extraction methods such as EDTA and $CaCl_2$ extractions. Moreover, it can be utilized to evaluate the long-term stability of contaminated soil (Ma et al., 2022). In a recent study conducted by Chen et al. (2021), a predictive model for Cd uptake in rice grains was successfully developed using the DGT technique and bioconcentration factor. The results demonstrated a strong linear correlation ($r = 0.99$) between the concentration assessed by DGT and the measured concentration in rice samples collected from three provinces of China, indicating that the DGT method holds promise as an effective tool for predicting Cd uptake in rice grains. Similarly, DGT has also been a reliable predictor for determining the bioavailable concentration of As in paddy soil from Bangladesh (Garnier et al., 2015).

Based on the aforementioned research experience, previous researchers have attempted to apply DGT technology for assessing the bioavailability of Hg in soil. Some early researchers posited that the effective root concentration measured by DGT was equivalent to the total Hg concentration in soil solution measured by HPLC-ICP-MS (Cattani et al., 2008). Also, previous studies demonstrated that DGT can predict the bioavailability of MeHg in paddy soil and can quantitatively describe the absorption rate of bioavailable MeHg (Liu et al., 2012). Moreover, recent investigations by Turull et al. (2019) substantiated that DGT technology can predict Hg uptake by the root of rosella in soil. Pelcova et al. (2019) discovered a significant positive correlation between Hg flux into DGT and its uptake in different tissues of pea plants, including roots ($r = 0.989$), leaves ($r = 0.985$), and stems ($r = 0.904$). In a typical Hg smelt region in northern France, Ridoskova et al. (2019) discovered a significantly positive correlation ($r = 0.77$) between the concentration of Hg in *Miscanthus giganteus* and soil Hg flux by DGT. Additionally, Turull et al. (2019) observed that DGT could indicate the bioavailable Hg pool for lettuce. Pelcova et al. (2021) investigated Hg bioavailability in soils surrounding a cinnabar mine using the DGT technique, and they observed significant positive correlations ($0.75 < r < 0.92$) between Hg concentrations in secondary roots, storage roots, and leaves of plants and soil Hg flux measured by DGT. All those studies demonstrated that DGT has proven to be a reliable indicator of Hg bioavailability in soils, as well as an effective predictor of Hg uptake from soil into plant tissues.

The DGT technique was employed not only for investigating the bioavailability of Hg to plants but also for assessing its bioavailability to animals. For example, Nguyen et al. (2019, 2021) found that Hg concentration in earthworms was well correlated with Hg flux by DGT, and this phenomenon is less affected by organic matter, pH, and soil Hg concentration.

8.4 SUMMARY AND FUTURE PERSPECTIVE

The DGT technique has been extensively employed for investigating the bioavailability of Hg in various environmental media. Numerous studies have MeHg measured in situ by DGT align with the levels of THg or MeHg found in organisms, indicating that DGT is a reliable predictor of Hg bioavailability in soil, sediment, and water. However, there are still certain limitations that need to be addressed. The presence of diverse binding sites and molecular structures of organic ligands introduces uncertainties regarding diffusion coefficients and stability of organic-Hg complexes, which may lead to inaccuracies in DGT measurements. Additionally, while DGT is commonly used for detecting soluble Hg fractions, it cannot effectively investigate nanoparticulated Hg specie—crucial components involved in Hg biogeochemical cycling (Tang et al., 2020). Therefore, integrating DGT with laser denudation, 3D nondestructive imaging techniques, and other high-resolution imaging methods would be essential for studying nanoparticulated Hg. It should be noted that although the application of DGT in assessing Hg bioavailability is still at the early stage, future research should combine ecological risk models specific to different environmental media with DGT to better manage and control risks associated with environmental mercury contamination. Furthermore, recent studies have utilized DGT for determining low-concentration isotopes (Yin et al., 2023), suggesting that employing DGT for analyzing Hg isotopes can provide novel insights into the biogeochemical cycling of mercury within the environment.

REFERENCES

Amirbahman, A., Massey, D.I., Lotufo, G., et al., 2013. Assessment of mercury bioavailability to benthic macroinvertebrates using diffusive gradients in thin films (DGT). Environmental Science: Processes & Impacts 15, 2104–2114.

Bloom, N.S., Preus, E., Katon, J., et al., 2003. Selective extractions to assess the biogeochemically relevant fractionation of inorganic mercury in sediments and soils. Analytica Chimica Acta 479, 233–248.

Borowska, M., Jankowski, K., 2020. Sensitive determination of bioaccessible mercury in complex matrix samples by combined photochemical vapor generation and solid phase microextraction coupled with microwave induced plasma optical emission spectrometry. Talanta 219, 121162.

Boszke, L., Kowalski, A., Astel, A., et al., 2008. Mercury mobility and bioavailability in soil from contaminated area. Environmental Geology 55, 1075–1087.

Bretier, M., Dabrin, A., Billon, G., et al., 2020. To what extent can the biogeochemical cycling of mercury modulate the measurement of dissolved mercury in surface freshwaters by passive sampling? Chemosphere 248, 126006.

Cattani, I., Spalla, S., Beone, G.M., et al., 2008. Characterization of mercury species in soils by HPLC–ICP-MS and measurement of fraction removed by diffusive gradient in thin films. Talanta 74, 1520–1526.

Cattani, I., Zhang, H., Beone, G.M., et al., 2009. The role of natural purified humic acids in modifying mercury accessibility in water and soil. Journal of Environmental Quality 38, 493–501.

Chen, R., Cheng, N., Ding, G., et al., 2021. Predictive model for cadmium uptake by maize and rice grains on the basis of bioconcentration factor and the diffusive gradients in thin-films technique. Environmental Pollution 289, 117841.

Clarisse O., Foucher, D., Hintelmann, H., 2008. Methylmercury speciation in the dissolved phase of a stratified lake using the diffusive gradient in thin film technique. Environmental Pollution 157(3), 987–993.

Clarisse, O., Hintelmann, H., 2006. Measurements of dissolved methylmercury in natural waters using diffusive gradients in thin film (DGT). Journal of Environmental Monitoring 8, 1242–1247.

Clarisse, O., Lotufo, G.R., Hintelmann H., et al., 2012. Biomonitoring and assessment of monomethylmercury exposure in aqueous systems using the DGT technique. Science of the Total Environment 416, 449–454.

Davison, W., Grime, G.W., Morgan, J.A., 1991. Distribution of dissolved iron in sediment pore waters at submillimetre resolution. Nature 352, 323–325.

Davison, W., Zhang, H., 1994. In situ speciation measurements of trace components in natural waters using thin-film gels. Nature 367, 546–548.

Diez, S., Giaggio, R., 2018. Do biofilms affect the measurement of mercury by the DGT technique? Microcosm and field tests to prevent biofilm growth. Chemosphere 210, 692–698.

Ding, S., Wang, Y., Zhang, L., et al., 2016. New holder configurations for use in the diffusive gradients in thin films (DGT) technique. Rsc Advances 6, 88143–88156.

Divis, P., Kadlecova, M., Ouddane, B., 2016. Mercury distribution in the Deule River (Northern France) measured by the diffusive gradients in thin films technique and conventional methods. Archives of Environmental Contamination &Toxicology 70, 700–709.

Divis, P., Leermakers, M., Docekalova, H., et al., 2005. Mercury depth profiles in river and marine sediments measured by the diffusive gradients in thin films technique with two different specific resins. Analytical and Bioanalytical Chemistry 382, 1715–1719.

Divis, P., Szkandera, R., Brulik, L., et al., 2009. Application of new resin gels for measuring mercury by diffusive gradients in a thin-films technique. Analytical Sciences 25, 575–578.

Docekalova, H., Divis, P., 2005. Application of diffusive gradient in thin films technique (DGT) to measurement of mercury in aquatic systems. Talanta 65, 1174–1178.

Fernandez-Gomez, C., Bayona, J.M., Diez, S., 2014. Comparison of different types of diffusive gradient in thin film samplers for measurement of dissolved methylmercury in freshwaters. Talanta 129, 486–490.

Fernandez-Gomez, C., Bayona, J.M., Diez, S., 2015. Diffusive gradients in thin films for predicting methylmercury bioavailability in freshwaters after photodegradation. Chemosphere 131, 184–191.

Fernandez-Gomez, C., Dimock, B., Hintelmann, H., et al., 2011. Development of the DGT technique for Hg measurement in water: Comparison of three different types of samplers in laboratory assays. Chemosphere 85, 1452–1457.

Gao, F., 2020. Assessment of Mercury Bioavailability in Soils Based on Diffusion Gradients in Thin Films Technique. MS diss., Guizhou University. (in Chinese)

Gao, Y., Craemer, S.D., Baeyens, W., 2014. A novel method for the determination of dissolved methylmercury concentrations using diffusive gradients in thin films technique. Talanta 120, 470–474.

Garmo, O.A., Royset, O., Steinnes, E., et al., 2003. Performance study of diffusive gradients in thin films for 55 elements. Analytical Chemistry 75, 3573–3580.

Garnier, J.M., Garnier, J., Didier, J., et al., 2015. Using DET and DGT probes (ferrihydrite and titanium dioxide) to investigate arsenic concentrations in soil porewater of an arsenic-contaminated paddy field in Bangladesh. Science of the Total Environment 536, 306–315.

Gu, Y., Huang, H., Jiang, S., et al., 2022. Appraising ecotoxicological risk of mercury species and their mixtures in sediments to aquatic biota using diffusive gradients in thin films (DGT). Science of the Total Environment 825, 154069.

Han, Y., Kingston, H.M., Boylan, H.M., et al., 2003. Speciation of mercury in soil and sediment by selective solvent and acid extraction. Analytical and Bioanalytical Chemistry 375, 428–436.

Hesslein, R.H., 1976. An in situ sampler for close interval pore water studies. Limnology and Oceanography 21, 912–914.

Hong, Y.S., Dan, N.P., Kim, E., et al., 2014. Application of diffusive gel-type probes for assessing redox zonation and mercury methylation in the Mekong Delta sediment. Environmental Science Processes & Impacts 16, 1799.

Hong, X., Inui, M., Matsusaka, T., et al., 2002. X-ray diffraction measurements for expanded fluid mercury using synchrotron radiation: from the liquid to dense vapor. Journal of Non-Crystalline Solids 312–314, 284–289.

Hong, Y.S., Rifkin, E., Bouwer, E.J., 2011. Combination of diffusive gradient in a thin film probe and IC-ICP-MS for the simultaneous determination of CH_3Hg^+ and Hg^{2+} in oxic water. Environmental Science & Technology 45, 6429–6436.

Leeuwen, H.P., Town, R.M., Buffle, J., et al., 2005. Dynamic speciation analysis and bioavailability of metals in aquatic systems. Environmental Science & Technology 39, 8545–8556.

Li, W., Teasdale, P.R., Zhang, S., et al., 2003. Application of a poly (4-styrenesulfonate) liquid binding layer for measurement of Cu^{2+} and Cd^{2+} with the diffusive gradients in thin-films technique. Analytical Chemistry 75, 2578–2583.

Liu, J., 2011. Determination of Methylmercury in Nature Water by DGT-Ethylation-GC-CVAFS and Application of DGT Method. PhD diss., Chinese Academy of Sciences. (in Chinese)

Liu, J., Feng, X., Qiu, G., et al., 2011. Intercomparison and applicability of some dynamic and equilibrium approaches to determine methylated mercury species in pore water. Environmental Toxicology and Chemistry 30, 1739–1744.

Liu, J., Feng, X., Qiu, G., et al., 2012. Prediction of methylmercury uptake by rice plants (*Oryza sativa* L.) using the diffusive gradient in thin films technique. Environmental Science & Technology 46, 11013–11020.

Luo, J., Wang, X., Zhang, H., et al., 2011. Theory and application of diffusive gradients in thin films in soils. Journal of Agro-Environment Science 30, 205–213. (in Chinese)

Marziali, L., Valsecchi, L., 2021. Mercury bioavailability in fluvial sediments estimated using *Chironomus riparius* and diffusive gradients in thin-films (DGT). Environments 8, 7–20.

Ma, P., Tian, T., Dai, Z., et al., 2022. Assessment of Cd bioavailability using chemical extraction methods, DGT, and biological indicators in soils with different aging times. Chemosphere 296, 133931.

Ma, Q., Zhao, W., Guan, D., et al., 2020. Comparing $CaCl_2$, EDTA and DGT methods to predict Cd and Ni accumulation in rice grains from contaminated soils. Environmental Pollution 260, 114042.

Morosini, C., Terzaghi, E., Raspa, G., et al., 2021. Mercury vertical and horizontal concentrations in agricultural soils of a historically contaminated site: Role of soil properties, chemical loading, and cultivated plant species in driving its mobility. Environmental Pollution 285, 117467.

Neal-Walthall, N., Ndu, U., Jr, Elias D. A.,, et al., 2022. Utility of diffusive gradient in thin-film passive samplers for predicting mercury methylation potential and bioaccumulation in freshwater wetlands. Environmental Science & Technology 56, 1743–1752.

Nguyen, V.H., Seon, J., Qasim, G.H., et al., 2021. Applying the diffusive gradient in thin films method to assess soil mercury bioavailability to the earthworm *Eisenia fetida*. Environmental Science and Pollution Research 28, 39840–39852.

Nguyen, V.H., Yee, S.K., Hong, Y., et al., 2019. Predicting mercury bioavailability in soil for earthworm *Eisenia fetida* using the diffusive gradients in thin films technique. Environmental Science and Pollution Research 26, 19549–19559.

Noh, S., Hong, Y., Han, S., 2016. Application of diffusive gradients in thin films and core centrifugation methods to determine inorganic mercury and monomethylmercury profiles in sediment porewater. Environmental Toxicology & Chemistry 35, 348–356.

Noh, S., Kim, Y., Kim, H., et al., 2020. The performance of diffusive gradient in thin film probes for the long-term monitoring of trace level total mercury in water. Environmental Monitoring and Assessment 192, 66.

O'Connor, D., Hou, D., Ok, Y.S., et al., 2019. Mercury speciation, transformation, and transportation in soils, atmospheric flux, and implications for risk management: A critical review. Environment International 126, 747–761.

Pelcova, P., Docekalova, H., Kleckerova, A., 2014. Development of the diffusive gradient in thin films technique for the measurement of labile mercury species in water. Analytica Chimica Acta 819, 42–48.

Pelcova, P., Docekalova, H., Kleckerova, A., 2015. Determination of mercury species by the diffusive gradient in thin film technique and liquid chromatography – atomic fluorescence spectrometry after microwave extraction. Analytica Chimica Acta 866, 21–26.

Pelcova, P., Kopp, R., Ridoskova, A., et al., 2022. Evaluation of mercury bioavailability and phytoaccumulation by means of a DGT technique and of submerged aquatic plants in an aquatic ecosystem situated in the vicinity of a cinnabar mine. Chemosphere 288, 132545.

Pelcova, P., Ridoskova, A., Hrachovinová, J., et al., 2020. Fractionation analysis of mercury in soils: A comparison of three techniques for bioavailable mercury fraction determination. Environmental Toxicology & Chemistry 39, 1670–1677.

Pelcova, P., Ridoskova, A., Hrachovinová, J., et al., 2021. Evaluation of mercury bioavailability to vegetables in the vicinity of cinnabar mine. Environmental Pollution 283, 117092.

Pelcova, P., Vicarova, P., Docekalova, H., et al., 2018. The prediction of mercury bioavailability for common carp (*Cyprinus carpio* L.) using the DGT technique in the presence of chloride ions and humic acid. Chemosphere 211, 1109–1112.

Pelcova, P., Vicarova, P., Ridoskova, A., et al., 2017. Prediction of mercury bioavailability to common carp (*Cyprinus carpio* L.) using the diffusive gradient in thin film technique. Chemosphere 187, 181–187.

Pelcova, P., Zouharova, I., Ridoskova, A., et al., 2019. Evaluation of mercury availability to pea parts (*Pisum sativum L.*) in urban soils: Comparison between diffusive gradients in thin films technique and plant model. Chemosphere 234, 373–378.

Pham, A.L., Johnson, C., Manley, D., et al., 2015. Influence of sulfide nanoparticles on dissolved mercury and zinc quantification by diffusive gradient in thin-film passive samplers. Environmental Science & Technology 49, 12897–12903.

Ridoskova, A., Pelfrene, A., Douay, F., et al., 2019. Bioavailability of mercury in contaminated soils assessed by the diffusive gradient in thin film technique in relation to uptake by *Miscanthus x giganteus*. Environmental Toxicology & Chemistry 38, 321–328.

Ruby, M.V., Davis, A., Link, T.E., et al., 1993. Development of an in vitro screening test to evaluate the in vivo bioaccessibility of ingested mine-waste lead. Environmental Science & Technology 27, 2870–2877.

Natasha, Shahid, M., Khalid, S., Bibi, I., et al., 2020. A critical review of mercury speciation, bioavailability, toxicity and detoxification in soil-plant environment: Ecotoxicology and health risk assessment. Science of the Total Environment 711, 134749.

Tang, W., Liu, Y., Guan, W., et al., 2020. Understanding mercury methylation in the changing environment: Recent advances in assessing microbial methylators and mercury bioavailability. Science of the Total Environment 714, 136827.

Turull, M., Fontàs, C., Díez, S., 2019. Conventional and novel techniques for the determination of Hg uptake by lettuce in amended agricultural peri-urban soils. Science of the Total Environment 668, 40–46.

Turull, M., Komarova, T., Noller, B., et al., 2018. Evaluation of mercury in a freshwater environment impacted by an organomercury fungicide using diffusive gradient in thin films. Science of the Total Environment. 621, 1475–1484.

Wang, C., Yao, Y., Wang, P., et al., 2016. In situ high-resolution evaluation of labile arsenic and mercury in sediment of a large shallow lake. Science of the Total Environment 541, 83–91.

Wang, X., Zhang, Y., Li, Z., et al., 2022. A review of the development and application of DGT technique in determination of mercury and its compounds. Journal of Agricultural Resources and Environment 39, 913–922. (in Chinese)

Wei, T., Guan, D., Fang, W., et al., 2018. Theory and application of diffusive gradients in thin films (DGT) in the environment. III: Theoretical basis and application potential in phytoavailability assessment. Journal of Agro-Environment Science 37, 841–849. (in Chinese)

Xiang, W., Li, X., Yan, J., et al., 2021. Bioavailability evaluation of heavy metals in Yulin coal gasification slag. Journal of Agro-Environment Science 40, 1097–1105. (in Chinese)

Xu, X., Bryan, A.L., Mills, G.L., et al., 2019. Mercury speciation, bioavailability, and bio-magnification in contaminated streams on the Savannah River Site (SC, USA). Science of the Total Environment 668, 261–270.

Yin, H., Yao, H., Yuan, W., et al., 2023. Determination of the isotopic composition of aqueous mercury in a paddy ecosystem using diffusive gradients in thin films. Analytical Chemistry 95, 12290–12297.

9 Mercury Accumulation in the Rice Plant

Bo Meng, Lei Zhao, Jiang Liu, and Xinbin Feng

9.1 INTRODUCTION

The mobility and toxicity of mercury (Hg) are largely dependent on its chemical speciation, in which the organic form of Hg, methylmercury (MeHg), can be bioaccumulated and biomagnified along the food chain, posing a potential threat to human health (Stein et al., 1996; Hasegawa et al., 2005). It is generally accepted that consumption of fish, fish products, and marine mammals is currently considered the main pathway of human exposure to MeHg, posing a worldwide human health threat (Clarkson, 1993). Recently, however, rice (*Oryza sativa* L.) has been identified as a bioaccumulator plant of MeHg (Qiu et al., 2008; Meng et al., 2010; Zhang et al., 2010a), and rice consumption can be the main pathway of MeHg exposure to humans in Hg mining areas and also in certain inland areas in the southwestern part of China (Feng et al., 2008; Zhang et al., 2010b; Li et al., 2015, 2017; Du et al., 2018). Since rice paddy is one of the most prevalent land uses throughout South and East Asia, where rice is the dominant staple food, MeHg-contaminated rice and the resulting MeHg exposure risks are recognized as a global issue. Therefore, research concerning Hg cycling in the paddy ecosystem has received considerable attention in past decades. This chapter highlights the issue of MeHg-contaminated rice globally, comprehensively and systematically summarizes the current understanding of sources, distribution patterns, and processes of inorganic Hg (IHg) and MeHg accumulation in rice plants, and then gives recommendations for future research.

9.2 ISSUES OF METHYLMERCURY-CONTAMINATED RICE IN THE WORLD

Horvat et al. (2003) first announced the MeHg-contaminated rice grain (140 µg/kg) collected from Wanshan Hg mining area in Guizhou Province, Southwestern China. Qiu et al. (2008) further demonstrated that the levels of MeHg detected in rice grain obtained at abandoned Hg mining sites can reach up to 180 µg/kg, which is approximately 100–1000 times higher than those in other local crops, including cabbage, tobacco, rape, and corn. MeHg-contaminated rice was also widely observed in other Hg mining sites in China, such as Xiushan in Chongqing, Wuchuan in Guizhou Province, Xunyang in Shannxi Province, and Xinhuang in Hunan Province (Qiu et al., 2006, 2012; Li et al., 2013; Xu et al., 2018) (Table 9.1). The Hg contamination in rice also exists in industrial areas, such as the compact fluorescent lamp manufacturing area (Liang et al, 2015), electronic waste recycling area in Zhejiang Province (Tang et al., 2015), chemical plant in Guizhou Province (Horvat et al., 2003), and coal-fired power

DOI: 10.1201/9781003404941-9

TABLE 9.1

Concentrations of Total Mercury (THg) and Methylmercury (MeHg) in Rice Grain in Different Areas of the World (Mean ± SD, Min~Max)

Locations	Hg Pollution Status	THg (µg kg⁻¹)	MeHg (µg kg⁻¹)	References
Commercial rice, Bangladesh	No	2.48 ± 1.41(0.42~14.4)	0.83 ± 0.60 (0.026~7.47)	Wang et al., 2020
Commercial rice, Sri Lanka	No	1.73 ± 0.89 (0.21~6.13)	0.51 ± 0.37 (0.03~3.81)	Xu et al., 2020
Niigata Prefecture, Japan	No	1.0 ± — (—~8.0)	—	Nakagawa and Yumita, 1998
15 provinces, China	No	4.7 ± — (1.1~23)	0.68 ± — (0.03~8.7)	Zhao et al., 2019
Guizhou, China	No	6.2 ± — (—)	2.9 ± 1.0 (1.8~4.5)	Meng et al., 2010
Guizhou, China	No	2.8 ± 0.97 (1.0~5.5)	2.0 ± 0.78 (0.37~3.3)	Rothenberg et al., 2012
Guizhou, China	No	2.3 ± 1.2 (1.3~6.4)	1.6 ± 0.40 (0.42~3.7)	Zhang et al., 2010a
Guizhou, China	No	3.2 ± 2.1 (1.2~7.7)	2.1 ± 1.7 (0.24~6.1)	Zhang et al., 2010a
83 rice products marketed in EU	No	3.04 ± 2.07 (0.53~11.1)	1.91 ± 1.07 (0.11~6.45)	Brombach et al., 2017
79 rice-based infant cereals, samples marketed in USA and China	No	3.8 ± 2.8 (1.5~16)	2.3 ± 2.5 (0.57~14)	Cui et al., 2017
Riyadh, Saudi Arabia	No	1.6 ± — (<3.0~3.31)	—	Al-Saleh and Shinwari, 2001
Egypt	No	1.63 ± — (0.51~2.75)	—	Al-Saleh and Shinwari, 2001
Arabia, Thailand	No	1.8 ± — (<3.0~3.5)	—	Al-Saleh and Shinwari, 2001
Valencia, Spain	No	2.1 ± — (1.6~3.3)	—	da Silva et al., 2010
Palma de Mallorca, Spain	No	4.48 ± — (2.15~7.25)	—	da Silva et al., 2013
Paris, France	No	5.0 ± — (—)	—	Leblanc et al., 2005
Western Italy	No	5.21 ± — (—)	0.86 ± — (—)	Horvat et al., 2003
Southern India	No	7.4 ± — (—)	—	Srikumar, 1993
Recife and Sao Paulo, Brazil	No	3.1 ± — (2.1~4.4)	—	da Silva et al., 2010
Salvador City, Brazil	No	8.36 ± — (4.1~13.7)	—	Silva et al., 2012
Kampong, Cambodia	No	8.14 ± — (6.16~11.7)	1.44 ± — (1.17~1.96)	Cheng et al., 2013

(Continued)

TABLE 9.1 *(Continued)*

Concentrations of Total Mercury (THg) and Methylmercury (MeHg) in Rice Grain in Different Areas of the World (Mean ± SD, Min~Max)

Locations	Hg Pollution Status	THg (µg kg^{-1})	MeHg (µg kg^{-1})	References
Kandal, Cambodia	No	10.2 ± — (5.9~15.1)	2.34 ± — (0.48~5.23)	Cheng et al., 2013
Guizhou, China	No	7.0 ± 2.8 (3.2~15.1)	2.5 ± 1.2 (0.8~4.3)	Feng et al., 2008
Zhejiang, China	No	9.0 ± — (—)	4 ± — (—)	Cheng et al., 2009
Guizhou, China	No	2.8 ± — (—)	1.3 ± — (—)	Li et al., 2008
Commercial rice (domestic), China	Not clear	4.03 ± 2.37 (0.64~31.7)	1.40 ± 1.21 (0.02~18.6)	Xu et al., 2020
Commercial rice (imported), China	Not clear	3.82 ± 1.56 (1.12~8.90)	1.02 ± 0.64 (0.07~3.29)	Xu et al., 2020
7 provinces, Nepal	Not clear	7.05 ± 7.71 (0.62~158)	0.82 ± 0.66 (0.19~8.50)	Wang et al., 2021
15 provinces, China	Not clear	23±— (6.3~39)	4.5 ± — (1.9~11)	Shi et al., 2005
Hunan, China	Coal-fired power plant	5.7 ± — (2.0~22)	2.4 ± 0.72 (1.7~3.8)	Xu et al., 2017a
Guizhou, China	Coal-fired power plant	14.6 ± 14.3 (2.5~34)	11.3 ± 12.8 (0.71~28)	Horvat et al., 2003
Guizhou, China	Hg mining	149 ± 178 (11.1~569)	38.9 ± 41.8 (8.03~144)	Horvat et al., 2003
Guizhou, China	Hg mining	26 ± — (13~52)	9.4 ± — (3.5~23)	Li et al., 2013
Hunan, China	Hg mining	29 ± — (11~58)	11 ± — (6.5~24)	Li et al., 2013
Guizhou, China	Hg mining	180 ± 160 (—)	7.0 ± 3.2 (3.8~18)	Meng et al., 2010
Guizhou, China	Hg mining	310 ± 170 (—)	32 ± 14 (18~62)	Meng et al., 2010
Guizhou, China	Hg mining	86 ± 44 (—)	21 ± 9.3 (—)	Meng M. et al., 2014
Guizhou, China	Hg mining	22 ± 5.3 (—)	12 ± 4.9 (—)	Meng M. et al., 2014
Guizhou, China	Hg mining	94 ± 114 (—~584)	30 ± 27 (—~132)	Meng M. et al., 2014
Guizhou, China	Hg mining	78 ± 100 (7.3~508)	9.3 ± 9.0 (1.2~44)	Zhang et al., 2010a
Guizhou, China	Coal-fired power plant	5.5 ± 4.9 (1.0~25)	2.2 ± 1.7 (0.12~9.0)	Zhang et al., 2010a
Guizhou, China	Hg mining	58.5 ± 39.9 (21.1~192)	14.6 ± 4.7 (7.5~27.6)	Feng et al., 2008
Guizhou, China	Hg mining	21.3 ± 16.8 (10~66.9)	5.7 ± 1.9 (3.3~10.2)	Feng et al., 2008
Guizhou, China	Hg mining	33.1 ± 57.4 (4.9~214.7)	4.0 ± 3.0 (1.9~14.7)	Feng et al., 2008
Guizhou, China	Hg mining	42.4 ± 52.7 (—)	11.7 ± 8.84 (—)	Li et al., 2015
Guizhou, China	Hg mining	26.8 ± 24.8 (6~113)	7.8 ± 3.6 (3.8~12.3)	Li et al., 2008
Guizhou, China	Hg mining	22 ± 9.5 (10~45)	11 ± 7.6 (3.2~39)	Qiu et al., 2013

(Continued)

TABLE 9.1 *(Continued)*

Concentrations of Total Mercury (THg) and Methylmercury (MeHg) in Rice Grain in Different Areas of the World (Mean ± SD, Min~Max)

Locations	Hg Pollution Status	THg (µg kg⁻¹)	MeHg (µg kg⁻¹)	References
Guizhou, China	Hg mining	120 ± 33 (72~190)	63 ± 19 (31~100)	Rothenberg et al., 2012
Guizhou, China	Hg mining	18 ± 4.3 (11~34)	9.9 ± 5.1 (1.5~18)	Rothenberg et al., 2012
Guizhou, China	Hg mining	12 ± 9.9 (2.4~38)	5.0 ± 3.8 (1.2~13)	Rothenberg et al., 2013
Zhejiang, China	Lamp manufacturing	13 ± 7.2 (1.3~41)	6.01 ± 3.6 (0.09~21.5)	Liang et al., 2015
Guangdong, China	Pb-Zn mining	15 ± — (1.5~52)	1.2 ± — (0.28~3.5)	Li et al., 2013
Guangdong, China	Pb-Zn mining	16 ± 4.1 (10~28)	2.0 ± 0.5 (—)	Meng M. et al. 2014
Zhejiang, China	E-waste recycling	81 ± 15 (—)	42 ± 10 (—)	Tang et al., 2015
Chongqing, China	Hg mining	48 ± 97 (4.8~384)	12 ± 15 (3.0 ~64)	Xu et al., 2018
Shaanxi, China	Hg mining	103 ± 54 (50~200)	22 ± 22 (8.2~80)	Qiu et al., 2012
Guizhou, China	Hg mining	608 ± 290 (49~1120)	62 ± 42 (22~174)	Qiu et al., 2008
Punjab and Sindh, Pakistan	Brick-making kilns	4.51 ± 8.56 (0.44~157)	3.71 ± 6.69 (0.16~67.9)	Aslam et al., 2020
Kratie, Cambodia	Gold mining	13 ± — (9.9~17)	1.5 ± — (1.1~2.3)	Cheng et al., 2013
Mindanao, Philippines	Gold mining	18 ± — (8~50)	—	Appleton et al., 2006
Rwamagasa, Tanzania	Gold mining	26 ± — (11~35)	—	Taylor et al., 2005
California, USA	Gold mining/ Hg mining	50 ± — (50~51)	4.6 ± — (4.1~5.0)	Windham-Myers et al., 2014
Phichit Province, Thailand	Gold mining	212 ± — (172~268)	—	Pataranawat et al., 2007
Lombok Island, Indonesia	Gold mining	—	58 ± 43 (11~115)	Krisnayanti et al., 2012
Mie prefecture, Japan	Chemical plant	23 ± — (3~60)	—	Morishita et al., 1982
Ganjam, India	Chemical plant	510 ± — (470~530)	—	Lenka et al., 1992

Note: "—" means data are unavailable.

plant in Hunan Province (Xu et al., 2017) (Table 9.1). Moreover, elevated levels of total Hg or MeHg in rice seeds were widely observed in other Hg-polluted areas around the world (Table 9.1), including Ganjam in India (associated with a chlor-alkali plant, Lenka et al., 1992), California in the United States (gold and mercury mining activities, Windham-Myers et al., 2014), Phichit Province in Thailand (gold mining activities, Pataranawat et al., 2007), Mindanao in the Philippines (artisanal gold mining, Appleton et al., 2006), Lombok Island in Indonesia (artisanal gold mining, Krisnayanti et al., 2012), Punjab and Sindh in Pakistan (brick-making kilns, Aslam et al., 2020), and Gandaki Province in Nepal (terrestrial sources, industrial sources, and biogenic combustion processes, Wang et al., 2021).

Zhao et al. (2019) investigated Hg concentration in rice grain in non-contaminated areas from 15 provinces across China and found relatively low total Hg (THg) and MeHg levels in rice grain (polished rice) in the majority of provinces, with geometric mean concentrations of 4.7 μg kg^{-1} (range: 1.1~23 μg kg^{-1}, $n = 560$) and 0.68 μg kg^{-1} (range: 0.03~8.7 μg kg^{-1}), respectively (Table 9.1). THg and MeHg concentrations in rice grain obtained from background areas (without a known point Hg source) are much lower than those from Hg-polluted areas in China, especially the Hg mining area (Table 9.1). Similarly, Chinese commercial rice (polished rice, domestic = 709 and abroad = 58) showed relatively low levels of THg and MeHg, with mean concentrations of 3.97 ± 2.33 μg kg^{-1} (range: 0.64~32 μg kg^{-1}) and 1.37 ± 1.18 μg kg^{-1} (range: 0.020~19 μg kg^{-1}), respectively (Xu et al., 2020), which are comparable to findings from an early study conducted in the background areas of China (Zhao et al., 2019). Therefore, Hg concentrations in rice grain from non-contaminated areas are low in China (Zhao et al., 2019). MeHg-contaminated rice is mainly found in Hg-polluted areas, especially Hg mining areas, and it needs to be paid more attention (Table 9.1).

Generally, Hg exists in inorganic form in crop plants (WHO, 1991). Consequently, food safety standards are recommended based on THg levels, and therefore, safe guidelines for MeHg in foodstuff are unavailable. However, MeHg levels in rice grain often exceed the permissible limit of 20 μg/kg issued by the Chinese National Standard Agency (Qiu et al., 2008; Meng B. et al., 2014). More importantly, the ratio of MeHg to THg in rice grain can be very high, reaching up to 72% (Meng et al., 2014). It has been confirmed that rice plants can bioaccumulate MeHg from soils in Hg-polluted areas (Table 9.1). Mercury concentrations in commercial market rice and rice-based products from the EU and the United States were studied. Results showed that both adults and infants in the EU and the United States face potential Hg exposure health risks through rice or rice-based product consumption (Brombach et al., 2017; Cui et al., 2017). Recently, a modeling simulation predicted that the Hg concentration in Chinese rice might be increased by 13% if there are no policies to control Hg emission (Kwon et al., 2018). The bioaccumulated MeHg in the paddy field ecosystem can migrate into the food chain via rice grain.

Rice serves as a primary nutrition source for nearly half of the world's population. Therefore, rice cultivation has an important position in agriculture throughout South and East Asia (FAO, 2002). The latest report from the Food and Agriculture Organization (FAO) of the United Nations indicates that the total area of land under rice cultivation is 163 million hectares globally, with ~50% of the land located in China (FAO, 2016). With its rapidly developing economy, China holds the leading position in Hg production, use, and emission in the world. As a result, the concentrations of atmospheric Hg in China are significantly higher than those in developed regions and countries like Europe and America (Fu et al., 2012). The high levels of Hg in the atmosphere may cause large-scale Hg pollution in rice once it is deposited into rice-planting areas. Additionally, there are many Hg ore deposits in China, and they are distributed in Guizhou Province, Hunan Province, Chongqing, Yunnan Province, and Shaanxi Province, which are also the main rice cultivation areas. Rice consumers who live in Hg-polluted regions are exposed to Hg to various extents. It has been reported that rice consumption has become a predominant route of MeHg exposure for its consumers in Southwestern China (Feng et al., 2008; Zhang et al., 2010b; Li et al., 2015, 2017; Du et al., 2018). In Hg-polluted regions, the daily exposure to MeHg reaches up to 1.8 µg/kg of body weight, which is nearly 200 times higher than the edible standard recommended by the US EPA (Qiu et al., 2008). Therefore, attention needs to be paid to the risks of mercury exposure for rice consumers in Hg-contaminated regions. Moreover, the scenario of MeHg contamination in paddy field ecosystems requires urgent intervention, especially in Hg-polluted areas. Therefore, an understanding of the sources and processes of Hg accumulation in rice plants is very important, as it can potentially provide guidance on remediation of Hg-contaminated paddy soil, reduction of MeHg uptake in rice plants, and MeHg exposure of local residents.

9.3 SOURCES OF INORGANIC Hg AND METHYLMERCURY IN RICE PLANTS

Rice grains can accumulate high levels of MeHg, posing a potential threat to people and wildlife (Feng et al., 2008; Zhang et al., 2010b; Li et al., 2015, 2017; Abeysinghe et al., 2017a, 2017b,; Du et al., 2018; Xu et al., 2019). Therefore, knowledge of the bioaccumulation processes of inorganic Hg and MeHg in rice plants can be helpful for building strategies to mitigate Hg risks from paddy fields. Horvat et al. (2003) attempted to show the source of Hg in rice based on the relationship between the Hg concentration in rice and that in the corresponding soil in the Wanshan Hg mining area. They failed to observe any relationship between THg or MeHg in rice and soil and attributed this phenomenon to the influence of diverse Hg contamination sources on Hg accumulation by rice. However, a positive correlation between MeHg in soil and rice from an industrial site in Guizhou Province in China was observed (Horvat et al., 2003). Meng et al. (2010, 2011, 2012) focused on the bioaccumulation pathways of inorganic Hg and MeHg in the tissues of rice plants. Results based on statistical analysis (e.g., regression analysis, principal components analysis, and factorial analysis) of Hg concentrations in the different parts of rice plants showed that the atmosphere is the principal source of inorganic Hg in the above-ground portions of rice plants. Specifically, both soil and ambient atmosphere provide inorganic Hg to the stalk, with the atmosphere being more pronounced. Soil has been confirmed to be a predominant source of IHg in roots and a unique bioaccumulation pathway of MeHg for tissues of rice plants (Meng et al., 2010, 2011, 2012). Recently, Aslam et al. (2022) reported that the above-ground tissues of rice plants, including grains, leaves, and stalks, can accumulate inorganic Hg from both the atmosphere and soil to varying degrees depending on the concentration gradient of each source. In vivo methylation of Hg in plant organs is unlikely, and thus paddy soil is a predominant source of MeHg in the tissues of rice plants (Aslam et al., 2022).

The diffusive gradient in thin films technique (Liu et al., 2012) and Hg isotope tracer technique (Strickman and Mitchell, 2017; Liu et al., 2021) have been used to quantify the contribution of different Hg contamination sources to the Hg in the tissues of rice plants. For example, by using Hg stable isotope tracers, Liu et al. (2021) found that, in addition to the atmosphere, soil is an important source of inorganic Hg to rice grains, which had been underestimated in previous studies. However, the contribution of MeHg from other sources to rice plants is still in debate more or less. It's worth mentioning that in vivo demethylation of MeHg, possibly via photolytic demethylation, in rice plants, especially the above-ground parts, was observed in previous studies (Li et al., 2016; Strickman and Mitchell, 2017; Liu et al., 2021). It's possible to mitigate MeHg accumulation in rice grains by promoting in vivo demethylation of MeHg (Liu et al., 2021). However, further work is needed to obtain solid evidence to support the in situ demethylation of MeHg in rice plants. In addition to soil MeHg, the atmospheric dimethylmercury (DMeHg), which is originally derived from paddy soil, can be a potential contributor to MeHg in rice plants (Wang et al., 2018).

9.4 THE DISTRIBUTION PATTERNS AND LOCALIZATION OF Hg IN RICE PLANTS

The distribution and localization characteristics of IHg and MeHg in rice plants have been studied under field conditions in different Hg-polluted areas (Meng B. et al., 2010, 2014). Generally, the distribution patterns of IHg in rice plants are largely dependent on the relative Hg levels in the soil compared to the atmosphere. From significant Hg contamination in the ambient air, the shoots of rice plants accumulated inorganic Hg, particularly in the leaves, at an artisanal Hg mining site (Meng et al., 2010). However, the elevated inorganic Hg concentration in rice root tissues at abandoned Hg mining sites could be sourced from Hg-contaminated rice paddies (Meng et al., 2010). In contrast, the highest concentrations of MeHg were generally observed in rice grain, regardless of sampling site, and then root, hull, stalk, and leaf (Meng et al., 2010; Zhang et al., 2010a) (Figure 9.1). Moreover, the majority of MeHg was stored in the rice seed, which confirmed that rice seed had

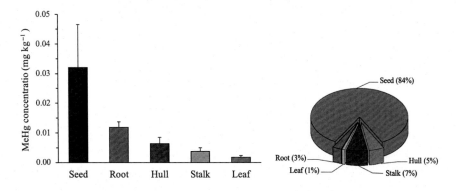

FIGURE 9.1 Concentrations and relative distribution of MeHg in tissues of rice plant from an artisanal Hg mining site in Guizhou Province, China. (Modified from Meng et al., 2010.)

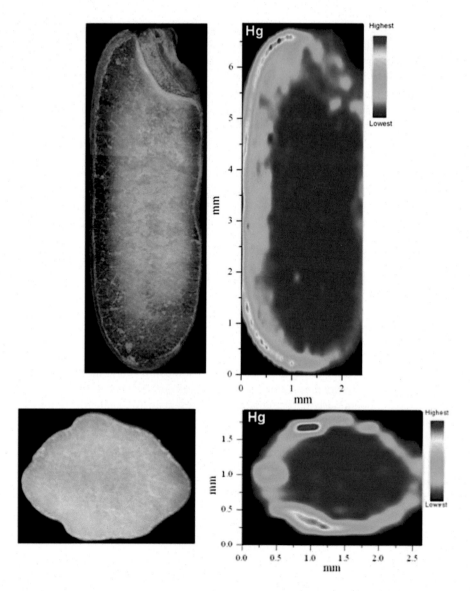

FIGURE 9.2 Mercury maps of longitudinal (top) and latitudinal (bottom) sections of rice grain (ventral side on right). (Modified from B. Meng et al., 2014.)

the greatest ability to bioaccumulate MeHg compared to other tissues (Meng et al., 2010; Zhang et al., 2010a) (Figure 9.2). The different distribution patterns between inorganic Hg and MeHg in the tissues of rice plants may be due to the differences in inorganic Hg and MeHg sources and accumulation mechanisms for rice plant tissues (Meng et al., 2010, 2011, 2012).

The speciation and localization of Hg species in different parts of rice grain (white rice, bran, and hull) have been studied (Rothenberg et al., 2011; Qiu et al., 2012;

Meng B. et al., 2014). Results showed that rice bran has the highest levels of IHg and MeHg, followed by hull and white rice (Meng B. et al., 2014). Moreover, most IHg in rice grain is observed in the bran and hull, while most of the MeHg is present in the white rice. Consequently, the majority of IHg is removed, but MeHg still remains in the edible parts (white rice) during the processing of rice grain (Meng B. et al., 2014).

MeHg, as a possible organic nutrient, can utilize membrane transport pathways in the endosperm more efficiently than inorganic Hg, leading to the accumulation of MeHg in the white rice (Rothenberg et al. (2011). Using synchrotron radiation-based microscopic X-ray fluorescence spectroscopy (μ-XRF), B. Meng et al. (2014) revealed the prominent localization of Hg at the surface of the brown rice grain, which corresponds to the pericarp and aleurone layers, and a gradient of Hg levels from surface layers of rice grain (pericarp and aleurone) to the center part (endosperm) (Figure 9.2). The accumulation of Hg in the surface layer of rice grain (pericarp and aleurone) is due to the high affinity of Hg to the protein-ligand side chains (Meng B. et al., 2014). Although the distribution and localization of Hg in rice grain have been studied, the mechanism of IHg and MeHg storage in different parts of rice grain has still yet to be studied.

9.5 THE PROCESSES OF Hg SPECIES ACCUMULATION IN RICE PLANTS

The processes of inorganic Hg and MeHg accumulation in the tissues of rice plants during the whole rice growing period have been studied (Meng B. et al., 2010, 2012, 2014; Zhang et al., 2010a; Liu et al., 2012; Cui et al., 2014). A steady increase in the concentration and mass of inorganic Hg in the above-ground parts of rice plants (e.g., the leaf and stalk) is generally observed during rice growing periods, especially for the rice plants grown in Hg mining areas that were exposed to highly elevated Hg vapor (Meng et al., 2010; Cui et al., 2014) (Figure 9.3). The stomatal and nonstomatal routes were hypothesized to be the potential pathways of the atmospheric Hg vapor exchange and uptake into above-ground parts of the rice plant

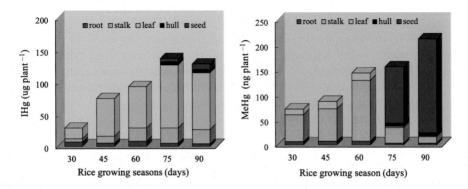

FIGURE 9.3 Inorganic mercury (IHg, left) and methylmercury (MeHg, right) mass in tissues of rice plants collected from an artisanal site paddy. (Modified from Meng et al., 2011, 2012.)

(foliage and stalk) (Meng et al., 2012; Cui et al., 2014). Therefore, the accumulated inorganic Hg from atmospheric Hg vapor could be fixed into leaf and stalk tissues and was hardly re-emitted to the atmosphere or translocated to other parts (i.e., seed, hull, and root) (Meng et al., 2012, 2018; Cui et al., 2014). Recently, Aslam et al. (2022) suggested that atmospheric Hg accumulated by above-ground rice tissues could be partially translocated to below-ground tissues (roots). However, more evidence is still urgently needed to further confirm this alternative process (Aslam et al., 2022). In contrast, the rice root (iron plaque) may represent a potential barrier to inorganic Hg absorption and accumulation, which potentially sequestrates inorganic Hg and consequently reduces the Hg uptake through the root to the above-ground parts (Zhang et al., 2010a; Meng et al., 2012; Cui et al., 2014). Moreover, the formation of Hg–phytochelatin complexes was observed in the rice root, which can trap inorganic Hg in the rice root system to inhibit its translocation to above-ground parts (Krupp et al., 2009).

The bioavailability and toxicity of Hg are largely dependent on its chemical speciation (Hasegawa et al., 2005). Therefore, the chemical speciation of Hg in rice grain was further studied based on X-ray absorption near-edge spectroscopy (XANES). B. Meng et al. (2014) proposed that inorganic Hg in rice grain was predominantly bound to cysteine and associated with phytochelatins, which possibly explained why the majority of Hg was located in surface layers of rice grain (pericarp and aleurone) and not in the center part (endosperm) (Rothenberg et al., 2011). The localization of inorganic Hg in different parts of rice grain and the chemical speciation of inorganic Hg in rice grain were recognized as mechanisms of self-detoxification or self-protection when the rice plant was exposed to atmospheric Hg^0 (Rothenberg et al., 2011; Cui et al., 2014; Meng B. et al., 2014).

The mechanism and process of inorganic Hg accumulation in rice plants were shown to be different from those of MeHg (Meng B. et al., 2011, 2012, 2014). Generally, the bioaccumulation and translocation of MeHg from the root to the above-ground parts are described as a dynamic process (Figure 9.3). Rice roots can absorb MeHg from soil, which suggested that the processes (absorption) within the plant-soil interface occurred more easily than those of inorganic Hg (Krupp et al., 2009; Meng et al., 2011). Phytochelatins, small peptides that detoxify heavy metals in plants, were observed in rice plants and could sequester Hg^{2+} but not MeHg (Krupp et al., 2009). Therefore, MeHg can pass through the physical barrier on the rice root surface (iron plaque). It is speculated that MeHg in roots behaves like a mobile plant nutrient and then is translocated to the above-ground parts of the rice plant (Krupp et al., 2009; Meng B. et al., 2014) (Figure 9.3). Consequently, a very limited amount of MeHg was maintained in the rice root during the rice growing season. During rice growing periods, most of the MeHg was stored in the leaf and stalk of the premature plant; however, MeHg that was temporarily located in the leaf and stalk was further transported and accumulated into ripening rice seeds during the grain filling period (Meng et al., 2011) (Figure 9.3). Recently, researchers suggested that the process of MeHg uptake by roots is impacted by the types and levels of thiols in the soil-rice plant system during the rice growing periods (Hao et al., 2022). Specially, the presence of cysteine can facilitate MeHg uptake by the root and then translocation from root to shoot. Glutathione seems only to facilitate MeHg uptake by the root, while the influence of glutathione on the translocation of MeHg from root to shoot is less pronounced (Hao et al., 2022). On the opposite side, it's very interesting that penicillamine significantly inhibits MeHg uptake by the root and translocation to the shoot (Hao et al., 2022). XANES and HPLC-ICP-MS analysis confirmed that the MeHg in rice ripening seeds was exclusively in the form of the MeHg-S compound (MeHg-cysteine), which is responsible for the transfer of MeHg across the blood-brain and placental barriers (Li et al., 2010; Meng B. et al., 2014). Therefore, it is speculated that free MeHg-cysteine can be recognized as a movable compound and acts in a similar way to free cysteine or amino acid. This MeHg complex might be associated with proteins in rice grain (Meng B. et al., 2011, 2014).

9.6 FUTURE PERSPECTIVE

Future research on the impacts of rice production on MeHg release to the environment and rice consumption on human Hg exposure should examine geographically diverse areas, including Asian countries beyond China as well as other major continents (e.g., Africa, South America, and North America) where rice production and consumption are substantial. Such data are critical in understanding the global issue of MeHg-contaminated rice and the potential health risks associated with rice consumption in areas with Hg-contaminated soils. While the source, distribution patterns, and processes of MeHg accumulation in rice plants, as well as the potential transformation of Hg species in rice plants, have been previously studied, the mechanism of MeHg accumulation in rice plants, as well as its controlling factors, is very complex and far from being fully understood; an example is the in vivo demethylation of MeHg within rice plants and its underlying mechanism. Furthermore, the absorption pathways of MeHg through the rice root and the loci and genes associated with MeHg uptake in rice plants are still unknown. Remediation measures are urgently needed to reduce the MeHg accumulation in rice and exposure of local residents, especially in Hg-polluted areas.

REFERENCES

Abeysinghe, K. S., Qiu, G. L., Goodale, E., et al. 2017a. Mercury flow through an Asian rice-based food web. Environmental Pollution 229, 219–228.

Abeysinghe, K. S., Yang, X. D., Goodale, E., et al. 2017b. Total mercury and methylmercury concentrations over a gradient of contamination in earthworms living in rice paddy soil. Environmental Toxicology and Chemistry 36, 1202–1210.

Al-Saleh, I., Shinwari, N. 2001. Report on the levels of cadmium, lead, and mercury in imported rice grain samples. Biological Trace Element Research 131, 43–54.

Appleton, J. D., Weeks, J. M., Calvez, J. P. S., et al. 2006. Impacts of mercury contaminated mining waste on soil quality, crops, bivalves, and fish in the Naboc River area, Mindanao, Philippines. Science of the Total Environment 354, 198–211.

Aslam, M. W., Ali, W., Meng, B., et al. 2020. Mercury contamination status of rice cropping system in Pakistan and associated health risks. Environmental Pollution 263, 114625.

Aslam, W. M., Meng, B., Abdelhafiz, M. A., et al. 2022. Unravelling the interactive effect of soil and atmospheric mercury influencing mercury distribution and accumulation in the soil-rice system. Science of the Total Environment 803, 149967.

Brombach, C. C., Manorut, P., Kolambage-Dona, P. P. P., et al. 2017. Methylmercury varies more than one order of magnitude in commercial European rice. Food Chemistry 214, 360–365.

Cheng, J. P., Gao, L. L., Zhao, W. C., et al. 2009. Mercury levels in fisherman and their household members in Zhoushan, China: Impact of public health. Science of the Total Environment 407, 2625–2630.

Cheng, Z., Wang, H. S., Du, J., et al. 2013. Dietary exposure and risk assessment of mercury via total diet study in Cambodia. Chemosphere 92, 143–149.

Clarkson, T. W. 1993. Mercury: Major issues in environmental health. Environmental Health Perspectives 100, 31–38.

Cui, L. W., Feng, X. B., Lin, C. J., et al. 2014. Accumulation and translocation of [198]Hg in four crop species. Environmental Toxicology and Chemistry 33, 334–340.

Cui, W. B., Liu, G. L., Bezerra, M., et al. 2017. Occurrence of methylmercury in rice-based infant cereals and estimation of daily dietary intake of methylmercury for infants. Journal of Agricultural and Food Chemistry 65, 9569–9578.

da Silva, D. G., Portugal, L. A., Serra, A. M., et al. 2013. Determination of mercury in rice by MSFIA and cold vapour atomic fluorescence spectrometry. Food Chemistry 137, 159–163.

da Silva, M. J., Paim, A. P. S., Pimentel, M. F., et al. 2010. Determination of mercury in rice by cold vapor atomic fluorescence spectrometry after microwave-assisted digestion. Analytica Chimica Acta 667, 43–48.

Du, B. Y., Feng, X. B., Li, P., et al. 2018. Use of mercury isotopes to quantify mercury exposure sources in inland populations, China. Environmental Science & Technology 52, 5407–5416.

FAO. 2002. Rice Information, December 2002, Volume 3. Rome, Italy. (http://www.fao.org/docrep/005/Y4347E/y4347e00.htm)

FAO. 2016. Rice Market Monitor, December 2016, Volume XIX, Issue No. 4. Rome, Italy. (http://www.fao.org/economic/est/publications/rice-publications/rice-market-monitor-rmm/en/)

Feng, X. B., Li, P., Qiu, G. L., et al. 2008. Human exposure to methylmercury through rice intake in mercury mining areas, Guizhou province, China. Environmental Science & Technology 42, 326–332.

Fu, X. W., Feng, X. B., Sommar, J., et al. 2012. A review of studies on atmospheric mercury in China. Science of the Total Environment 421, 73–81.

Hao, Y. Y., Zhu, Y. J., Yan, R. Q., et al. 2022. Important roles of thiols in methylmercury uptake and translocation by rice plants. Environmental Science & Technology 56, 6765–6773.

Hasegawa, T., Asano, M., Takatani, K., et al. 2005. Speciation of mercury in salmon egg cell cytoplasm in relation with metallomics research. Talanta 68, 465–469.

Horvat, M., Nolde, N., Fajon, V., et al. 2003. Total mercury, methylmercury and selenium in mercury polluted areas in the province Guizhou, China. Science of the Total Environment 304, 231–256.

Krisnayanti, B. D., Anderson, C. W. N., Utomo, W. H., et al. 2012. Assessment of environmental mercury discharge at a four-year-old artisanal gold mining area on Lombok Island, Indonesia. Journal of Environmental Monitoring 14, 2598–2607.

Krupp, E. M., Mestrot, A., Wielgus, J., et al. 2009. The molecular form of mercury in biota: Identification of novel mercury peptide complexes in plants. Chemical Communications 28, 4257–4259.

Kwon, S. Y., Selin, N. E., Giang, A., et al. 2018. Present and future mercury concentrations in Chinese rice: Insights from modeling. Global Biogeochemical Cycles 32, 437–462.

Leblanc, J. C., Guérin, T., Noël, L., et al. 2005. Dietary exposure estimates of 18 elements from the 1st French total diet study. Food Additives & Contaminants: Part B 22, 624–621.

Lenka, M., Panda, K. K., Panda, B. B. 1992. Monitoring and assessment of mercury pollution in the vicinity of a chloralkali plant. IV. Bioconcentration of mercury in in situ aquatic and terrestrial plants at Ganjam, India. Archives of Environmental Contamination and Toxicology 22, 195–202.

Liang, P., Feng, X. B., Zhang, C., et al. 2015. Human exposure to mercury in a compact fluorescent lamp manufacturing area: By food (rice and fish) consumption and occupational exposure. Environmental Pollution 198, 126–132.

Li, P., Du, B. Y., Maurice, L., et al. 2017. Mercury isotope signatures of methylmercury in rice samples from the Wanshan mercury mining area, China: Environmental implications. Environmental Science & Technology 51, 12321–12328.

Li, P., Feng, X. B., Chan, H. M., et al. 2015. Human body burden and dietary methylmercury intake: The relationship in a rice-consuming population. Environmental Science & Technology 49, 9682–9689.

Li, P., Feng, X. B., Qiu, G. L., et al. 2008. Mercury exposure in the population from Wuchuan mercury mining area, Guizhou, China. Science of the Total Environment 395, 72–79.

Li, B., Shi, J. B., Wang, X., et al. 2013. Variations and constancy of mercury and methylmercury accumulation in rice grown at contaminated paddy field sites in three provinces of China. Environmental Pollution 181, 91–97.

Li, L., Wang, F. Y., Meng, B., et al. 2010. Speciation of methylmercury in rice grown from a mercury mining area. Environmental Pollution 158, 3103–3107.

Li, Y. Y., Zhao, J. T., Zhang, B. W., et al. 2016. The influence of iron plaque on the absorption, translocation and transformation of mercury in rice (*Oryza sativa* L.) seedlings exposed to different mercury species. Plant and Soil 398, 87–97.

Liu, J. L., Feng, X. B., Qiu, G. L., et al. 2012. Prediction of methyl mercury uptake by rice plants (*Oryza sativa* L.) using the diffusive gradient in thin films technique. Environmental Science & Technology 46, 11013–11020.

Liu, J., Meng, B., Poulain, A. J., et al. 2021. Stable isotope tracers identify sources and transformations of mercury in rice (*Oryza sativa* L.) growing in a mercury mining area. Fundamental Research 1, 259–269.

Meng, B, Feng, X. B, Qiu, G. L., et al. 2010. Distribution patterns of inorganic mercury and methylmercury in tissues of rice (*Oryza sativa* L.) plants and possible bioaccumulation pathways. Journal of Agricultural and Food Chemistry 58, 4951–4958.

Meng, B., Feng, X. B., Qiu, G. L., et al. 2011. The process of methylmercury accumulation in rice (*Oryza sativa* L.). Environmental Science & Technology 45, 2711–2717.

Meng, B., Feng, X. B., Qiu, G. L., et al. 2012. Inorganic mercury accumulation in rice (*Oryza sativa* L.). Environmental Toxicology and Chemistry 31, 2093–2098.

Meng, B., Feng, X. B., Qiu, G. L., et al. 2014. Localization and speciation of mercury in brown rice with implications for pan-Asian public health. Environmental Science & Technology 48, 7974–7981.

Meng, B., Li, Y. B., Cui, W. B., et al. 2018. Tracing the uptake, transport, and fate of mercury in sawgrass (*Cladium jamaicense*) in the Florida Everglades using multi-isotope technique. Environmental Science & Technology 52, 3384–3391.

Meng, M., Li, B., Shao, J. J., et al. 2014. Accumulation of total mercury and methylmercury in rice plants collected from different mining areas in China. Environmental Pollution 184, 179–186.

Morishita, T., Kishino, K., Idaka, S. 1982. Mercury contamination of soils, rice plants, and human hair in the vicinity of a mercury mine in Mie prefecture, Japan. Soil Science and Plant Nutrition 28, 523–534.

Nakagawa, R., Yumita, Y. 1998. Change and behavior of residual mercury in paddy soils and rice of Japan. Chemosphere 377, 1483–1487.

Pataranawat, P., Parkpian, P., Polprasert, C., et al. 2007. Mercury emission and distribution: Potential environmental risks at a small-scale gold mining operation, Phichit Province, Thailand. Journal of Environmental Science and Health, Part A 42, 1081–1093.

Qiu, G. L., Feng, X. B., Li, P., et al. 2008. Methylmercury accumulation in rice (*Oryza sativa L.*) grown at abandoned mercury mines in Guizhou, China. Journal of Agricultural and Food Chemistry 56, 2465–2468.

Qiu, G. L., Feng, X. B., Meng, B., et al. 2012. Methylmercury in rice (*Oryza sativa L.*) grown from the Xunyang Hg mining area, Shaanxi province, northwestern China. Pure and Applied Chemistry 84, 281–289.

Qiu, G. L., Feng, X. B., Meng, B., et al. 2013. Environmental geochemistry of an abandoned mercury mine in Yanwuping, Guizhou Province, China. Environmental Research 125, 124–130.

Qiu, G. L., Feng, X. B., Wang, S. F., et al. 2006. Environmental contamination of mercury from Hg-mining areas in Wuchuan, northeastern Guizhou, China. Environmental Pollution 142, 549–558.

Rothenberg, S. E., Feng, X. B., Dong, B., et al. 2011. Characterization of mercury species in brown and white rice (*Oryza sativa L.*) grown in water-saving paddies. Environmental Pollution 159, 1283–1289.

Rothenberg, S. E., Feng, X. B, Zhou, W. J, et al. 2012. Environment and genotype controls on mercury accumulation in rice (*Oryza sativa L.*) cultivated along a contamination gradient in Guizhou, China. Science of the Total Environment 426, 272–280.

Rothenberg, S. E., Yu, X. D., Zhang, Y. M. 2013. Prenatal methylmercury exposure through maternal rice ingestion: Insights from a feasibility pilot in Guizhou Province, China. Environmental Pollution 180, 291–298.

Shi, J. B., Liang, L. N., Jiang, G. B. 2005. Simultaneous determination of methylmercury and ethylmercury in rice by capillary gas chromatography coupled on-line with atomic fluorescence spectrometry. Journal of AOAC International 88, 665–669.

Silva, L. O. B., da Silva, D. G., Leao, D. J., et al. 2012. Slurry sampling for the determination of mercury in rice using cold vapor atomic absorption spectrometry. Food Analytical Methods 5, 1289–1295.

Srikumar, T. S. 1993. The mineral and trace element composition of vegetables, pulses and cereals of southern India. Food Chemistry 46, 163–167.

Stein, E. D., Cohen, Y., Winer, A. M. 1996. Environmental distribution and transformation of mercury compounds. Critical Reviews in Environmental Science and Technology 26, 1–43.

Strickman, R. J., Mitchell, C. P. 2017. Accumulation and translocation of methylmercury and inorganic mercury in *Oryza sativa*: An enriched isotope tracer study. Science of the Total Environment 574, 1415–1423.

Tang, W., Cheng, J. P., Zhao, W. C., et al. 2015. Mercury levels and estimated total daily intakes for children and adults from an electronic waste recycling area in Taizhou, China: Key role of rice and fish consumption. Journal of Environmental Sciences 34, 107–115.

Taylor, H., Appleton, J. D., Lister, R., et al. 2005. Environmental assessment of mercury contamination from the Rwamagasa artisanal gold mining centre, Geita District, Tanzania. Science of the Total Environment 343, 111–133.

Wang, Y. J., Habibullah-Al-Mamun, M., Han, J. L., et al. 2020. Total mercury and methylmercury in rice: Exposure and health implications in Bangladesh. Environmental Pollution 265, 114991.

Wang, L., Han, J. L., Katuwal, H. B., et al. 2021. Occurrence of total mercury and methylmercury in rice: Exposure and health implications in Nepal. Ecotoxicology and Environmental Safety 228, 113019.

Wang, Z. W., Sun, T., Driscoll, C. T., et al. 2018. Mechanism of accumulation of methylmercury in rice (*Oryza sativa L.*) in a mercury mining area. Environmental Science & Technology 52, 9749–9757.

WHO. 1991. Inorganic Mercury. Environmental health criteria 118. International Program on Chemical Safety, World Health Organization, Geneva.

Windham-Myers, L., Marvin-DiPasquale, M., Kakouros, E., et al. 2014. Mercury cycling in agricultural and managed wetlands of California, USA: Seasonal influences of vegetation on mercury methylation, storage, and transport. Science of the Total Environment 484, 308–318.

Xu, X. H., Han, J. L., Pang, J., et al. 2020. Methylmercury and inorganic mercury in Chinese commercial rice: Implications for overestimated human exposure and health risk. Environmental Pollution 258, 113706.

Xu, X. H., Lin, Y., Meng, B., et al. 2018. The impact of an abandoned mercury mine on the environment in the Xiushan region, Chongqing, southwestern China. Applied Geochemistry 88, 267–275.

Xu, X. H., Meng, B., Zhang, C., et al. 2017. The local impact of a coal-fired power plant on inorganic mercury and methyl-mercury distribution in rice (*Oryza sativa* L.). Environmental Pollution 223, 11–18.

Xu, Z. D., Abeysinghe, K. S., Xu, X. H., et al. 2019. New insights into the chemical forms of extremely high methylmercury in songbird feathers from a contaminated site. Chemosphere 225, 803–809.

Zhang, H., Feng, X. B., Larssen, T., et al. 2010a. Bioaccumulation of methylmercury versus inorganic mercury in rice (*Oryza sativa* L.) grain. Environmental Science & Technology 44, 4499–4504.

Zhang, H, Feng, X. B., Larssen, T., et al. 2010b. In inland China, rice, rather than fish is the major pathway for methylmercury exposure. Environmental Health Perspectives 118, 1183–1188.

Zhao, H. F., Yan, H. Y., Zhang, L. M., et al. 2019. Mercury contents in rice and potential health risks across China. Environment International 126, 406–412.

10 Mercury Stable Isotope Fractionation in the Paddy Field Ecosystem

Chongyang Qin, Runsheng Yin, Ping Li, and Xinbin Feng

10.1 INTRODUCTION

The unique flooded anaerobic environment in paddy fields is conducive to mercury (Hg) methylation, affected by biogeochemical factors, such as redox potential, pH, and dissolved organic carbon, sulfur, and iron, and dissolved Hg contents. Although fish consumption has been identified as one of the dominant exposure pathways of methylmercury (MeHg) worldwide, recent studies have confirmed rice consumption as another significant exposure route for residents in Hg-contaminated areas in Southwestern China (Feng et al., 2008; Zhang et al., 2010; Li et al., 2015; Li et al., 2017; Du et al., 2018). The paddy field is a complicated ecosystem, of which atmosphere, rainfall, irrigation water, overlying water, soil, and rice are important components. Understanding the mechanisms and processes of Hg transformation and accumulation in rice paddies is very important, as it could potentially guide remediation of mercury-contaminated paddy soil, inhibition of MeHg uptake in rice plants, and reduction of Hg exposure for residents.

With the development of MC–ICP–MS, it has become a reality to use Hg stable isotope ratios to identify the sources and fate of Hg in the environment. Mercury has seven natural stable isotopes, ^{196}Hg, ^{198}Hg, ^{199}Hg, ^{200}Hg, ^{201}Hg, ^{202}Hg, and ^{204}Hg, which undergo both mass-dependent fractionation (MDF, reported as δ^{202}Hg) and mass-independent fractionation (MIF, reported as Δ^{199}Hg, Δ^{200}Hg, and Δ^{201}Hg) via various physical-chemical and biological processes (Bergquist and Blum, 2007; Blum et al., 2014). Recent studies have demonstrated that Hg isotope compositions differ significantly among different source materials (Blum et al., 2014) and that Hg isotopes can be systematically fractionated during specific transformation reactions (Bergquist and Blum, 2007; Yang and Sturgeon, 2009; Zheng and Hintelmann, 2010; Qin et al., 2018). MDF occurred in most environmental processes, such as microbial methylation and demethylation (Janssen et al., 2016), abiotic methylation (Jimenez-Moreno et al., 2013), and Hg uptake by plants (Yin et al., 2013a). MIF is caused by the magnetic isotope effect (MIE) and the nuclear volume effect (NIE), while biotic and dark abiotic reactions do not produce significant amounts of MIF (Kwon et al., 2012; Blum et al., 2014). A negative MDF shift of 2.89‰ was observed during the uptake of Hg by foliage from the atmosphere (Yin et al., 2013a; Yuan et al., 2019); however, significant MIF was unlikely to occur during Hg metabolism processes in plants.

DOI: 10.1201/9781003404941-10

The absence of MIF during metabolism processes suggests that an Hg stable isotope can be a geochemical tool to trace the sources of Hg in paddy field ecosystems.

10.2 ATMOSPHERE

Atmospheric Hg plays a crucial role in the global Hg cycle. Hg in the atmosphere is defined in three major forms, namely gaseous elemental mercury (GEM), gaseous oxidized mercury (GOM), and particulate bound mercury (PBM), with the sum of GEM and GOM known as total gaseous mercury (TGM). At present, there are three methods to collect TGM for isotope measurement, gold trapping (Rolison et al., 2013), solution trapping (Yin et al., 2013a), and activated carbon trapping (Fu et al., 2014), of which solution trapping and activated carbon trapping are applied in rice paddy ecosystems for studying the Hg isotope of TGM (Yin et al., 2013a; Qin et al., 2020). For example, the solution trapping system was equipped with a vacuum pump with a flow rate of 2.5 L min^{-1}. The reactor vessel (glass bubbler, 100 mL) was loaded with 40 mL of trapping solution. Trapping solutions were prepared fresh daily by dissolving 0.1% $KMnO_4$ in 10% H_2SO_4. A 47-mm-diameter quartz fiber filter was utilized at the entrance of the glass bubbler to remove particulate matter. These preconcentration methods make it possible to determine the isotope of low atmospheric Hg concentrations.

The Hg isotope composition of atmospheric Hg is complex, derived from both anthropogenic and natural sources. The $\Delta^{199}Hg$ value is about 0 in a fumarole plume from an active volcano in Italy (Zambardi et al., 2009). However, the Hg^0 in Grand Bay, United States, displayed a significant negative $\Delta^{199}Hg$ value, from $-0.41‰$ to $-0.03‰$ (Gratz et al., 2010).Yin et al. (2013a) observed that the ambient atmosphere above the paddy water surface showed both negative MDF ($-2.32‰$ to $-1.85‰$ in $\delta^{202}Hg$) and negative MIF ($-0.34‰$ to $-0.24‰$ in $\Delta^{199}Hg$), which results from the multiple sources of the air samples, such as evaporation of GEM from the soil and vegetation, local anthropogenic emissions, and long-range transport of Hg from other areas. Qin et al. (2020) found less negative Hg isotope composition in the same area ($-0.95‰$ to $-0.37‰$ in $\delta^{202}Hg$, $-0.09‰$ to $-0.02‰$ in $\Delta^{199}Hg$), which was similar to the Hg isotope composition of mining wastes. Atmospheric Hg isotope characteristics are closely related to the source and may change with time. Therefore, to study the effect of atmospheric Hg on a rice paddy system, it is necessary to conduct a sampling of atmospheric mercury and the rice paddy system at the same time.

10.3 SOIL

Due to seasonable irrigation during the rice growing periods, rice paddy fields are recognized as an intermittent wetland ecosystem. Flooded paddy soils form an anaerobic environment that is conducive to microbial activity. The methylation/demethylation is largely controlled by the abundance and activity of microorganisms (Meng et al., 2014). The MeHg concentration in paddy soil is the consequence of both methylation and demethylation (Zhao et al., 2016). In Hg methylation experiments, sulfate-reducing bacteria in a pure culture caused MDF of stable Hg isotopes and generated MeHg enriched with lighter Hg isotopes (Rodriguez-Gonzalez et al., 2009; Perrot et al., 2015). The demethylation process results in the opposite isotopic fractionation. MeHg remaining in the reactors became progressively heavier (increasing the δ^{202}Hg value) over time as MeHg was degraded to volatile elemental Hg (Hg^0), similar to what has been found during the photo-decomposition of dissolved MeHg (Kritee et al., 2009; Malinovsky et al., 2010). By comparing sediment/soil sample MeHg isotopes with inorganic mercury (IHg) isotopes, it is possible to determine whether methylation or demethylation is dominant (Qin et al., 2018; Janssen et al., 2015).

MeHg stable isotopes are obtained by extracting MeHg from total mercury (THg), while IHg isotopes are obtained by calculating based on THg and MeHg stable isotopes. Approximately 0.2-g soil samples were digested in a water bath (95°C) using 5 mL of fresh mixture of HCl and HNO$_3$ (3:1, v/v) for THg isotope measurement (Yin et al., 2013a). A combination of gas chromatography column and solenoid valve was applied to separate MeHg from THg and enable researchers to measure MeHg isotopic composition eventually (Qin et al., 2018). Soil samples were digested with HNO$_3$ leaching solvent extracted method. The solutions were then ethylated and purged, with the vapor passing through a tenax tube. The trapped compounds were then released and went through a gas chromatography column and solenoid valve. The MeHg extraction was collected by a gold trap. The Hg in the gold trap was released by heating to 500°C for 3 min and subsequently trapped in a solution containing 20% HNO$_3$ and HCl (3:1, v/v). Hg trapped in the solution was subjected to MeHg isotope analysis. The IHg isotope values were calculated according to Eqs. 10.1 and 10.2:

$$\delta^{202}\text{Hg}_{\text{THg}} = \delta^{202}\text{Hg}_{\text{MeHg}} \times R + \delta^{202}\text{Hg}_{\text{IHg}} \times (1 - R) \tag{10.1}$$

$$\Delta^{199}\text{Hg}_{\text{THg}} = \Delta^{199}\text{Hg}_{\text{MeHg}} \times R + \Delta^{199}\text{Hg}_{\text{IHg}} \times (1 - R) \tag{10.2}$$

where R represents the ratio of MeHg to THg in the sample; $\delta^{202}\text{Hg}_{\text{THg}}$, $\delta^{202}\text{Hg}_{\text{MeHg}}$, and $\delta^{202}\text{Hg}_{\text{IHg}}$ represent the δ^{202}Hg values of THg, MeHg, and IHg, respectively; and $\Delta^{199}\text{Hg}_{\text{THg}}$, $\Delta^{199}\text{Hg}_{\text{MeHg}}$, and $\Delta^{199}\text{Hg}_{\text{IHg}}$ represent the Δ^{199}Hg values of THg, MeHg, and IHg, respectively.

MeHg is elevated in rice paddies, where flooded conditions enhance microbial activity and promote the conversion of less toxic IHg to MeHg, which can be taken up by the rice plant. The Hg in paddy soil in the Wanshan mercury mining (WSMM) area has been studied. There was no significant MIF of THg observed in paddy soil, as well as the two bioavailable Hg species, water–soluble Hg and (NH$_4$)$_2$S$_2$O$_3$– extractable Hg (Yin et al., 2013a). A similar result was found in Qin et al. (2018) research. The values of δ^{202}Hg and Δ^{199}Hg of THg in paddy soil averaged $-1.30 \pm 0.27‰$ and $-0.05 \pm 0.01‰$, respectively. Because of the extremely high proportion of IHg in THg (~99.98%) in soil, the calculated results for δ^{202}Hg and Δ^{199}Hg of IHg were equivalent to the THg measurements. However, a positive MIF signature was observed in the MeHg of paddy soil. The values of δ^{202}Hg and Δ^{199}Hg of MeHg in paddy soil averaged $-1.55 \pm 0.47‰$ and $0.13 \pm 0.03‰$, respectively. Methylation dominates the reaction between MeHg and IHg in paddy soil rather than demethylation, resulting in lighter Hg isotopes in the product MeHg (δ^{202}Hg of MeHg < δ^{202}Hg of IHg).

10.4   RICE PLANT

It has been found that rice paddies are a hotspot of Hg methylation. MeHg in paddy soils is absorbed by the roots of rice plants and translocated to the leaves, stalks, and grains. In contrast, IHg in rice plants originates from soil or/and the atmosphere. Meanwhile, MeHg and IHg exhibit distinct isotopic signatures of MDF and MIF. The selective extraction method (SEM) for compound-specific stable isotope analysis (CSIA) was applied to separate MeHg from IHg in biota samples, which demonstrated significantly different isotopic signatures between MeHg and IHg (Masbou et al., 2013). Li et al. (2017) applied a modified SEM for CSIA to paddy rice grain samples in WMMA and verified that atmospheric Hg contributed 31% ± 16% of IHg and 17% ± 11% of THg in rice grains and IHg in soil contributed to the remaining Hg in the grain.

The calculation of isotope values of IHg is based on the THg and MeHg isotope values, followed by Eqs. 10.1 and 10.2. About 5-g rice tissue samples were digested with a 5-mL mixture of HNO_3 and H_2SO_4 (4:1, v/v) for 3 h or digested in 5 mL of HNO_3 at 120°C for 6 h. The digest was then diluted with Milli–Q water to 15–25 vol % acid and adjusted to yield a reverse *aqua regia* solution (3:1 v/v HNO_3 and HCl) with a THg concentration of 1 ng/g for THg isotope analysis (Li et al., 2017).

A modified SEM was applied to extract MeHg from THg in rice tissue samples for MeHg isotope measurements (Li et al., 2017). An appropriate amount of rice sample (0.25–0.5 g) was extracted with 5 mL of acidic sodium bromide (30% w/w NaBr in 4 mol/L H_2SO_4), 10 mL of aqueous cupric sulfate (2.5% w/w $CuSO_4$), and 10 mL of toluene in a 50-mL centrifuge tube. The tube was shaken at 420 rpm for 1 h, and the toluene phase was then removed and back–extracted with aqueous sodium thiosulfate solution (0.005 mol/L). An aliquot of the aqueous phase (containing MeHg–thiosulfate complex) was transferred to a 5-mL tube and kept at 4°C until analysis for the MeHg isotope. The recovery and purity were used to determine the efficiency of the extraction process. Based on the results of previous measurement of THg and MeHg concentrations, the MeHg recovery was calculated from the ratio of THg in the purified solution to the initial MeHg concentration in rice tissues. The purity of MeHg in the extract was calculated from the percentage of MeHg in the THg concentration in each solution. Each purified MeHg–thiosulfate solution was diluted with a 3:1 v/v mixture of HNO_3 and HCl to give a final Hg concentration of 1 ng/g before the measurement of MeHg isotope compositions.

The values of $\delta^{202}Hg$ and $\Delta^{199}Hg$ of THg of the leaf were –3.28 ± 0.07‰ and –0.18± 0.05‰ in the artisanal mercury mining area. The root showed more positive THg isotope values, –1.86 ± 0.12‰ of $\delta^{202}Hg$ and –0.01 ± 0.05‰ of $\Delta^{199}Hg$ (Yin et al., 2013a). Although the Hg isotope compositions of rice plant tissues in different paddy fields are different, they all follow the same trend: leaf < stalk/grain < root (Chang et al., 2021). The difference in the isotope values of different plant tissues was mainly caused by different Hg sources. A study was carried out by sampling rice plants throughout the whole growing season, including the tilling stage (15 days), elongation stage (45 days), heading stage (75 days), and ripening stage (105 days), to show the biochemical cycle of MeHg and IHg by the isotope method (Qin et al., 2020). Similar regulation was found in IHg isotope values during the whole rice plant growing period, in which the values of $\delta^{202}Hg$ and $\Delta^{199}Hg$ followed the order

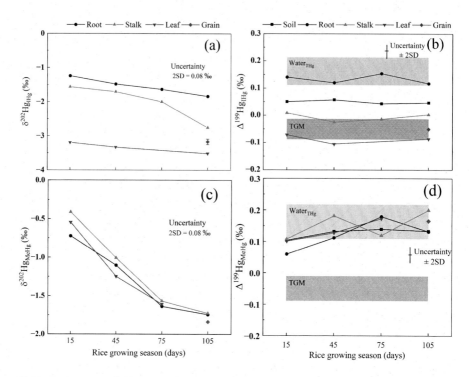

FIGURE 10.1   The δ^{202}Hg (a) and Δ^{199}Hg (b) values of IHg and the δ^{202}Hg (c) and Δ^{199}Hg (d) values of MeHg in different rice tissues and paddy ecosystems throughout the rice growing season. (Adapted with permission from Qin et al., 2020.)

of leaf < stalk/grain < root (Figure 10.1a and b). However, the characteristics of the MeHg isotope showed a different pattern (Figure 10.1c and d). Similar δ^{202}Hg values of MeHg were observed among roots, stalks, leaves, and grain at the same growth stage (Figure 10.1c). The decreasing of the δ^{202}Hg of MeHg in rice tissues might be caused by the mixing of isotopic signatures with that of rhizosphere soil before transplantation. The values of Δ^{199}Hg of MeHg in roots, stalks, leaves, and grains averaged 0.12 ± 0.10‰, 0.15 ± 0.09‰, 0.13 ± 0.07‰, and 0.17‰, respectively (Figure 10.1d). Compared to the results of THg isotope study, the isotopic character of IHg and MeHg in rice tissues showed that the unique adsorption of IHg and MeHg in rice plants should be taken into consideration.

10.5   QUANTIFYING MERCURY SOURCES IN RICE TISSUES USING MIF

Mass-independent fractionation of the Hg isotope is generally understood to be caused by the nuclear volume effect (NVE) and/or the magnetic isotope effect (MIE) (Schauble, 2007; Sonke, 2011). The NVE has been observed during abiotic dark Hg reduction (Zheng and Hintelmann, 2010), elemental Hg volatilization (Estrade et al., 2009), and equilibrium Hg^{II}–thiol complexation (Wiederhold et al., 2010).

The MIE has been documented during photochemical reactions of aqueous Hg species (e.g., MeHg and Hg^{2+}), during which the odd mass number isotopes were preferentially reduced and lost as Hg^0 (Bergquist and Blum, 2007). When $\Delta^{199}Hg$ vs. $\Delta^{201}Hg$ is plotted for each of these photochemical reduction processes, a slope of 1.36 is observed for MeHg and 1.00 for Hg^{2+} photoreduction (Bergquist and Blum, 2007). The $\Delta^{199}Hg/\Delta^{201}Hg$ ratio of ~1 observed in paddy plants demonstrated that a fraction of Hg had undergone a photoreduction process before being retained by the tissues of rice plants (Yin et al., 2013a; Chang et al., 2021). In paddy fields, flooding regimes are manipulated. From the water layer with high DOC contents in rice paddies arises the possibility of the photoreduction of aqueous Hg species.

The atmosphere and soil were considered the two main sources of rice plants. Hence, a "two–dimensional" model was used to calculate the fraction of atmospheric Hg^0 in the tissues of rice, as shown in Eqs. 10.3 and 10.4 (Yin et al., 2013a):

$$\delta^{202}Hg_{tissue} = f_A\Delta^{199}Hg_{atm} + (1 - f_A)\Delta^{199}Hg_{soil} \quad (10.3)$$

$$f_A(\%) = (\Delta^{199}Hg_{tissue} - \Delta^{201}Hg_{soil}) \times 100 / (\Delta^{199}Hg_{atm} - \Delta^{199}Hg_{soil}) \quad (10.4)$$

where $\Delta^{199}Hg_{tissue}$ is the $\Delta^{199}Hg$ value of tissues in rice plants; $\Delta^{199}Hg_{tissue}$ and $\Delta^{199}Hg_{tissue}$ are the $\Delta^{199}Hg$ values of the atmospheric Hg and soil Hg, respectively; and $f_A(\%)$ is the fraction of atmospheric Hg source. The calculation results are shown in Figure 10.2. As the results indicate, rice leaves predominantly incorporate Hg^0 from the atmosphere, whereas the uptake of Hg from the root to the leaf is believed to be of less importance. The $f_A(\%)$ in the leaves is 111.7 ± 26.7% and

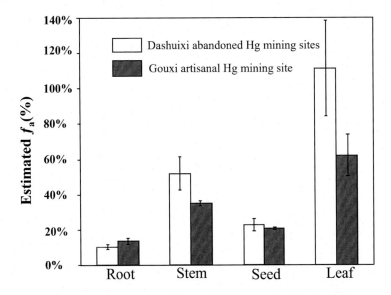

FIGURE 10.2 Estimated fraction of atmospheric Hg in different tissues of rice plants collected from the Dashuixi abandoned Hg mining site and the Gouxi artisanal Hg mining site. (Adapted) with permission from Yin et al., 2013a.)

$61.7 \pm 12.1\%$, and the fraction in roots is as low as $10.3 \pm 1.1\%$ and $12.4 \pm 2.9\%$. Atmospheric elemental Hg is mildly lipophilic in nature and can diffuse through the cuticle. The THg isotope signature was well applied to quantify the Hg source in the rice plant, but the differential behaviors of IHg and MeHg in the rice plant were not considered.

In the results of Qin et al. (2020), the characters of MDF and MIF of MeHg and IHg were significantly different in paddy soil and rice plants. Although rice plants continuously absorbed MeHg from the surrounding environment during the growth period, the Δ^{199}Hg values of MeHg were very similar in different rice tissues and did not change with the growing period (Figure. 10.1d). The Δ^{199}Hg values can be used as an effective tracer to understand the influence of different Hg sources in biota because no MIF occurred during the metabolism process (Gehrke et al., 2011). The consistency of positive Δ^{199}Hg values of MeHg between paddy soil ($0.13 \pm 0.03\text{‰}$) and rice tissues ($0.14 \pm 0.08\text{‰}$) indicated that MeHg in soil was the main source of MeHg in rice plants, as had also been confirmed previously (Meng et al., 2011; Strickman and Mitchell, 2017). Additionally, Δ^{199}Hg values of MeHg in soil were wihin the range of those of irrigation water ($0.17 \pm 0.09\text{‰}$). Higher MeHg concentrations were observed in the pore water than in the surface water (Rothenberg and Feng, 2012), indicating that IHg methylation mainly occurred in the soil subsurface. Hg with a positive Δ^{199}Hg signal in paddy water might be methylated by microorganisms (sulfate-reducing bacteria, iron-reducing bacteria, methanogens, and so on) in the soil and taken up by rice plants (Qin et al., 2020). The consistency of MeHg isotope values of irrigation water and soil indicated that the Hg–methylation process played an important role in the rice paddy system. However, there is a lack of study of the compound-specific Hg isotopes of the water–soil system in the paddy field. More Hg isotope measurements are needed for investigating methylation and/ or demethylation processes in paddy soil and water.

In order to identify the relative contributions to IHg in rice tissues from air, soil, and water, a mixing model was applied based on Δ^{199}Hg data (Eqs. 10.5, 10.6, 10.7, and 10.8) (Qin et al., 2020).

$$\Delta^{199}\text{Hg}_{\text{IHg-root}} = \Delta^{199}\text{Hg}_{\text{air}} \times f_{\text{water}} + \Delta^{199}\text{Hg}_{\text{IHg-soil}} \times f_{\text{soil}} \tag{10.5}$$

$$f_{\text{water}} + f_{\text{soil}} = 1 \tag{10.6}$$

$$\Delta^{199}\text{Hg}_{\text{IHg-tissue}} = \Delta^{199}\text{Hg}_{\text{air}} \times f_{\text{air}} + \Delta^{199}\text{Hg}_{\text{IHg-soil}} \times f_{\text{root}} \tag{10.7}$$

$$f_{\text{ATM}} + f_{\text{root}} = 1 \tag{10.8}$$

where $\Delta^{199}\text{Hg}_{\text{IHg-tissue}}$ represents the Δ^{199}Hg of IHg of leaf, stalk, and grain; $\Delta^{199}\text{Hg}_{\text{air}}$ and $\Delta^{199}\text{Hg}_{\text{water}}$ represent the Δ^{199}Hg value of THg in the ambient atmosphere and water, respectively; $\Delta^{199}\text{Hg}_{\text{IHg-soil}}$ represents Δ^{199}Hg of IHg in rhizosphere soil; and f_{air}, f_{water}, f_{root}, and f_{soil} are fractions of IHg from ambient air, water, roots, and soil, respectively.

In the results of Qin et al. (2020), IHg in leaves ($-0.07 \pm 0.02\text{‰}$), grain (-0.05‰), stalk ($0.02 \pm 0.02\text{‰}$), and roots ($0.13 \pm 0.03\text{‰}$) showed different Δ^{199}Hg values. However, Δ^{199}Hg values in each rice tissue remained consistent during the whole rice

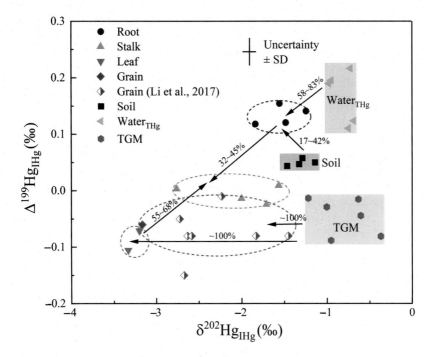

FIGURE 10.3 δ^{202}Hg and Δ^{199}Hg values of IHg of the paddy ecosystem and source appointment results. The squares represent the isotopic characteristics of each end-member. The circles represent the isotopic characteristics of rice tissues. The arrow indicates the direction of IHg transportation and the percentage represents the proportion of transportation. (Adapted with permission from Qin et al., 2020.)

growing season (Figure 10.1b). Water was considered one of the important sources of Hg in roots because the isotopic evidence showed that the average Δ^{199}Hg of IHg in roots (0.13 ± 0.03‰) fell in between those of water (0.17 ± 0.09‰) and soil (0.05 ± 0.01‰). Assuming that roots received IHg exclusively from paddy water and soil, the mixing model (Eqs. 10.5 and 10.6) would predict 58–83% and 17–42% contributions to the IHg in rice roots from water and soil, respectively (Figure 10.3). The average Δ^{199}Hg of IHg in leaves, grains, and stalks was much lower than that in roots. Therefore, these tissues also received IHg from the atmosphere because only TGM showed a negative Δ^{199}Hg signal among the three potential sources. The calculation results indicated that nearly ~100% of the IHg in leaves and grains was from the atmosphere. Similar results were received from the enriched isotope tracing experiment, in which Strickman and Mitchell (2017) indicated that rice leaves and grains uptake IHg entirely from the atmosphere. According to the contributions from water and soil to the IHg in roots (Eqs. 10.5, 10.6, 10.7, and 10.8), it was calculated that 12–24%, 5–10%, and 66–83% of the IHg in stalks was from water, soil, and atmosphere, respectively (Figure 10.3). The individual isotopic characteristics of IHg in each tissue of the rice plants indicated that the transport of IHg between tissues was restricted. The tissues under the water (roots, a small part of stalks) were controlled by the IHg in soil and water, and the parts above water (leaves, grains, and most parts of the stalks) were controlled by the IHg in the atmosphere. Measurement of the specific stable Hg isotope is a powerful tool for tracking the sources and procedures of Hg and certainly has increased our understanding of the biogeochemical cycle of MeHg and IHg in the paddy ecosystem.

10.6 MASS-DEPENDENT FRACTIONATION OF Hg IN RICE PLANTS

MDF occurs during biogeochemical processes, such as micro-reduction (Kritee et al., 2008), methylation (Rodriguez-Gonzalez et al., 2009), photoreduction (Bergquist and Blum, 2007), volatilization (Zheng et al., 2007), and adsorption-desorption (Wiederhold et al. 2010; Yin et al. 2013b), and results in a relatively lower δ^{202}Hg in the products. The mean δ^{202}Hg values of rice leaves were much lower than those of ambient air at both an abandoned Hg mining site and an artisanal Hg mining site, and the mean δ^{202}Hg values of rice roots were much lower than those of paddy soil (Yin et al., 2013a). In another study, δ^{202}Hg values of IHg in roots (–1.53 ± 0.49‰), stalks (–2.01 ± 1.07‰), leaves (–3.26 ± 0.08‰), and grains (–3.16‰) were significantly lower than those in paddy soil, paddy water, and the atmosphere (Qin et al., 2020). δ^{202}Hg values of IHg decreased in varying degrees with the growing season (Figure 10.1a), suggesting the bioaccumulation of lighter Hg isotopes in rice tissues. A negative shift of δ^{202}Hg in IHg (~0.21‰) was observed between rhizosphere soil and roots, suggesting that significant MDF occurred during the uptake of IHg by roots. Light isotopes were preferentially absorbed by plants because transport through ion channels and/or electrogenic pumps in root cell membranes preferred the uptake of the lighter isotope due to its greater diffusion coefficient (Kiczka et al., 2010). Unlike roots, leaves mostly take up IHg from Hg^0 in the ambient air (Qin et al., 2020). A shift of –2.4‰ in δ^{202}Hg between leaf IHg and that of the atmosphere was observed, which was consistent with the previous results that negative shifts of –3.0‰ to –1.0‰ in δ^{202}Hg occurred between air and leaves. In the harvest season, the consistency of δ^{202}Hg of MeHg between rhizosphere soil and rice tissues after the heading stage suggested that MDF had not occurred during the uptake of MeHg from soil by rice plants and the transfer process in plants (Figure 10.1c), which was different from the uptake of IHg in rice tissues. The absence of fractionation of Hg has been observed during the trophic transfer of MeHg to freshwater fish. More research on Hg isotope fractionation is needed in the future.

10.7 SUMMARY

Rice consumption is one of the major pathways of MeHg exposure in the inland areas of South China. It is an emerging concern because rice is an important dietary component not only in China but also in many other parts of the world. The observations of MeHg and IHg fractions in rice are isotopically different. Further studies of Hg specific isotopes in the paddy ecosystem will improve our understanding of the biogeochemical cycle of Hg.

REFERENCES

Bergquist, B. A. and Blum, J. D., 2007. Mass-dependent and -independent fractionation of hg isotopes by photoreduction in aquatic systems. Science (New York, N.Y.) 318(5849): 417–420.

Blum, J., Sherman, L. S., and Johnson, M. W., 2014. Mercury isotopes in earth and environmental sciences. Annual Review of Earth and Planetary Sciences 42: 249–269.

Chang, C., Yin, R., Huang, F., et al., 2021. Understanding the bioaccumulation of mercury in rice plants at the Wanshan mercury mine, China: Using stable mercury isotopes. Journal of Geophysical Research-Biogeosciences 126(2): e2020JG006103.

Du, B., Feng, X., Li, P., et al., 2018. Use of mercury isotopes to quantify mercury exposure sources in inland populations, China. Environmental Science & Technology 52(9): 5407–5416.

Estrade, N., Carignan, J., Sonke, J. E., et al., 2009. Mercury isotope fractionation during liquid–vapor evaporation experiments. Geochimica et Cosmochimica Acta 73(10): 2693–2711.

Feng, X., Li, P., Qiu, G., et al., 2008. Human exposure to methylmercury through rice intake in mercury mining areas, Guizhou Province, China. Environmental Science & Technology 42(1): 326–332.

Fu, X., Heimbürger, L. E., and Sonke, J. E., 2014. Collection of atmospheric gaseous mercury for stable isotope analysis using iodine- and chlorine-impregnated activated carbon traps. Journal of Analytical Atomic Spectrometry 29(5): 841–852.

Gehrke, G. E., Blum, J. D., Slotton, D. G., et al., 2011. Mercury isotopes link mercury in San Francisco Bay forage fish to surface sediments. Environmental Science & Technology 45(4): 1264–1270.

Gratz, L. E., Keeler, G. J., Blum, J. D., et al., 2010. Isotopic composition and fractionation of mercury in Great Lakes precipitation and ambient air. Environmental Science & Technology 44(20): 7764–7770.

Janssen, S. E., Johnson, M. W., Blum, J. D., et al., 2015. Separation of monomethylmercury from estuarine sediments for mercury isotope analysis. Chemical Geology 411: 19–25.

Janssen, S. E., Schaefer, J. K., Barkay, T., et al., 2016. Fractionation of mercury stable isotopes during microbial methylmercury production by iron- and sulfate-reducing bacteria. Environmental Science & Technology 50(15): 8077–8083.

Jimenez-Moreno M., Maria, P., Vincent, E., et al., 2013. Chemical kinetic isotope fractionation of mercury during abiotic methylation of Hg(II) by methylcobalamin in aqueous chloride media. Chemical Geology 336: 26–36.

Kiczka, M., Wiederhold, J. G., Kraemer, S. M., et al., 2010. Iron isotope fractionation during Fe uptake and translocation in alpine plants. Environmental Science & Technology 44(16): 6144–6150.

Kritee, K., Barkay, T., and Blum, J. D., 2009. Mass dependent stable isotope fractionation of mercury during mer mediated microbial degradation of monomethylmercury. Geochimica et Cosmochimica Acta 73(5): 1285–1296.

Kritee, K., Blum, J. D., and Barkay, T., 2008. Mercury stable isotope fractionation during reduction of Hg(II) by different microbial pathways. Environmental Science & Technology 42(24): 9171–9177.

Kwon, S. Y., Blum, J. D., Carvan, M. J., et al., 2012. Absence of fractionation of mercury isotopes during trophic transfer of methylmercury to freshwater fish in captivity. Environmental Science & Technology 46(14): 7527–7534.

Li, P., Du, B., Maurice, L., et al., 2017. Mercury isotope signatures of methylmercury in rice samples from the Wanshan mercury mining area, China: Environmental implications. Environmental Science & Technology 51(21): 12321–12328.

Li, P., Feng, X., Chan, H., et al., 2015. Human body burden and dietary methylmercury intake: The relationship in a rice-consuming population. Environmental Science & Technology 49(16): 9682–9689.

Malinovsky, D., Latruwe, K., Moens, L., et al., 2010. Experimental study of mass-independence of Hg isotope fractionation during photodecomposition of dissolved methylmercury. Journal of Analytical Atomic Spectrometry 25: 950–956.

Masbou, J., Point, D., and Sonke, J. E., 2013. Application of a selective extraction method for methylmercury compound specific stable isotope analysis (MeHg-CSIA) in biological materials. Journal of Analytical Atomic Spectrometry 28(10): 1620–1628.

Meng, B., Feng, X., Qiu, G., et al., 2011. The process of methylmercury accumulation in rice (*Oryza sativa* L.). Environmental Science & Technology 45(7): 2711–2717.

Meng, B., Feng, X., Qiu, G., et al., 2014. Localization and speciation of mercury in brown rice with implications for pan-Asian public health. Environmental Science & Technology 48(14): 7974–7981.

Perrot, V., Bridou, R., Pedrero, Z., et al., 2015. Identical Hg isotope mass dependent fractionation signature during methylation by sulfate-reducing bacteria in sulfate and sulfate-free environment. Environmental Science & Technology 49(3): 1365–1373.

Qin, C., Chen, M., Yan, H., et al., 2018. Compound specific stable isotope determination of methylmercury in contaminated soil. Environmental Science & Technology 644: 406–412.

Qin, C., Du, B., Yin, R., et al., 2020. Isotopic fractionation and source appointment of methylmercury and inorganic mercury in a paddy ecosystem. Environmental Science & Technology 54(22): 14334–14342.

Rodriguez G., Pablo, E., Vladimir N., et al., 2009. Species-specific stable isotope fractionation of mercury during Hg(II) methylation by an anaerobic bacteria (*Desulfobulbus propionicus*) under dark conditions. Environmental Science & Technology 43(24): 9183–9188.

Rolison, J. M., Landing, W. M., Luke, W., et al., 2013. Isotopic composition of species-specific atmospheric Hg in a coastal environment. Chemical Geology 336: 37–49.

Rothenberg, S. E. and Feng, X., 2012. Mercury cycling in a flooded rice paddy. Journal of Geophysical Research-Biogeosciences 117: G03003.

Schauble, E. A., 2007. Role of nuclear volume in driving equilibrium stable isotope fractionation of mercury, thallium, and other very heavy elements. Geochimica et Cosmochimica Acta 71(9): 2170–2189.

Sonke, J. E., 2011. A global model of mass independent mercury stable isotope fractionation. Geochimica et Cosmochimica Acta 75(16): 4577–4590.

Strickman, R. J. and Mitchell, C. P. J., 2017. Accumulation and translocation of methylmercury and inorganic mercury in *Oryza sativa*: An enriched isotope tracer study. Science of the Total Environment 574: 1415–1423.

Wiederhold, J. G., Cramer, C. J., Daniel, K., et al., 2010. Equilibrium mercury isotope fractionation between dissolved Hg(II) species and thiol-bound Hg. Environmental Science & Technology 44(11): 4191–4197.

Yang, L. and Sturgeon, R. E., 2009. Isotopic fractionation of mercury induced by reduction and ethylation. Analytical and Bioanalytical Chemistry 393(1): 377–385.

Yin, R., Feng, X., and Meng, B., 2013a. Stable mercury isotope variation in rice plants (*Oryza sativa* L.) from the Wanshan mercury mining district, SW China. Environmental Science & Technology 47(5): 2238–2245.

Yin, R., Feng, X., Wang, J., et al., 2013b. Mercury isotope variations between bioavailable mercury fractions and total mercury in mercury contaminated soil in Wanshan mercury mine, SW China. Chemical Geology 336: 80–86.

Yuan, W., Sommar, J., Lin, C., et al., 2019. Stable isotope evidence shows re-emission of elemental mercury vapor occurring after reductive loss from foliage. Environmental Science & Technology 53(2): 651–660.

Zambardi, T., Sonke, J. E., Toutain, J. P., et al., 2009. Mercury emissions and stable isotopic compositions at Vulcano Island (Italy). Earth and Planetary Science Letters 277(1–2): 236–243.

Zhang, H., Feng, X., Larssen, T., et al., 2010. In inland China, rice, rather than fish, is the major pathway for methylmercury exposure. Environmental Health Perspectives 118(9): 1183–1188.

Zhao, L., Anderson, C. W. N., Qiu, G., et al., 2016. Mercury methylation in paddy soil: Source and distribution of mercury species at a Hg mining area, Guizhou Province, China. Biogeosciences 13(8): 2429–2440.

Zheng, W. and Hintelmann, H., 2010. Nuclear field shift effect in isotope fractionation of mercury during abiotic reduction in the absence of light. The Journal of Physical Chemistry. A 114(12): 4238–4245.

Zheng, W., Foucher, D., Hintelmann, H., 2007. Mercury isotope fractionation during volatilization of Hg(0) from solution into the gas phase. Journal of Analytical Atomic Spectrometry 22(9): 1097–1104.

11 Impact of Sulfur on Biogeochemical Transformation of Mercury in Paddy Fields and Its Uptake by Rice

Jiating Zhao, Qingliang Chen, Yuxi Gao, and Yufeng Li

11.1 INTRODUCTION

Mercury (Hg) is a toxic element and ubiquitous in the environment. Mercury in soils originates from parent rocks, atmospheric Hg deposition, the irrigation of sewage, the use of pesticides and fertilizers, Hg mining and retorting activities, etc. The paddy field is a human-made wetland ecosystem because of the alternating processes of flooding and drainage periodically. The paddy field is favorable for Hg methylation after flooding, as an anaerobic environment stimulates the activities of Hg-methylation microorganisms (Porvari and Verta, 1995; Murase et al., 2006). Therefore, the paddy field is a hotspot of methylmercury (MeHg) in terrestrial ecosystems (Steffan et al., 1988; Roulet et al., 2001). There is a potential for the transfer of MeHg into the food chain through rice. Mercury contamination in rice attracts global concern, as over half of the world's population relies on rice as their primary source of food.

Mercury in rice plants is sourced from both soil and the atmosphere. A plant's leaves can take up Hg^0 from the atmosphere, and its roots can accumulate Hg from soil. Mercury in rice leaves primarily originates in the atmosphere, while Hg in rice roots largely derives from soil. Mercury in rice stalks comes from both the atmosphere and soil. As for MeHg, it primarily originates in soil. According to Meng et al. (2011), the concentration of MeHg in different tissues of rice mainly depends on the content of MeHg in soil. The accumulation of MeHg by rice is dynamic during the rice growing season. MeHg in soil is accumulated by roots and subsequently translocated to stalks, where it is stored until filling stage, and finally moved to grain at the maturing stage (Meng et al., 2011). The migration and transformation of Hg in paddy fields are affected by various factors, including atmospheric Hg dry and wet depositions, agricultural irrigation, the content and speciation of mercury in soil, etc.

Agricultural activities such as fertilization can enhance the mobilization of Hg in soils. For example, the application of organic fertilizer can reduce the adsorption of

 DOI: 10.1201/9781003404941-11

Hg^{2+} in soil, resulting in the release of Hg^{2+} and facilitating its uptake by rice, thereby enhancing its bioavailability.

Sulfur is not only an important biogenic element in soil but also an essential nutrient for plants. Sulfur is involved in numerous vital biochemical reactions in plants, including photosynthesis and promoting plant growth, development, metabolism, and other physiological processes. A deficiency of sulfur can inhibit the growth of plants, even resulting in wilting and death. Therefore, the application of adequate sulfur fertilizer is crucial for promoting plant growth.

Being Group IV elements in the periodic table, sulfur and selenium share similar physical and chemical properties. Soil amended with selenium substantially increases rice yield, while it reduces the translocation of inorganic Hg (IHg) and MeHg to the above-ground tissues, as well as the accumulation of total Hg (THg) and MeHg in rice plants (Zhang et al., 2012; Li et al., 2015; Zhao et al., 2020; Liu et al., 2022). Despite the ability of Se amendment to decrease Hg accumulation in rice, the scale-up of this method of soil remediation is limited. As an alternative, sulfur has potential in Hg remediation. Sulfur has a close geochemical association with Hg, and it can react with Hg to form HgS, by which Hg bioavailability is reduced. Sulfur-containing compounds are suitable amendments for remediation of Hg-polluted paddy soil, as they can both reduce Hg bioavailability and provide nutrients to plants. Knowledge of the impact of sulfur-containing compounds on the bioavailability of mercury and methylmercury in soil is important for using these compounds in Hg remediation.

Therefore, it is of great significance to investigate the influence of sulfur amendment on the bioavailability and uptake of Hg by rice plants. Results are important for using sulfur-containing compounds as an amendment in remediation of Hg-polluted soil and reducing the associated risk of Hg exposure.

11.2 PRINCIPLE OF THIOMERCURIC REACTION

Sulfur in soil is derived from various sources, including sulfur-containing minerals, organic matter, the precipitation of sulfur-containing acid rain, and the application of sulfur-containing fertilizer (Figure 11.1) (Li et al., 2023a). Sulfur in soil mainly exists in the organic or inorganic form, with the former being dominant. Organic sulfur can be categorized into sulfate in which sulfur is bonded to organic groups via –O– or –N– bonds and sulfur bonded directly to carbon through carbon-sulfur bonds (C-S). Inorganic sulfur can be operationally defined as water-soluble sulfur, adsorption sulfur, and hydrochloric acid-soluble sulfur (Nriagu and Soon, 1985; Roberts and Bettany, 1985).

Sulfur and its compounds can undergo transformations with the help of microorganisms under different environmental conditions, promoting the biogeochemical cycle of sulfur. The sulfur cycle in soil substantially impacts the biogeochemical processes of heavy metals. Under aerobic conditions, soil-dwelling sulfur-oxidizing bacteria (SOB) are capable of oxidizing elemental sulfur, resulting in the formation of SO_4^{2-} (Gao and Fan, 2023). This process is coupled to the mobilization of heavy metals, resulting in an increase of the bioavailability of heavy metals to plants. Under anaerobic conditions, sulfate is subjected to reduction to form sulfide (S^{2-}),

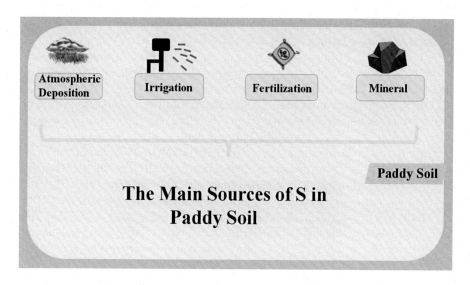

FIGURE 11.1   The main sources of sulfur in soil. (Modified from Li et al., 2023a.)

which can then react with heavy metals such as Hg^{2+}, Cu^{2+}, and Cd^{2+}, resulting in the formation of metal sulfides (Xu and Chen, 2020). This process immobilizes heavy metals, reducing their uptake by plants. Hence, the addition of sulfate in order to promote the formation of sulfide can mitigate the bioavailability of heavy metals by forming metal sulfides. Knowledge of the mechanism of the Hg transformation mediated by sulfur is crucial for assessing the fate of Hg and developing strategies by amendment of sulfur to mitigate Hg risks.

Sulfur is an important component of soil organic matter. Although sulfur is less abundant in soil than oxygen and nitrogen, Hg has a preferential affinity for sulfur. Hesterberg et al. (2001) investigated the binding of Hg to sulfur of humic acid using both X-ray near edge absorption spectroscopy (XANES) and extended X-ray absorption fine structure spectroscopy (EXAFS). They found that Hg preferentially binds to sulfhydryl groups by forming stable covalent compounds with these groups over the oxygen-containing and nitrogen-containing functional groups. The stable covalent bonds formed between Hg(II) and sulfhydryl groups remain stable even during the LC-MS/MS process (Guo et al., 2008). Therefore, the use of inorganic or organic sulfur compounds to precipitate, complex, or chelate with Hg is possible to reduce the mobility and bioavailability of Hg.

The prevalent process of Hg transformation in soil is regarded as the formation of stable complexes through the interaction between soil Hg(II) and reduced sulfur (-S) or sulfhydryl groups of soluble organic matter (Yin et al., 1997; Skyllberg et al., 2006; Skyllberg, 2008). The reduced sulfur groups of humic acids (HA) and dissolved organic matter (DOM) influence the chemical speciation of Hg. Under anaerobic conditions, when the concentration of reduced HA is lower than 0.2 mg/L, it can reduce Hg(II) to Hg^0, and the effect of Hg(II) reduction becomes weaker with the increasing of HA concentration. When the concentration of HA is greater than 0.2 mg/L, it can mediate Hg^0 oxidation to form stable covalent compounds

(Gu et al., 2011). The oxidation rate of Hg(0) is predominantly influenced by factors including the chemical structure of the sulfhydryl group, sulfhydryl/Hg ratio, short fatty sulfhydryl groups, etc. For example, the high mercaptoethanol and sulfhydryl/ Hg ratios are more conducive to the oxidation of Hg(0) (Zheng et al., 2013). All these transformation processes can affect the speciation of Hg in soil and sediment and thus impact the Hg availability for bacteria-mediated Hg methylation.

The reduced sulfur, such as sulfide from the reduction of sulfate mediated by SRBs or from the decomposition of organic sulfur by sulfur-containing amino acid degrading bacteria, can combine with Hg(II) to form HgS precipitates (Figure 12.2). The bioavailability of HgS to SRBs is weaker than that of soluble Hg, and thus the presence of sulfide may limit Hg methylation (Benoit et al., 1999a; Hintelmann et al., 2000). Earlier studies suggested that HgS has limited bioavailability for methylation (Winfrey and Rudd, 1990a). However, the presence of DOM can affect the binding of Hg to sulfide by forming $HgHS^{2-}$, $Hg(HS)_2^{0}$, HgS_2^{2-}, and $HgS^0_{(aq)}$, among which the neutral Hg-containing complexes such as $HgS^0_{(aq)}$ can diffuse across membranes into bacteria for methylation. The presence of excess S^{2-} can lead to the formation of charged Hg(I) S_2 and other complexes, which are difficult crossing the microbial cell membrane for methylation (Benoit et al., 1999b). However, certain fat-soluble neutral Hg polysulfide molecules are bioavailable to microorganisms to some extent (Figure 11.2) (Jay et al., 2000). Under oxidization conditions, sulfur-oxidizing bacteria can oxidize S^{2-}, by which HgS can be partially mobilized (Figure 11.2). Therefore, one should be aware of the potential mobilization of HgS under oxidization conditions.

In addition to inducing Hg speciation transformation in soil, sulfur can also affect the iron plaque of rice plants. Iron plaque, primarily composed of iron oxides, on the surface of the root of aquatic plants can affect the mobility and availability of

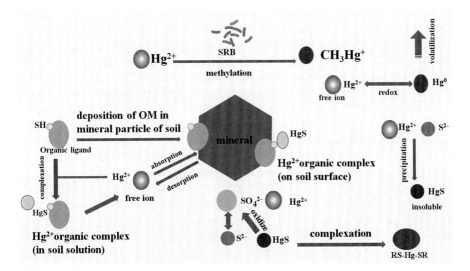

FIGURE 11.2 The coupled transformation of mercury and sulfur in the environment. (Modified from Hu et al., 2023.)

heavy metals through adsorption and/or co-precipitation (Li et al., 2016a; Fan et al., 2023). The formation of iron plaque on the root surface is closely associated with the geochemical cycle of sulfur. The addition of sulfur-containing amendment to paddy soil can impact the formation of iron plaque on the root surface of rice, which in turn will affect the accumulation of heavy metals in rice.

In contrast to immobilization, several studies have shown that the presence of elemental sulfur can enhance the mobilization of heavy metals in soil by lowering soil pH, thereby enhancing plants' uptake of heavy metals. Also, pyrite (FeS_2) can be oxidized by microorganisms such as *acidithiobacillus thiooxidans, ferrooxidans,* and other acidophilic bacteria to produce sulfite or sulfuric acid. This process can cause acidification of soil, enhancing the mobilization of heavy metals (Dopson and Johnson, 2012). These studies highlight the potential of sulfur and its compounds in the mobilization of heavy metals. Further, it is necessary to evaluate the potential environmental risks induced by application of sulfur.

It is clear that sulfur plays a complicated and important role in controlling the transformation and migration of Hg. More research is needed to explore the effect and mechanism of sulfur addition on Hg speciation transformation and bioavailability in the soil-rice system for controlling Hg uptake by rice.

11.3   THE EFFECT OF SULFUR ON Hg TRANSFORMATION, UPTAKE, AND ACCUMULATION IN RICE

Sulfate in soil is sourced from acid deposition, soil fertilization, irrigation, etc. The presence of sulfur strongly affects the transformation of Hg in soils, thereby influencing Hg toxicity and its accumulation by rice.

The formation of MeHg is closely associated with the sulfur cycle. Previous studies have demonstrated that MeHg in sediment primarily originates from microbial methylation processes involving Hg(II) and elemental Hg under anaerobic conditions (Graham et al., 2012; Small and Hintelmann, 2014; Wang et al., 2014; Strickman and Mitchell, 2017). Sulfate-reducing bacteria (SRBs) presenting in anaerobic sediments serve as the primary producer of MeHg (Gilmour et al., 1992; Achá et al., 2011) (Figure 11.3), as revealed by a positive correlation between the methylation rate of Hg in the sediment column and the concentrations of sulfate ($r = 0.97$) and organic matter ($r = 0.83$) and the sulfate reduction rate ($r = 0.99$). Also, the methylation of inorganic Hg and elemental Hg exhibited a positive correlation with the rate of sulfate reduction in sediment (Gilmour et al., 1992; King et al., 2000; Achá et al., 2011). Indeed, the addition of SO_4^{2-} increases the number and type of SRBs and thus affects the methylation of Hg (Yu et al., 2012, 2013). Rothenberg and Feng (2012) studied the dynamic of MeHg in pore water of a paddy field during the rice growing season, and they found that the level of MeHg was positively correlated with the concentration of sulfate. The above studies suggested that sulfate could enhance the formation of MeHg. Further studies demonstrated that the effect of sulfate on MeHg formation is dependent on the concentration of sulfate. Gilmour and Henry (1991) found that in a freshwater lake with a low sulfate concentration, an increase of SO_4^{2-} was favorable for the production of MeHg in sediments. They speculated that a 0.2–0.5 mM

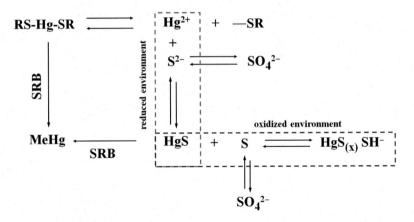

FIGURE 11.3   Reaction of different species of sulfur with Hg. (Modified from Hu et al., 2023.)

concentration of SO_4^{2-} favors the Hg methylation. When excessive SO_4^{2-} was added, the methylation of Hg by SRBs was inhibited.

Moreover, experimental results from SRBs cultured in freshwater sediment showed that the addition of sulfate produced more MeHg than non-sulfate and excessive sulfate treatments (Shao et al., 2012). The high concentration of SO_4^{2-} inhibits MeHg formation (Benoit et al., 2001; Ullrich et al., 2001; Skyllberg and Drott, 2010). In a soil polluted by the discharge of Hg-containing sewage, etc., the effect of elemental sulfur and sulfate addition on Hg accumulation depends on the amount of elemental sulfur or sulfate. The decrease of Hg methylation by sulfate is attributed to the fact that the reduction of sulfate produces sulfide, polysulfide, or sulfhydryl, all of which can bind with Hg^{2+} to form Hg sulfide complexes (Benoit et al., 2001; Skyllberg and Drott, 2010), which are often less bioavailable to microorganisms (Benoit et al., 1999b) (Figure 11.3). However, sulfide can also react with HgS to form highly active polysulfides, which are bioavailable to SRBs to some extent. Therefore, the amount of sulfate input into soil is critical for controlling MeHg in soil (Shao et al., 2012). Furthermore, laboratory study has shown that excessive sulfides can promote the transformation of MeHg into volatile dimethylmercury (Me_2Hg) (Baldi et al., 1995). However, it is unclear whether this conversion occurs in the natural environment.

Sulfate can also affect plant uptake of Hg by regulation of thiol-containing molecules in plants. Plants can accumulate sulfate to assimilate it to thioglycolic-rich glutathione and metallothionein, which can chelate and sequester with Hg^{2+} to reduce the toxicity of Hg^{2+}. Thus, the addition of sulfate can enhance the tolerance of plants to Hg stress.

The influence of elemental sulfur amendment on methylmercury (MeHg) accumulation in rice and the chemical form of Hg in the rhizosphere were investigated under water-logged conditions in a pot experiment (Li et al., 2019b). Results showed that the proportion of residual Hg fraction in soil decreases with an increase of elemental sulfur amendment (50–2000 mg/kg), while the proportion of organic bound Hg shows the opposite trend, indicating that S(0) input might mobilize the non-bioavailable Hg in the rhizospheric soil and enhance the net Hg methylation. This change of Hg speciation by sulfur amendment can affect Hg mobility and its uptake by rice.

The application of an appropriate amount of sulfur can significantly reduce the accumulation of Hg in rice. For example, the addition of 0 to 500 mg/kg of either elemental sulfur or sulfate can significantly reduce the Hg concentration in rice, with the effect of elemental sulfur being more significant. When the concentration of sulfur was higher than 1000 mg/kg, the accumulation of Hg by rice was promoted (Li et al., 2023b). The application of sulfur to inhibit the accumulation of MeHg by rice plants has been studied. The amendment of sulfur did not significantly reduce the total concentration of MeHg in soil compared to the non-treated control. Further, the concentration of MeHg in the root of sulfur-treated rice plants was higher than that in the non-treated control, but its concentrations in the stem, leaf, and grain were lower than those in the non-treated control. This phenomenon suggests that sulfur amendment inhibits Hg accumulation in rice grain by blocking MeHg in the root of rice (Li et al., 2023b). The increase of MeHg in the root of rice is thought to be related to iron plaque. Iron plaque has the ability to absorb heavy metals to inhibit their translocation to the above-ground tissue of rice plants (Hussain et al., 2020; Li et al., 2021). However, in other case studies, an increase of total Hg and MeHg concentration in rice grain was observed in sulfur-amended soil. It is interpreted that sulfur mobilizes HgS in soil and thus promotes Hg methylation (Li et al., 2019a). MeHg levels increased by 40–86% and 30–96% in soils under various types of sulfur input [(i.e., 200 mg/kg elemental sulfur, ammonium sulfate, sulfur-coated urea, and potassium sulfate (K_2SO_4)] and different amounts (e.g., 100, 200, and 400 mg/kg K_2SO_4) of sulfur input. The enhanced MeHg production could be explained by increased Hg mobility but not changes in microbial Hg methylators (Lei et al., 2021). An Hg L_{III} XANES further showed that S(0) addition increased the proportion of Hg in the form of RS-Hg-SR and decreased the proportion of Hg in the form of HgS, indicating that S(0) input may reactivate the non-bioavailable Hg in the rhizosphere and improve the net Hg methylation (Li et al., 2019b).

The input of sulfur-containing amendments can increase the biomass of plants. A study has shown that the co-application of elemental sulfur and gypsum significantly increases rice biomass and reduces grain cadmium (Cd) accumulation by reducing the labile Cd content in paddy soils (Zhang et al., 2019). Similarly, the growth of rice plants is inhibited by Hg stress but can be improved by S(0) supplementation (Huang et al., 2024).

11.4 IMPACT OF SULFATE APPLICATION TIME ON Hg ACCUMULATION IN RICE

The application of sulfate at different rice growing periods can affect rice uptake of Hg (Figure 11.4). At the early stage of rice growth, the addition of sulfate results in the decrease of E_h and the increase of soluble Fe and DOC, by which Hg is mobilized. This would enhance Hg risks in soil by promoting the accumulation of MeHg in rice grains (Li et al., 2022). At the post stage of rice growth, the net yield of MeHg

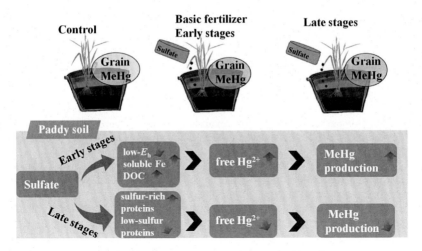

FIGURE 11.4 The concentration of MeHg in rice plants varied with the time of sulfur amendment. (Modified from Li et al., 2022.)

in soil and MeHg accumulation in rice are significantly reduced by sulfate addition, compared with their values at the early stage. One of the detoxification mechanisms of Hg in organisms is the binding of Hg to sulfhydryl groups of proteins (Carvalho et al., 2008). The application of sulfur at the post growing stage has been reported to increase the expression of sulfur-rich proteins and decrease the expression of non-sulfur proteins in plants (Zörb et al., 2009). This change in sulfur-containing protein might be involved in Hg detoxification and the decrease of Hg bioaccumulation in rice plants (Li et al., 2016b). The accumulation of Hg in rice by sulfate application is closely related to the timing of sulfate application to Hg-contaminated soil. It is recommended to amend sulfate to paddy fields at the post stage of the rice growth period, rather than the early stage, in order to reduce the production of MeHg in the soil and its accumulation in rice.

11.5 PERSPECTIVE

Although much progress has been achieved in the field of immobilization of Hg in soil by sulfur, most understandings were obtained under flooding conditions. However, paddy fields are seasonally flooded, with periodic alternation of wet and dry conditions (redox). This shift in redox conditions may affect the transformation of sulfur in soil and thereby the effect of sulfur amendment on Hg uptake by rice. Also, in order to reduce the concentration of Hg in rice grain below the guideline value, the combination of sulfur amendment and other agronomy practices, such as water management, to control rice uptake of Hg is recommended. Future studies should focus on the above aspects. The knowledge can be useful for developing strategies to mitigate Hg contamination risks and to protect human health.

REFERENCES

Achá, D., Hintelmann, H., & Yee, J. 2011. Importance of sulfate reducing bacteria in mercury methylation and demethylation in periphyton from Bolivian Amazon region. Chemosphere 82(6), 911–916.

Baldi, F., Parati, F., & Filippelli, M. 1995. Dimethylmercury and dimethylmercury-sulfide of microbial origin in the biogeochemical cycle of Hg. Water, Air, and Soil Pollution 80, 805–815.

Benoit, J. M., Gilmour, C. C., Mason, R. P., et al. 1999b. Sulfide controls on mercury speciation and bioavailability to methylating bacteria in sediment pore waters. Environmental Science & Technology 33, 951–957.

Benoit, J. M., Gilmour, C. C., & Mason, R. P. 2001. The influence of sulfide on solid-phase mercury bioavailability for methylation by pure cultures of Desulfobulbus propionicus (1pr3). Environmental Science & Technology 35, 127–132.

Benoit, J. M., Mason, R. P., & Gilmour, C. C.. Estimation of mercury-sulfide speciation in sediment pore waters using octanol-water partitioning and implications for availability to methylating bacteria. Environmental Chemistry and Ecotoxicology 18, 2138–2141.

Carvalho, C. M. L., Chew, E. H., Hashemy, S. I., et al. 2008. Inhibition of the human thioredoxin system - A molecular mechanism of mercury toxicity. Journal of Biological Chemistry 283, 11913–11923.

Dopson, M., & Johnson, D. B. 2012. Biodiversity, metabolism and applications of acidophilic sulfur-metabolizing microorganisms. Environmental Microbiology 14, 2620–2631.

Fan, Y., Sun, S., & He, S. 2023. Iron plaque formation and its effect on key elements cycling in constructed wetlands: Functions and outlooks. Water Research 235, 119837.

Gao, P., & Fan, K. 2023. Sulfur-oxidizing bacteria (SOB) and sulfate-reducing bacteria (SRB) in oil reservoir and biological control of SRB: A review. Archives of Microbiology 205, 162.

Gilmour, C. C., & Henry, E. A. 1991. Mercury methylation in aquatic systems affected by acid deposition. Environmental Pollution 71, 131–169.

Gilmour, C. C., Henry, E. A., & Mitchell, R. 1992. Sulfate stimulation of mercury methylation in freshwater sediments. Environmental Science & Technology 26, 2281–2287.

Graham, A. M., Aiken, G. R., & Gilmour, C. C. 2012. Dissolved organic matter enhances microbial mercury methylation under sulfidic conditions. Environmental Science & Technology 46, 2715–2723.

Gu, B., Bian, Y., Miller, C. L., et al. 2011. Mercury reduction and complexation by natural organic matter in anoxic environments. Proceedings of the National Academy of Sciences of the United States of America 1084, 1479–1483.

Guo, Y., Chen, L., Yang, L., et al. 2008. Counting sulfhydryls and disulfide bonds in peptides and proteins using mercurial ions as an MS-tag. Journal of the American Society for Mass Spectrometry 19, 1108–1113.

Hesterberg, D., Chou, J. W., Hutchison, K. J., et al. 2001. Bonding of Hg(II) to reduced organic sulfur in humic acid as affected by S/Hg ratio. Environmental Science & Technology 35, 2741–2745.

Hintelmann, H., Keppel-Jones, K., & Evans, R. D. 2000. Constants of mercury methylation and demethylation rates in sediments and comparison of tracer and ambient mercury availability. Environmental Chemistry and Ecotoxicology 19, 2204–2211.

Huang, Y., Yi, J., Li, X., et al. 2024. Transcriptomics and physiological analyses reveal that sulfur alleviates mercury toxicity in rice (Oryza sativa L.). Journal of Environmental Sciences 135, 10–25.

Hu, H., Gao, Y., Yu, H., et al. 2023. Mechanisms and biological effects of organic amendments on mercury speciation in soil–rice systems: A review. Ecotoxicology and Environmental Safety 251, 114516.

Hussain, B., Li, J., Ma, Y., et al. 2020. Effects of Fe and Mn cations on Cd uptake by rice plant in hydroponic culture experiment. PLOS ONE 15, e0243174.

Jay, J. A., Morel, F. M., & Hemond, H. F. 2000. Mercury speciation in the presence of polysulfides. Environmental Science & Technology 34, 2196–2200.

King, J. K., Kostka, J. E., Frischer, M. E., et al. 2000. Sulfate-reducing bacteria methylate mercury at variable rates in pure culture and in marine sediments. Applied and Environmental Microbiology 66, 2430–2437.

Lei, P., Tang, C., Wang, Y., et al. 2021. Understanding the effects of sulfur input on mercury methylation in rice paddy soils. Science of the Total Environment 778, 146325.

Li, Y., Dai, S. S., Zhao, J., et al. 2023a. Amendments of nitrogen and sulfur mitigate carbon-promoting effect on microbial mercury methylation in paddy soils. Journal of Hazardous Materials 448, 130983.

Li, Y., Lu, C., Zhu, N., et al. 2022. Mobilization and methylation of mercury with sulfur addition in paddy soil: Implications for integrated water-sulfur management in controlling Hg accumulation in rice. Journal of Hazardous Materials 430, 128447.

Li, Y., Wang, Y., Zhang, Q., et al. 2019b. Elemental sulfur amendment enhances methylmercury accumulation in rice (*Oryza sativa* L.) grown in Hg mining polluted soil. Journal of Hazardous Materials 379, 120701.

Li, Y., Zhao, J., Li, Y. F., et al. 2016b. Comparative metalloproteomic approaches for the investigation of proteins involved in the toxicity of inorganic and organic forms of mercury in rice (*Oryza sativa* L.) roots. Metallomics 8, 663–671.

Li, Y., Zhao, J., Zhang, B., et al. 2016a. The influence of iron plaque on the absorption, translocation and transformation of mercury in rice (*Oryza sativa* L.) seedlings exposed to different mercury species. Plant and Soil 398, 87–97.

Li, Y., Zhao, J., Zhong, H., et al. 2019a. Understanding enhanced microbial MeHg production in mining-contaminated paddy soils under sulfate amendment: Changes in Hg mobility or microbial methylators? Environmental Science & Technology 53, 1844–1852.

Li, Y., Zhu, N., Hu, W., et al. 2023b. New insights into sulfur input induced methylmercury production and accumulation in paddy soil and rice. Journal of Hazardous Materials 455, 131602.

Li, Y. F., Zhao, J., Li, Y., et al. 2015. The concentration of selenium matters: A field study on mercury accumulation in rice by selenite treatment in Qingzhen, Guizhou, China. Plant and Soil 391, 195–205.

Li, Z., Liang, Y., Hu, H., et al. 2021. Speciation, transportation, and pathways of cadmium in soil-rice systems: A review on the environmental implications and remediation approaches for food safety. Environment International 156, 106749.

Liu, Y., Chen, H., Zhu, N., et al. 2022. Detection and remediation of mercury contaminated environment by nanotechnology: Progress and challenges. Environmental Pollution 293, 118557.

Meng, B., Feng, X., Qiu, G., et al. 2011. The process of methylmercury accumulation in rice (*Oryza sativa* L.). Environmental Science & Technology 45, 2711–2717.

Murase, J., Noll, M., & Frenzel, P. 2006. Impact of protists on the activity and structure of the bacterial community in a rice field soil. Applied and Environmental Microbiology 72, 5436–5444.

Nriagu, J. O., & Soon, Y. K. 1985. Distribution and isotopic composition of sulfur in lake sediments of northern Ontario. Geochimica et Cosmochimica Acta 49, 823–834.

Porvari, P., & Verta, M. 1995. Methylmercury production in flooded soils: A laboratory study. Water, Air, and Soil Pollution 80, 765–773.

Roberts, T. L., & Bettany, J. R. 1985. The influence of topography on the nature and distribution of soil sulfur across a narrow environmental gradient. Canadian Journal of Soil Science 65, 419–434.

Rothenberg, S. E., & Feng, X. 2012. Mercury cycling in a flooded rice paddy. Journal of Geophysical Research: Biogeosciences 117, 184–192.

Roulet, M., Guimarães, J. R. D., & Lucotte, M. 2001. Methylmercury production and accumulation in sediments and soils of an Amazonian floodplain—Effect of seasonal inundation. Water, Air, and Soil Pollution 128, 41–60.

Shao, D., Kang, Y., Wu, S., et al. 2012. Effects of sulfate reducing bacteria and sulfate concentrations on mercury methylation in freshwater sediments. Science of the Total Environment 424, 331–336.

Skyllberg, U. 2008. Competition among thiols and inorganic sulfides and polysulfides for Hg and MeHg in wetland soils and sediments under suboxic conditions: Illumination of controversies and implications for MeHg net production. Journal of Geophysical Research: Biogeosciences 113, 285–295.

Skyllberg, U., Bloom, P. R., Qian, J., et al. 2006. Complexation of mercury(II) in soil organic matter: EXAFS evidence for linear two-coordination with reduced sulfur groups. Environmental Science & Technology 40, 4174–4180.

Skyllberg, U., & Drott, A. 2010. Competition between disordered iron sulfide and natural organic matter associated thiols for mercury(II)—An EXAFS study. Environmental Science & Technology 44, 1254–1259.

Small, J. M., & Hintelmann, H. 2014. Sulfide and mercury species profiles in two Ontario boreal shield lakes. Chemosphere, 111, 96–102.

Steffan, R. J., Korthals, E. T., & Winfrey, M. R. 1988. Effects of acidification on mercury methylation, demethylation, and volatilization in sediments from an acid-susceptible lake. Applied and Environmental Microbiology 54, 2003–2009.

Strickman, R. J., & Mitchell, C. P. J. 2017. Accumulation and translocation of methylmercury and inorganic mercury in *Oryza sativa*: An enriched isotope tracer study. Science of the Total Environment 574, 1415–1423.

Ullrich, S. M., Tanton, T. W., & Abdrashitova, S. A. 2001. Mercury in the aquatic environment: A review of factors affecting methylation. Critical Reviews in Environmental Science and Technology 31, 241–293.

Wang, X., Ye, Z., Li, B., et al. 2014. Growing rice aerobically markedly decreases mercury accumulation by reducing both Hg bioavailability and the production of MeHg. Environmental Science & Technology 48, 1878–1885.

Winfrey, M. R., & Rudd, J. W. M. 1990. Environmental factors affecting the formation of methylmercury in low pH lakes. Environmental Chemistry and Ecotoxicology 9, 853–869.

Xu, Y. N., & Chen, Y. 2020. Advances in heavy metal removal by sulfate-reducing bacteria. Water Science & Technology 81(9), 1797–1827.

Yin, Y., Allen, H. E., Huang, C. P., et al. 1997. Kinetics of mercury(II) adsorption and desorption on soil. Environmental Science & Technology 31, 496–503.

Yu, R. Q., Flanders, J. R., Mack, E. E., et al. 2012. Contribution of coexisting sulfate and iron reducing bacteria to methylmercury production in freshwater river sediments. Environmental Science & Technology 46, 2684–2691.

Yu, R. Q., Reinfelder, J. R., Hines, M. E., et al. 2013. Mercury methylation by the methanogen *Methanospirillum* hungatei. Applied and Environmental Microbiology 79, 6325–6330.

Zhang, D., Du, G., Chen, D., et al. 2019. Effect of elemental sulfur and gypsum application on the bioavailability and redistribution of cadmium during rice growth. Science of The Total Environment 657, 1460–1467.

Zhang, H., Feng, X., Zhu, J., et al. 2012. Selenium in soil inhibits mercury uptake and translocation in rice (*Oryza sativa* L.). Environmental Science & Technology 46, 10040–10046.

Zhao, J., Liang, X., Zhu, N., et al. 2020. Immobilization of mercury by nano-elemental selenium and the underlying mechanisms in hydroponic-cultured garlic plant. Environmental Science: Nano 7, 1115–1125.

Zheng, W., Lin, H., Mann, B. F., et al. 2013. Oxidation of dissolved elemental mercury by thiol compounds under anoxic conditions. Environmental Science & Technology 47, 12827–12834.

Zörb, C., Steinfurth, D., Seling, S., et al. 2009. Quantitative protein composition and baking quality of winter wheat as affected by late sulfur fertilization. Journal of Agricultural and Food Chemistry 57, 3877–3885.

12 Remediation of Hg-Contaminated Soil Using Carbon-Based Amendments

Ilia Mironov, Jianxu Wang, and Xinbin Feng

12.1 INTRODUCTION

According to a survey report released by the Chinese government, Hg pollution in soil is becoming one of the top threats to the safety of food in China (Figure 12.1). This situation is even worse in the southwestern part of China, where large areas of land are contaminated with Hg. It should be noted that most Hg in those soils is sourced from parent rocks due to the development of Hg deposits and mineral belts. Many efforts have been made to remediate Hg-contaminated soils, such as thermal

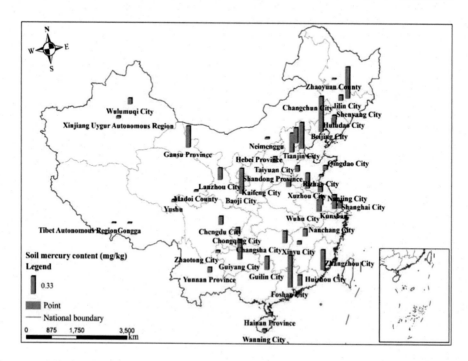

FIGURE 12.1 Spatial distribution of soil mercury content in provinces, cities, and autonomous regions in China. (Reprinted with permission from Liu et al., 2021.)

 DOI: 10.1201/9781003404941-12

desorption, soil washing, immobilization, bioremediation, and nanotechnologies (He et al., 2015; Xu et al., 2015; Teng et al., 2020; Liu et al., 2022). Amongst those methods, immobilization is often recommended due to its in-situ nature, low cost, low impact on soil fertility, etc. Carbon-based amendments, including biochar and activated carbon, are used for Hg remediation due to their high efficiency in immobilization of Hg and affordability. In this chapter, we review literature on the use of carbon-based amendments in Hg remediation. The knowledge will be helpful for engineers and scientists who work on the remediation of Hg-polluted soils.

12.2   THE PRODUCTION OF BIOCHAR AND ITS ADVANTAGES IN SOIL REMEDIATION

Biochar is produced by direct thermal decomposition of biomass in the absence of oxygen, resulting in a mixture of solids (biochars), liquids (bio-oils), and gaseous products ($CO + H_2$). Gasification is often used for production of biochar (Akhtar et al., 2018), and it includes oxidation, drying, pyrolysis, and reduction processes. Pyrolysis temperature in gasifiers is often set at 250–550°C (Rollinson, 2016). The pyrolysis product highly depends not only on the initial material but also on the process conditions, such as temperature, residence time, and heating rate. An increase in the heating rate results in a decrease in biochar yield (Aysu and Küçük, 2014), which in turn increases the liquid and gaseous products. Also, microwave-based thermo-catalytic depolymerization is used to produce biochar. The biochar produced this way has a high carbon content and calorific value compared to that obtained by traditional pyrolysis (Beneroso et al., 2017). Physical and chemical properties of biochar are dependent on the raw material and on production technology. The same raw material can yield different products under different production set-ups. Biochar properties are often characterized by studying proximate and elemental composition, porosity, pH value, and sorption capabilities. The H/C and O/C atomic ratios of biochar correlate with molecular structural properties of organic compounds, such as polarity and aromaticity (Crombie et al., 2012).

Biochar is a stable solid compound rich in pyrogenic carbon that can persist in soil for many hundreds of years due to its relatively low chemical activity. The application of biochar can increase the fertility of soils and overall agricultural productivity. Therefore, biochar is regarded as an environmentally friendly material for remediation of heavy metal-polluted soil.

12.3   THE EFFECT OF BIOCHAR ON Hg IMMOBILIZATION IN SOLUTION AND SOIL/SEDIMENT

It has been well documented that biochar is efficient in adsorption of heavy metals in water through physical and chemical processes (ion exchange, electrostatic attraction, surface and inner sphere complexation, precipitation, etc.). Several groups have studied the ability of different biochars on Hg removal from solution. Liu et al. (2016) used different feedstocks to produce biochars, including mulch, pine bark, corn stovers, corn cob, cocoa husk, cotton seed husk, wheat shaft, spent hops, switchgrass, cow manure,

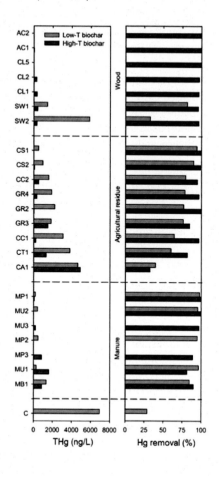

Abbreviation	Feedstock	T (°C)
Wood		
AC1	activated carbon A	-
AC2	activated carbon B	-
CL1	Wicked Good Charcoal	~700
CL2	Cowboy Charcoal	~700
CL5	Biochar Engineering Charcoal	~700
SW1H	mulch	600
SW1L	mulch	300
SW2H	pine bark	600
SW2L	pine bark	300
Agricultural residue		
CS1H	corn stovers	600
CS1L	corn stovers	300
CS2H	corn stovers	600
CS2L	corn stovers	300
CC1H	corn cob	600
CC1L	corn cob	300
CC2H	corn cob	600
CC2L	corn cob	300
CA1H	cocoa husk	600
CA1L	cocoa husk	300
CT1H	cotton seed husk	600
CT1L	cotton seed husk	300
GR2H	wheat shaft	600
GR2L	wheat shaft	300
GR3H	spent hops	600
GR3L	spent hops	300
GR4H	switchgrass	600
GR4L	switchgrass	300
Manure		
MB1H	cow manure	600
MB1L	cow manure	300
MP1H	chicken manure	600
MP1L	chicken manure	300
MP2L	chicken manure	300
MP3H	chicken manure	600
MU1H	mushroom soil	600
MU1L	mushroom soil	300
MU2H	mushroom soil	600
MU2L	mushroom soil	300
MU3H	mushroom soil	600

FIGURE 12.2 Liu et al. (2016) biochar amendments for Hg remediation. Left: abbreviations of biochar amendments, sources of feedstock, and pyrolysis production temperatures. L and H represent low-T and high-T biochar, respectively. Right: THg concentrations of Hg spiked waters treated by the biochars and the biochars' Hg removal efficiency. The single C abbreviation represents the control.

chicken manure, and mushroom soil, and they tested the efficiency of these biochars on Hg removal from solution. Results showed that over 80% of Hg was removed from solution by the biochars (Figure 12.2). The removal of Hg(II) (as ionic Hg^{2+}) by biochar was due to high porosity, surface functional groups (Cl-containing, S-containing, and O-containing groups) that complex with Hg(II), and its highly aromatic structure enabling Hg–π binding (Deng et al., 2020; Chaudhuri et al., 2022).

In other studies, various feedstocks have been used for production of biochar for remediation of Hg-contaminated soils/sediments, including plant biomass-based biochars (Bussan et al., 2016; Liu et al., 2017; Liu et al., 2018; O'Connor et al., 2018; Wang et al., 2019; Xing et al., 2019; Wei et al., 2022), animal waste-based biochars (Liu et al., 2018; Betts et al., 2021), and other organic waste material-based biochars (Zhang et al.,

2019). Among these, plant biomass-based biochars are most popular, as plant biomass is more available than other feedstocks. Wei et al. (2022) spiked cassava straw biochar into Hg-polluted soil at a mass ratio of 1% and then planted with spinach for 30 days. Results showed that the fractional amount of bioavailable Hg in the biochar-treated soil decreased by 11.5%, and Hg concentration in spinach was reduced by approximately 65%, compared to the control. Bussan et al. (2016) used a single enriched Hg stable isotope approach to study Hg methylation and demethylation in sediment with biochar amendment. The pinewood biochar was spiked into Hg-polluted sediment at a mass ratio of 5%, and the sediment was incubated under dark conditions for 14 days. The results showed that the methylation rate of Hg decreased by 88% in sediment, while Hg dimethylation rates remained unchanged. The reduction of the Hg methylation rate was attributed to the decrease of Hg availability by biochar.

Biochars produced at different pyrolysis temperatures have different effects on Hg in soil. In a case study, the amendment of switchgrass biochar pyrolyzed at 300°C to soil for 440 days significantly decreased dissolved total Hg and MeHg, while that pyrolyzed at 600°C also decreased dissolved total Hg content but increased MeHg concentration in soil (Liu et al., 2017). Similar to that of 600°C switchgrass biochar, application of oak biochar produced at 700°C to Hg-polluted sediment reduced the concentration of dissolved Hg by 20–60%; however, it stimulated MeHg production during a long-term incubation (Liu et al., 2018). This case study showed that when switchgrass was used as feedstock, the biochar produced at high pyrolysis temperature was less efficient in immobilization of MeHg.

Prior studies have mainly focused on bath experiments which were performed in the laboratory. In a field study, Xing et al. (2019) used rice husk biochar at ratios of 24 to 72 t/ha to remediate Hg-polluted paddy fields. The concentration of Hg in the pore water of soil was decreased by up to 44%, and this decrease was attributed to the immobilization of Hg by the formation of HgS induced by biochar. Mercury concentration in the biochar-treated rice plants was reduced by up to 62% in the bran, 43% in the hull, and 70% in the polished rice, all relative to the control. This field study shows a promising result that the amendment of biochar in Hg-polluted paddy fields can significantly reduce Hg concentration in rice grain.

In addition to plant biomass-based biochar, animal-based biochars are also used for Hg remediation. Betts et al. (2021) used both poultry litter and swine solids as feedstocks to produce biochars. They used both original biochars and washed biochars to treat Hg-polluted soils, and they found that original biochars were more efficient in immobilization of Hg than washed biochars. This phenomenon is attributed to the fact that original poultry litter and swine solid biochars contain more sulfur compounds than the washed biochars, and these sulfur compounds promote Hg immobilization via the formation of HgS complexes. Potential users should be aware that organic molecules from poultry litter also have the potential to stimulate microorganisms, the activities of which may enhance Hg mobilization and methylation. The use of sewage sludge as feedstock for production of biochar has the big advantage of recycling solid wastes. Zhang et al. (2019) used sewage sludge biochar to remediate Hg-polluted soil and found that the biochar enhanced Hg methylation in acidic soil but did not enhance rice uptake of total Hg and MeHg from soil. It appears that the increased MeHg in soil brought about by sewage sludge biochar amendment has limited availability for rice plants.

The mechanisms of immobilization of MeHg by biochar are complicated. Biochar can affect both Hg-methylation microorganism activities and Hg availability in soil. Both the inhibition and the promotion of Hg-methylation microorganisms have been reported by different studies. In one case study, biochar inhibits the microbial methylation of Hg^{2+}, resulting in reduced MeHg production (Yang et al., 2021), and consequently reduces the accumulation of MeHg by rice plants. However, in another study (Man et al., 2021), biochar increases the relative abundance of hgcA-carrying methylating bacteria, leading to a high microbial methylation rate. But in this case study, MeHg bioavailability is reduced by the biochar. Biochar has a certain ability to reduce the availability of Hg and MeHg in soils. It has been reported that biochar can promote the reduction of Fe^{3+} to Fe^{2+}, SO_4^{2-} to S^{2-}, and SO_3H^+ to HS^- (in organic compounds) (Liu et al., 2018; Xing et al., 2020; Yang et al., 2021). This can result in the presence of polysulfides $Fe^{2+}(S)_n$, thiols R-HS, and sulfides, which are able to immobilize both MeHg and Hg^{2+} through chemisorption by S groups. Table 12.1 summarizes the effect of addition of different biochars on immobilization of Hg in soils and sediments and Hg immobilization mechanisms.

TABLE 12.1

Impact of Biochar Amendments on Hg Immobilization in Soils/Sediments

Feedstocks (Pyrolysis Temperature, °C)	Matrix	Added Dose	Effects	Mechanisms	References
Bamboo (600)	Soil	0.5% weight	25–59% reduction in soil CH_3Hg^+ 82–87% reduction in brown rice grain CH_3Hg^+	formation of CH_3Hg^+ complexes on the biochar surface	Wang et al. (2019)
Cassava straw (550)	Soil	1% weight	Bioavailable Hg^{2+} fraction decrease (in comparison to THg) from 18.5% to 7%	adsorption	Wei et al. (2022)
Pinewood (~830)	Sediment	5% weight	88% reduction in the methylation rate	complexation, electrostatic interactions, ion exchange	Bussan et al. (2016)
Poultry litter (unwashed biochar) (700)	Soil	2.5% weight	Approx. 54% reduction in water-extracted Hg	formation of sulfur-complexes (higher total sulfur resulted in greater Hg immobilization)	Betts et al. (2021)

(Continued)

TABLE 12.1 *(Continued)*
Impact of Biochar Amendments on Hg Immobilization in Soils/Sediments

Feedstocks (Pyrolysis Temperature, °C)	Matrix	Added Dose	Effects	Mechanisms	References
Reed straw (550)	Soil	1% weight	Bioavailable Hg fraction decrease (in comparison to THg) from 18.5% to 8%	Adsorption	Wei et al. (2022)
Rice husks and elemental sulfur (550)	Soil	Up to 5% weight	Up to 99.3% reduction in Hg^{2+} bioavailability	Formation of low-solubility HgS (cinnabar)	O'Connor et al. (2018)
Rice shells (480–660)	Soil	24–72 t/ha	Reduction of THg content of up to 62% in bran, up to 43% in hull, up to 70% in polished rice seed; and up to 44% in pore water	Combination of sulfide with Hg to form Hg sulfides	Xing et al. (2019)
Swine solids (unwashed biochar) (900)	Soil	2.5% weight	Approx. 46% reduction in water-extracted Hg	Formation of sulfur-complexes (higher total sulfur resulted in greater Hg immobilization)	Betts et al. (2021)
Switchgrass (300 and 600)	Water and sediment	1:20:160 (biochar, sediment, water)	Reduction in aqueous THg of up to 92.5%	Adsorption	Liu et al. (2017)
Oak (700)	Sediment	5% weight	THg concentration in soil waters decreased by 20% to 60% (mean 46%)	Adsorption, formation of Hg-sulfide minerals and precipitation	Liu et al. (2018)
Sewage sludge (600)	Soil	approx. 5% weight	73.4% decrease in CH_3Hg^+, 81.9% decrease in THg (rice grain)	Adsorption	Zhang et al. (2019)

(Continued)

TABLE 12.1 *(Continued)*

Impact of Biochar Amendments on Hg Immobilization in Soils/Sediments

Feedstocks (Pyrolysis Temperature, °C)	Matrix	Added Dose	Effects	Mechanisms	References
Wheat straw (350–450)	Soil	72 t/ha	Reduction of THg content of up to 31% in bran, up to 36% in hull, up to 37.5% in polished rice seed, and up to 26% in pore water	Immobilization through formation of Hg sulfides	Xing et al. (2019)

Note: Augmented version of Yang et al. (2021).

The modification of biochar with sulfur compounds promotes the immobilization of Hg. O'Connor et al. (2018) utilized 5% sulfur-modified rice husk biochar to treat Hg-polluted soil. The result showed that Hg concentration in soil leachates decreased by 99.3%. This promotion is due to the enhanced adsorption of Hg^{2+} by S-groups of sulfur-modified biochar. Prior studies mainly focused on the amendment of biochar in original Hg-polluted soil. In a case study, the effect of biochar amendment on soil treated with selenium was studied. Wang et al. (2019) pyrolyzed bamboo (Phyllostachys edulis) at 600°C for 1 h. The produced bamboo biochar was spiked in polluted soil preliminarily spiked with Se at a mass ratio of 0.5% and then the soil was planted with rice. Results showed that the concentration of MeHg decreased by 25–59% in the biochar-treated soil compared to the control. Further, the concentration of MeHg was decreased by 82–87% in the grain, 71–84% in the straw, and 2–38% in the root of the biochar-treated rice, all relative to the control. The decrease of availability of MeHg was due to the formation of Hg-Se complexes on the biochar surface.

12.4   THE PRODUCTION OF ACTIVATED CARBON AND ITS APPLICATION IN REMEDIATION OF Hg-POLLUTED SOLUTION AND SOIL/SEDIMENT

Activated carbon (active carbon, activated charcoal, AC) is produced from carbon-containing raw materials such as coal, petroleum pitch, plants, or animals (basically produced from biochar materials). Activated carbon is divided into four main classes: powdered activated carbon, granular activated carbon, fibrous activated carbon, and activated carbon fabrics (Asif and Tauseef, 20C19). The carbonized material is converted into activated carbon by using hot gases. The introduced air burns gases, creating a sorted, sifted, dust-free form of activated carbon. The steps below are involved in the process (Hendrawan et al., 2019):

- *Dehydration:* Water is removed from the raw material in order to avoid byproducts.
- *Carbonization:* C-containing raw material is carbonized at different temperatures ($300+°C$).
- *Activation:* After dehydration and carbonization, activation is performed. The activation can be carried out both physically using non-reactive gases (for example, steam or carbon dioxide), or chemically with the help of chemically active liquid or solid reagents (hydroxides, carbonates, chlorides, sulfates, phosphates, organic and inorganic acids). (Mohan et al., 2001; Zhou et al., 2018).

Activated carbon is a synthetic porous solid material containing 85–95% carbon (Hendrawan et al., 2019). It has high microporosity, which makes it an extremely capable sorption material. Activated coal usually has an internal surface area of around 900–2000 or more m^2/g, whereas non-activated carbons have a surface area of 400–800 m^2/g only (Liu, 2016). For instance, Dillon et al. (1989) reported two activated carbons with surface areas of 1500–3000 m^2/g.

The microspores of AC act similar to sponges that contain an extremely large amount of holes which can trap dust and other substances (Muzarpar et al., 2020). The London dispersion force is the force responsible for physical adsorption on micropores of activated carbon (Muzarpar et al., 2020). This is a form of Van der Waals force as a result of intermolecular interaction. Nevertheless, the sorption process also depends on properties of the sorbates. As a result, chemisorption (the process of chemical reaction of adsorbent surfaces with free or adsorbed molecules of adsorbate) can occur, which also leads to immobilization of pollutants, such as sorption of gaseous Hg^0 (Rodriguez et al., 2021). The chemisorption forces are much stronger than the London dispersion forces, which leads to more efficient immobilization. The physical adsorption forces are significant only if the gaps/voids within the microporous structure are less than 4–5 molecular layers.

Activated carbon can be reactivated by removing contaminants, such as Hg^0 and Hg^{2+}, from its porous surface (Chen et al., 2019). The most commonly used and effective reactivation technique for Hg sorbed activated carbon is thermal reactivation due to gaseous Hg^0 release under high temperature conditions (Chen et al., 2019). This process requires no extra reagents besides no-oxidizing gases, like CO_2, or steam. The thermal regeneration process usually consists of three stages (Sabio et al., 2004): drying of the activated carbon, high temperature-based decomposition, and desorption of contaminants from activated carbon micropores. However, it should be noted that the extraction of activated carbon from soils for the reactivation process is extremely difficult.

Sedimite® (Bundschuh et al., 2015), bituminous particulate AC (Gilmour et al., 2013), coconut shell AC and sulfur-modified coconut shell AC (Ch'ng et al., 2020), Siemens Water Technologies Corp. AC (Bessinger and Marks, 2010), and nano AC (Wang et al., 2020) have been used for Hg remediation (Table 12.2). Coconut shell activated carbon and sulfur-modified coconut shell activated carbon were tested for Hg remediation by spiking into Hg-polluted sediment at a mass ratio of 3% (Ch'ng et al., 2020). Results showed that the concentrations of total Hg and MeHg in soil

TABLE 12.2

Impact of Activated Carbon Amendments on Hg Immobilization in Soils/ Sediments

AC Type	Matrix	Added Dose	Effects	Mechanisms	References
Sedimite (AC 50%, clay, starch binders, and quartz sand mix)	Sediment	1.11 g Sedimite/10 g sediment	Up to 60% reduction in THg bioavailability	Adsorption	Bundschuh et al. (2015)
Bituminous particulate AC (TOG 80 × 235 mesh; particle size 75–300 μm)	Sediment	5% weight	Up to 90% reduction in CH_3Hg^+ bioaccumulation, up to 95% CH_3Hg^+ reduction in pore waters	Reduced CH_3Hg^+ production from Hg^{2+} due to sorption/enhanced CH_3Hg^+ degradation or flux	Gilmour et al. (2013)
Coconut shell AC	Sediment	3% weight	Up to 82% and 78% reduction of THg mobility for AC and its S-modified AC	Adsorption for activated carbon Adsorption + chemisorption (due to S-groups) for S-modified AC	Ch'ng et al. (2020)
Nano AC	Paddy soil	1–3% weight	Reduction of THg content in pore water by 61–76% and in polished rice by 47–63%	Induced change in Hg^{2+} binding from organic matter to formation of nano-HgS	Wang et al. (2020)
Siemens Water Technologies Corp. (Warrendale) AC (no feedstock information), granular, fine, and powdered	Soil	2.5–7.5% wet weight	Decrease in Hg concentration in soil solution from 2.5–34.2 μg/L (control) to 1.5–3.8 (granular), 0.34–1.6 (fine), and 0.07–0.55 (powdered)	(1) The formation of stable Hg complexes on powdered AC surfaces and (2) the direct adsorption of dissolved organic matter responsible for Hg dissolution	Bessinger and Marks (2010)

solution decreased by 82% and 94% in coconut shell activated carbon-treated soil and by 78% and 92% in sulfur-modified coconut shell activated carbon-treated soil, relative to corresponding controls. The modification of sulfur did not improve, or even lower, the performance of coconut shell activated carbon, and this is likely because the modification process blocked active sorption centers of activated carbon. Gilmour et al. (2013) spiked 5% bituminous particulate activated carbon (w/w) into Hg-polluted sediment populated with *Lumbriculus variegatus* worms and incubated it for 14 days. Results showed that the MeHg concentration in pore water of sediment decreased by 95% relative to the control. Further, the MeHg concentration in *L. variegatus* worms was decreased by up to 90%. This case study showed that the amendment of activated carbon could reduce the risk of biotic MeHg accumulation from the contaminated environment and subsequent contamination of food chains.

Bundschuh et al. (2015) added about 10% Sedimite® activated carbon into Hg-polluted sediment to test the efficiency of this amendment on Hg accumulation by amphipod crustacean Hyalella azteca. The bioaccumulation of Hg in Hyalella azteca was reduced by 60–96% in activated carbon-treated sediment relative to the control. Sedimite® can impact Hyalella azteca by covering the amphipods' integument, adsorbing Hg from the water phase, or it can cause a shift in amphipod ingestion toward the Sedimite® amendment instead of the normal food source. Also, Sedimite® activated carbon showed an ability to reduce the bioavailability of sediment-bound Hg. Bessinger and Marks (2010) studied the particle size effect of AC on remediation of Hg pollution. They tested the efficiency of granular, fine, and powdered AC at a spiking ratio of 2.5–7.5% in a short-term incubation experiment. Results showed that the concentration of Hg in soil solution decreased from 2.5–34.2 µg/L in the control to 1.5–3.8 µg/L in the granular AC treatment, to 0.34–1.6 µg/L in the fine AC treatment, and to 0.07–0.55 µg/L in the powdered form treatment. Clearly, the larger the reactive surface area, the greater the immobilization efficiency of Hg. Wang et al. (2020) tested the efficacy of nano AC on the bioavailability of Hg in paddy fields and its uptake by rice plants. The total carbon content of the amendment was 99.5%, and its surface area was 500 m2/g. Results showed that 1–3% of the nano AC addition to paddy soil was capable of reducing Hg content in pore water by 61–76%. Additionally, Hg bioaccumulation in rice plant tissues was reduced by 15–63%, relative to the control. Specifically, nano AC reduced the Hg concentration of polished rice by 47–63% compared to the control, to a level lower than the maximum allowable Hg concentration in rice grain (20 ng/g) defined by the Chinese government.

The mechanism of immobilization of Hg by AC includes the formation of stable Hg^{2+} complexes on powdered AC surfaces and the direct adsorption of dissolved organic matter (DOM) responsible for Hg^{2+} dissolution in sediments (Bessinger and Marks, 2010). Further, AC can promote the reduction reaction of sulfur in soil to produce more reduced sulfur compounds, which can react with Hg to form Hg sulfide complexes.

12.5   SUMMARY

The main advantages of biochar and AC in soil remediation are their cheap feedstock material cost, relatively high efficiency in Hg immobilization, and environmental friendliness. Amongst the reviewed amendments [except Liu et al. (2016) biochars], Hg remediation efficiency in soils or sediments varies from 37.5% to 99.3% (Figure 12.3). The difference is mostly attributable to amendment porosity and the amount of Hg immobilizing groups, which are highly dependent on feedstock and production temperatures. The most effective amongst biochars is rice husk biochar, showing up to 99.3% Hg immobilization. The leader amongst activated carbons reaches up to 98.4% immobilization. The amendment of biochar and activated

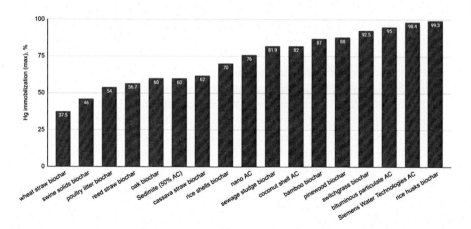

FIGURE 12.3 Amendments' maximum remediation effectiveness. Note: The figure only shows maximum achieved Hg^{2+} or CH_3Hg^+ reduction without taking into account concentrations of the amendments.

carbon into paddy fields showed a significant decrease of Hg bioavailability and subsequently reduced Hg concentration in rice grain (Wang et al., 2019; Wang et al., 2020; Xing et al., 2019). The long-term incubation and field studies showed promising results of carbon-based amendments on Hg immobilization in soil and its uptake by rice plants (Liu et al., 2018; Xing et al., 2019).

Most biochars and ACs share two mechanisms for immobilization of Hg (Tables 12.1, 12.2). First is the physical adsorption of Hg by biochar, which is highly related to the porosity of the biochar. Second is the chemical sorption by S-containing groups (thiol, sulfide, etc.), which have a strong affinity for Hg^{2+} compounds (including CH_3Hg^+) and produce insoluble immobile Hg compounds. In addition to S-containing groups, N- and O-containing groups are also involved in the Hg immobilization process (Kabiri et al., 2015; Ma et al., 2018). The impact of biochar and AC on soil microorganisms can influence the methylation of Hg. Some biochars can enhance the activity of Hg-methylation microorganisms, as a certain group of carbon molecules of biochar may serve as a food source for microorganisms. Therefore, assessment of the impact of biochars on Hg methylation microorganisms is needed before the large-scale application of biochar. However, it should be noted that the bioavailability of MeHg still gets reduced.

In previous studies, biochars and ACs were added into different soils/sediments at various ratios, and thus it is difficult to do a cost-effective analysis for those biochars to select the optimal one. Therefore, more studies are needed to study the performance of those biochars that were efficient in immobilization of Hg in soil in Hg-polluted paddy fields under the same experimental conditions. Further, it is necessary to study the impact of the amendment of different amounts of biochars on Hg mobilization and methylation in soils, as this would be helpful for obtaining the optimal amount of biochar for mitigation of Hg risks. Most of the previous studies were performed under laboratory conditions. To fully understand the efficiency of the carbon-based amendments, more studies should focus on field studies.

REFERENCES

Akhtar A., Krepl V., Ivanova T., 2018. A combined overview of combustion, pyrolysis, and gasification of biomass. Energy & Fuels 32, 7294–7318.

Asif A., Tauseef A., 2019. 4 - Water purification technologies. Bottled and Packaged Water 4, 83–120.

Aysu T., Küçük M. M., 2014. Biomass pyrolysis in a fixed-bed reactor: Effects of pyrolysis parameters on product yields and characterization of products. Energy 64, 1002–1025.

Beneroso D., Monti T., Kostas E. T., 2017. Microwave pyrolysis of biomass for bio-oil production: Scalable processing concepts. Chemical Engineering Journal 316, 481–498.

Bessinger B. A., Marks C. D., 2010. Treatment of mercury-contaminated soils with activated carbon: A laboratory, field, and modeling study. Remediation Journal 21, 115–135.

Betts A., Millard G., Plunkett S., et al., 2021. Effect of Biochar Type on Immobilization of Mercury (Hg) from a Mercury-Spiked Soil. 2021 ASA, CSSA, SSSA International Annual Meeting.

Bundschuh M., Zubrod J.P., Seitz F., et al., 2015. Effects of two sorbents applied to mercury-contaminated river sediments on bioaccumulation in and detrital processing by Hyalella azteca. Journal of Soils and Sediments 15, 1265–1274.

Bussan D. D., Sessums R. F., Cizdziel J. V., 2016. Activated carbon and biochar reduce mercury methylation potentials in aquatic sediments. Bulletin of Environmental Contamination and Toxicology 96, 536–539.

Ch'ng, B. L., Hsu C. J., Ting Y., et al., 2020. Aqueous mercury removal with carbonaceous and iron sulfide sorbents and their applicability as thin-layer caps in mercury-contaminated estuary sediment. Water 12, 1991.

Chaudhuri S., Sigmund G., Bone S. E., et al., 2022. Mercury removal from contaminated water by wood-based biochar depends on natural organic matter and ionic composition. Environmental Science & Technology 56, 11354–11362.

Chen C., Duan Y., Zhao S., et al., 2019. Experimental study on mercury removal and regeneration of SO_2 modified activated carbon. Industrial & Engineering Chemistry Research 5, 13190–13197.

Crombie K., Mašek O., Sohi S. P., et al., 2012. The effect of pyrolysis conditions on biochar stability as determined by three methods. Global Change Biology Bioenergy 5, 122–131.

Deng R., Huang D., Wan J., et al., 2020. Recent advances of biochar materials for typical potentially toxic elements management in aquatic environments: A review. Journal of Cleaner Production 255, 119523.

Dillon E. C., Wilton J. H., Barlow J. C., Watson W. A., 1989. Large surface area activated charcoal and the inhibition of aspirin absorption. Annals of Emergency Medicine 18, 547–552.

Gilmour C. C., Riedel G. S., Riedel G., et al., 2013. Activated carbon mitigates mercury and methylmercury bioavailability in contaminated sediments. Environmental Science & Technology 47, 13001–13010.

He F., Gao J., Pierce E. et al., 2015. In situ remediation technologies for mercury-contaminated soil. Environmental Science and Pollution Research 22, 8124–8147.

Hendrawan Y., Sajidah N., Umam C., et al., 2019. Effect of carbonization temperature variations and activator agent types on activated carbon characteristics of Sengon wood waste (*Paraserianthes falcataria* (L.) Nielsen). IOP Conference Series: Earth and Environmental Science 23 9012006.

Kabiri S., Tran D. N. H., Azari S., Losic D., 2015. Graphene-diatom silica aerogels for efficient removal of mercury ions from water. ACS Applied Materials & Interfaces 7, 11815–11823.

Liu. E., 2016. Activated charcoal. Science & Food, Discover Magazine.

Liu J., Lin L., Wang K., et al., 2022. Concentrations and species of mercury in municipal sludge of selected Chinese cities and potential mercury emissions from sludge treatment and disposal. Frontiers in Environmental Science 10, 895075.

Liu P., Ptacek C. J., Blowes D. W., Landis R. C., 2016. Mechanisms of mercury removal by biochars produced from different feedstocks determined using X-ray absorption spectroscopy. Journal of Hazardous Materials 308, 233–242.

Liu P., Ptacek C. J., Blowes D. W., Finfrock Y. Z., Gordon R. A., 2017. Stabilization of mercury in sediment by using biochars under reducing conditions. Journal of Hazardous Materials 325, 120–128.

Liu, P., Ptacek, C. J., Elena, K. M. A., et al., 2018. Evaluation of mercury stabilization mechanisms by sulfurized biochars determined using X-ray absorption spectroscopy. Journal of Hazardous Materials 347, 114–122.

Liu S., Wang X., Guo G., Yan Z., 2021. Status and environmental management of soil mercury pollution in China: A review. Journal of Environmental Management 277, 111442.

Ma C. B., Du Y., Du B., Wang H., Wang E., 2018. Investigation of an eco-friendly aerogel as a substrate for the immobilization of MoS_2 nanoflowers for removal of mercury species from aqueous solutions. Journal of Colloid and Interface Science 525, 251–259.

Man Y., Wang B., Wang J., et al., 2021. Use of biochar to reduce mercury accumulation in *Oryza sativa* L: A trial for sustainable management of historically polluted farmlands. Environment International 153, 106527.

Mohan, D., Gupta, V., Srivastava, S., Chander, S., 2001. Kinetics of mercury adsorption from wastewater using activated carbon derived from fertilizer waste. Colloids and Surfaces A: Physicochemical and Engineering Aspects 177, 169–181.

Muzarpar M. S., Leman A. M., Maghpor N., Hassan N. N. M., Misdana N., 2020. The adsorption mechanism of activated carbon and Its application - A review. IJATEC 1, 3.

O'Connor D., Peng T., Li G., et al., 2018. Sulfur-modified rice husk biochar: A green method for the remediation of mercury contaminated soil. Science of the Total Environment 621, 819–826.

Rodriguez R., Contrino D., Mazyck D., 2021. Role of activated carbon precursor for mercury oxidation and removal: Oxidized surface and carbene site interaction. Processes 9, 1190.

Rollinson A.N., 2016. Gasification reactor engineering approach to understanding the formation of biochar properties. Proceedings of the Royal Society A - Mathematical Physical and Engineering Sciences 472, 20150841.

Sabio E., González E., González J.F., González-García C. M., Ramiro A., Gañan J., 2004. Thermal regeneration of activated carbon saturated with p-nitrophenol. Carbon 42, 2285–2293.

Teng D., Mao K., Ali W., et al., 2020. Describing the toxicity and sources and the remediation technologies for mercury-contaminated soil. RSC Advances 10, 23221–23232.

Wang Y., Dang F., Zheng X., Zhong H., 2019. Biochar amendment to further reduce methylmercury accumulation in rice grown in selenium-amended paddy soil. Journal of Hazardous Materials 365, 590–596.

Wang J., Shaheen M. S., Anderson W. N. C., et al., 2020. Nanoactivated carbon reduces mercury mobility and uptake by *Oryza sativa* L: Mechanistic investigation using spectroscopic and microscopic techniques. Environmental Science & Technology 54, 2698–2706.

Wei Y., Li R., Lu N., Zhang B., 2022. Stabilization of soil co-contaminated with mercury and arsenic by different types of biochar. Sustainability 14,13637.

Xing Y., Wang J., Shaheen S. M., et al., 2020. Mitigation of mercury accumulation in rice using rice hull-derived biochar as soil amendment: A field investigation. Journal of Hazardous Materials 388, 121747.

Xing Y., Wang J., Xia J., et al., 2019. A pilot study on using biochars as sustainable amendments to inhibit rice uptake of Hg from a historically polluted soil in a Karst region of
China. Ecotoxicology and Environmental Safety 170, 18–24.

Xu J., Bravo A. G., Lagerkvist A., et al., 2015. Sources and remediation techniques for mercury contaminated soil. Environment International 74, 42–53.

Yang Q., Wang Y., Zhong H., 2021. Remediation of mercury-contaminated soils and sediments using biochar: A critical review. Biochar 3, 23–35.

Zhang J., Wu S., Xu Z., et al., 2019. The role of sewage sludge biochar in methylmercury
formation and accumulation in rice. Chemosphere 218, 527–533.

Zhou J., Luo A., Zhao Y., 2018. Preparation and characterisation of activated carbon from
waste tea by physical activation using steam. Journal of the Air & Waste Management
Association 68, 1269–1277.

Index

Note: *Italic* page numbers refer to *figures* and **bold** page numbers refer to **tables**.

For Product Safety Concerns and Information please contact our
EU representative GPSR@taylorandfrancis.com Taylor & Francis
Verlag GmbH, Kaufingerstraße 24, 80331 München, Germany